Leckie × Leckie
Scotland's leading educational publishers

National 4 & 5 DESIGN & MANUFACTURE
COURSE NOTES

N4 & 5 DESIGN & MANUFACTURE COURSE NOTES

Jill Connolly

001/10082015

10 9 8 7 6 5 4 3 2

ISBN 9780007504787

Published by

Leckie & Leckie Ltd

An imprint of HarperCollins*Publishers*

Westerhill Road, Bishopbriggs, Glasgow, G64 2QT

T: 0844 576 8126 F: 0844 576 8131

leckieandleckie@harpercollins.co.uk

www.leckieandleckie.co.uk

Special thanks to

Delphine Phin (copy-edit); Jill Laidlaw (proofread); Roda Morrison (proofread); Anna Clark (editorial project management); Ken Vail Graphic Design (layout)

Printed in the Italy by Grafica Veneta S.P.A.

A CIP Catalogue record for this book is available from the British Library.

Acknowledgements

We would like to thank the following for permission to reproduce photographs.

P6 Victoria and Albert Museum, London; P10a Herman Miller; P13 Mark Newson Ltd and Magis; P14 Graham Murdoch and Real Wood Studios; P15a Skye Soap Company; P17a Loft Furniture Ltd; P21a Charlotte Tangye Design; P23b and P23c Steelcase Inc; P29b Adidas; P30a KardBoardz; P30c Maja and Nico Backström; P33 Estudio Mariscal; P42a Desu Design; P44b Suck UK; P45c Branca, Lisboa; P53a British Standards Institution; P53b International Organisation for Standardisation; P53c European Commission; P54 Carrera; P61 Lakeland; P63 Orla Kiely; P65b www.doiydesign.com; P73 Ikea; P95 gallery: lapas77 / Shutterstock.com, iPad: manaemedia / Shutterstock.com, concert: Christian Bertrand / Shutterstock.com; P97a and P97b James Dyson Foundation; P120b Snug. Studio, Germany; P125a Forestry Commission Scotland; P152f Draper tools; P154a–P154f Draper tools; P155e Draper tools; P156f Draper tools; P166c Draper Tools; P168a–P168b Draper tools; P168c HPC Laser Ltd; P168d Umbra; P172b–P172d Draper Tools; P172e Bowers Group; P172f Draper Tools; P182a Draper Tools; P182c Draper Tools; P182h Draper tools; P182i HME Technology Ltd; P193b and P193c One Foot Taller; P194a and P194b Bonnie Bling; P208 Draper Tools; P212 Joseph Joseph Ltd; P216a Edward Barber & Jay Osgerby, Vitra AG; P216b Suck UK; P217a www.doiydesign.com; P217b BSH Home Appliances Limited; P218a Estudio Mariscal; P218b KardBoardz

All other images © Shutterstock.com, © Thinkstock.com or Author's own.

Introduction

About this book

This book will provide you with the knowledge and understanding for the **National 4 and 5 qualifications in Design and manufacture**: **Unit 1**, **Design** and **Unit 2, Materials and manufacturing.**

As well as covering the learning that will prepare you for the N4 and N5 unit assessments and the N5 Design and manufacture question paper, it also leads you through the stages of the course assignment, helping you to design a product that is suitable for manufacture.

Features

CHAPTER SUMMARIES

Each chapter starts with a summary of the learning it contains.

In this chapter you will learn about:

- the design process and designing
- the members of a design team and their roles
- the term 'commercial products'
- the difference between needs and wants.

ACTIVITIES

The activities throughout the book aim to help you to develop your skills to become a successful designer.

Activity

Selecting evaluation factors for products

The Landscape Dinner Set takes inspiration from a child's drawing. It is made from melamine plastic, which is food and drink safe. It is aimed at children aged 12 months and over.

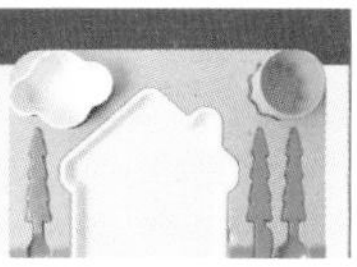

TEST YOUR KNOWLEDGE

These boxes contain questions to help you review your knowledge and understanding. Suggested answers can be found using the QR codes or by entering the web addresses into an internet browser.

Test your knowledge

Link to suggested answers
www.leckieandleckie.co.uk/tykanswers

Commercial manufacture of plastic products
A toy truck is manufactured from four different plastic components.

1. State the name of **one** method suitable for manufacturing all the plastic components of the toy truck.

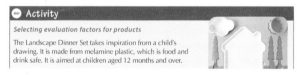

CASE STUDIES

These are real-life examples of relevant products and organisations, brilliant designers and exciting design projects.

Case study

Bonnie Bling laser cut plastic jewellery

Based on the Isle of Bute, Bonnie Bling is a range of quirky tongue-in-cheek acrylic jewellery and fashion accessories created by graphic designer Mhairi Mackenzie.

HINT

Hint boxes give extra support and make helpful suggestions for achieving success in your course.

Hint

When selecting materials for a product think of their properties as a menu – a list of possible choices. Ask yourself how much material you need, what properties you need and how much money you have to spend.

MAKE THE LINK

Design and manufacture is not a subject in isolation! Make-the-link boxes provide appropriate links to other subject areas. You are also encouraged to 'Make the link' between different parts of the course, and between your knowledge and understanding and your practical skills.

Make the Link

For enhanced performance, material properties should be matched to the needs of the product. Chapter 5 gives an introduction to materials and their properties.

CHECK YOUR PROGRESS

At the end of every chapter there is a checklist that enables you to rate your understanding of the key concepts, showing you where you need to target your efforts.

Check your progress

I can:	*HELP NEEDED*	*GETTING THERE*	*CONFIDENT*
• describe design activities	◯	◯	◯
• explain the ways in which the function of a product influences its design	◯	◯	◯

ASSESSMENT

Chapter 8 provides help and advice on the course assignment and written paper, along with example exam-style questions with suggested answers and marking commentary, and practice exam questions for you to try yourself.

Contents

CONTENTS

DESIGN SECTION OVERVIEW

The first four chapters of this book will provide you with the knowledge and understanding for **Unit 1**, **Design**, and will also be useful when you complete your course assignment. Combined with your classwork and the guidance of your teacher, these chapters will lead you through the stages of the design process, helping you to design a product that is suitable for manufacture. The activities in this section aim to help you to develop your skills to become a successful designer. The information in this section will also be useful throughout the course, along with other reference books and additional sources of information.

Chapter 1, **An introduction to designing**, explains the process of designing and introduces you to the various members of a design team. It explains the term 'commercial products' and sets out the reasons why we have these products in our lives. This chapter provides a foundation on which to build your knowledge and understanding of designing.

Chapter 2, **The factors that influence design**, focuses on the design of commercial products and the way in which they are influenced by function, performance, market, aesthetics and ergonomics. In this chapter you will develop an understanding of these five main factors which influence the design of commercial products.

The third chapter, **Evaluating products**, requires you to apply your understanding of design factors to evaluate products. This chapter begins by offering guidance about how to select a suitable commercial product for your evaluation, before looking at the seven different evaluation methods that can be used to research and evaluate products. Different approaches to structuring and planning your evaluation are shown, and tips for writing a conclusion to the evaluation are included.

The final chapter in this section is **Designing**. This chapter explains the tasks which designers work through, from identifying a need for a product, to reaching a final design proposal. There is a description of each stage of the design process, an exploration of the purpose of each stage and an elaboration of links between the stages. For those stages that involve the production of written work, such as the analysis and specification, helpful tips and suggestions are given to aid report structure and wording.

This chapter also explains the graphic and modelling techniques used to communicate and develop your ideas in 2D and 3D. Further support for the design development stage is provided, to help you to justify design decisions and apply relevant information regarding the design factors. The end of this section explains how to present the final design concept and make plans for the manufacture of your design.

SECTION 1
Design

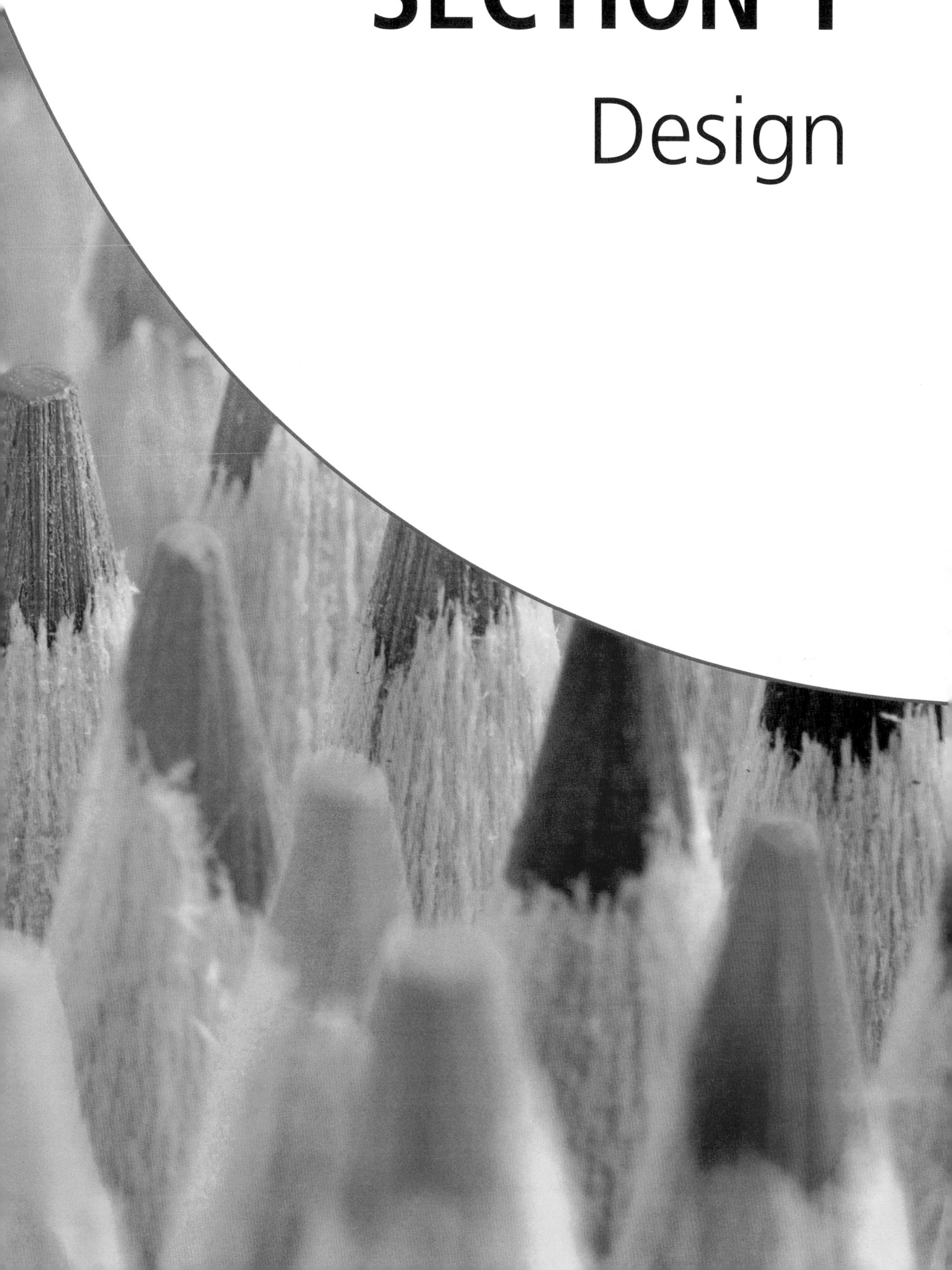

1 An introduction to designing

In this chapter you will learn about:

- the design process and designing
- the members of a design team and their roles
- the term 'commercial products'
- the difference between needs and wants.

Design

Designing is about developing an idea, or **concept**, and then fine tuning the details so that the concept can be brought to life. Designing involves sketching, drawing and modelling the concept until what you create becomes true to the vision in your head. This involves making decisions and compromises. Designing includes selecting appropriate materials and manufacturing methods, and then figuring out how all the pieces can be put together to make something useful or beautiful … or both.

The design process

The design process is a range of activities which allow designerly thinking to take place. These activities ensure all the various design aspects are considered in order to reach a final design proposal.

‘Have nothing in your house that you do not know to be useful, or believe to be beautiful.’

William Morris (leader of the Arts and Crafts design movement, 1834–96)

This diagram shows an overview of design activities and their relationships with one another.

Presenting and recording work

A folder or **portfolio of work** is gathered together as you work through the design activity. This will provide evidence of your thought processes, your decisions and your creativity, while allowing you to explain and justify the reasons why your final design is the best possible solution to the brief.

Hint

Keep your folio organised by making a checklist for the front.

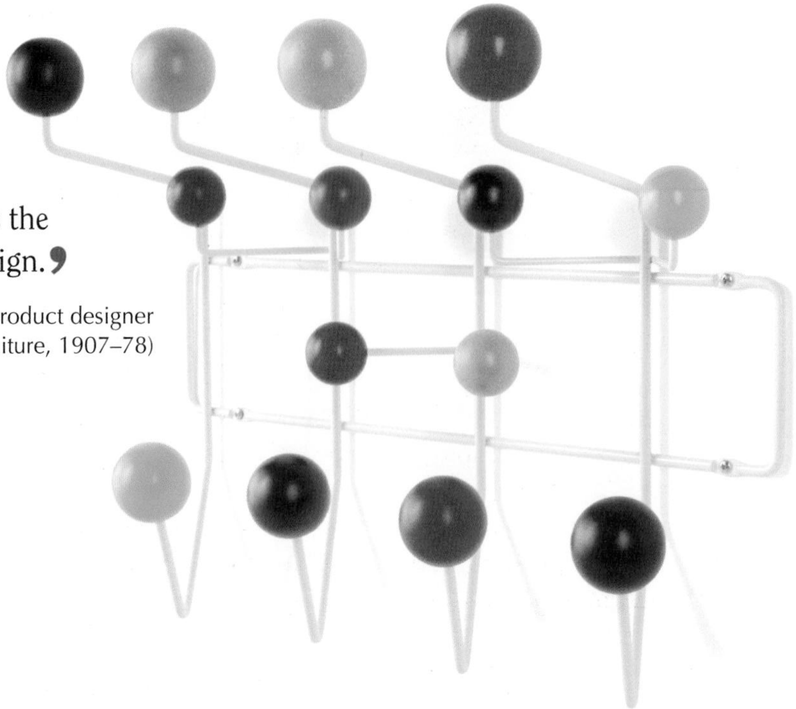

❛Recognising the need is the primary condition for design.❜

Charles Eames (revolutionary product designer of 20th-century furniture, 1907–78)

Each stage of the design process is recorded in various ways; from written pieces of work to drawings, sketches and 3D models. It is very important to record every part of the design process using an appropriate method. A digital camera, webcam or a voice recorder can be useful to record work that can't easily be presented on paper.

A completed folio includes work from the start of the design process to the end. Your folio may be recorded on various different media formats. It is important to keep your work organised. Keeping a good, clear and organised record of your work will help you to develop your designs.

During this course you may work on projects which involve all stages of the design process or you may work on projects which perhaps just take you through parts of the design process.

Hint

Often the shortened word 'folio' is used to refer to the portfolio folder.

Make the Link

English – Keeping a portfolio of written and verbal work.

Graphic communication – Keeping a variety of drawings and sketches clean and tidy in a folder.

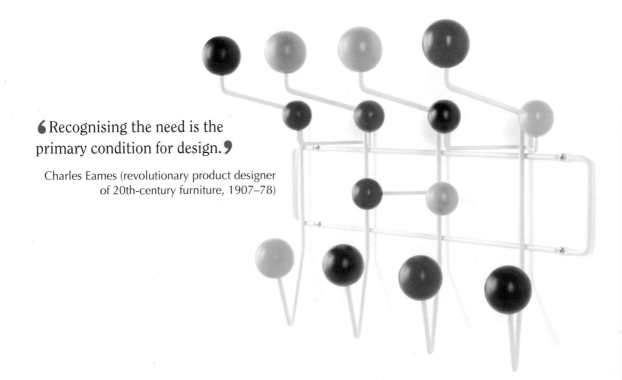

The design team

For every commercial design project there is a team of specialists, all of whom contribute towards the final product.

There are many people in a design team and they are often managed by a Senior Designer who has experience of designing, is knowledgeable about manufacturing and understands the design process. He or she must be a strong team leader who is good at delegating tasks and leading people. The Senior Designer takes responsibility for piecing all the parts of the project together, collecting information from the team and finalising the design.

Large companies can employ thousands of people in just one design team. The team may work on one product, but could potentially be developing several products at once. In a large design team, the product can be complex due to the team's combined depth and breadth of knowledge.

The design team for a car, for example, has sub-teams with their own designing or manufacturing expertise, for example in mechanics, interior fittings or electronics. Within these sub-teams will be specialists like ergonomists, designers and engineers who will work together, contributing on their specialist area and communicating with the other sub-teams to ensure every element of the product works.

Some design studios, however, are small enterprises and each team member is responsible for a wide variety of roles, working with specialists when required. For example, a small jewellery design company may employ five people. The designer may be responsible for the design, manufacturing and marketing of the jewellery.

Working in a design team

Communication is very important when working in a design team. Regular contact between design-team members allows the team to monitor the progress made, resolve any issues with the design, share their ideas, continually evaluate the design, contribute specialist knowledge and also discuss how the design can be improved.

The design team can meet in person or online through internet phone conferencing (Skype for example). This allows members of the design team in other countries or other locations to stay involved.

The design team

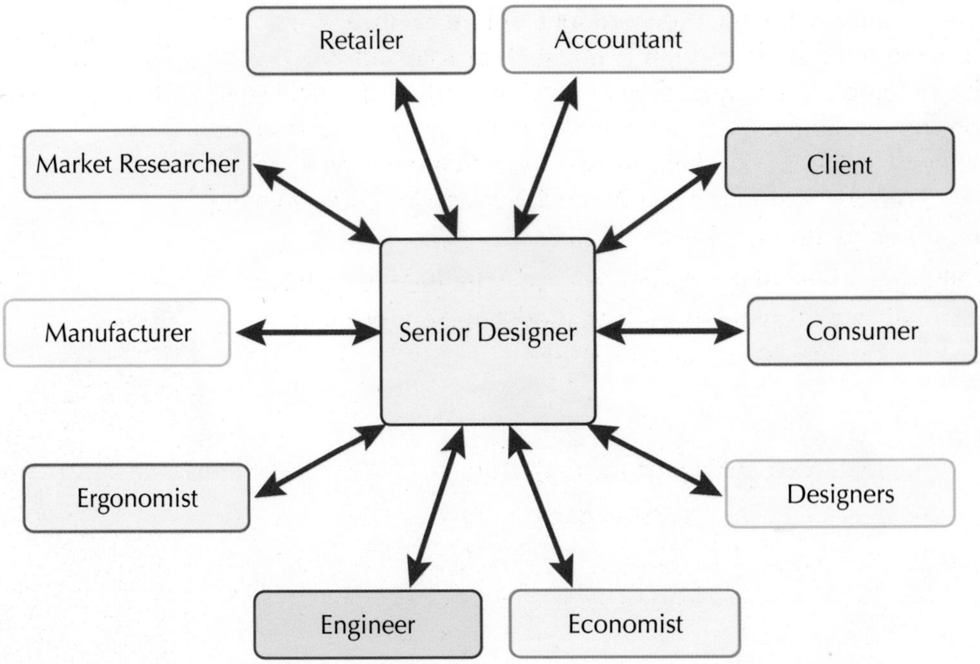

- **Accountant** – organises finances, controls cash-flow, organises staff wages to be paid and generally takes care of the project's incomings and outgoings.
- The **client** – sets the brief and asks for the product to be designed.
- **Consumer** – buys the product.
- The **designers** – develop the product.
- **Market researcher** – investigates current products on the market, the client, the target market and the brand. They also forecast the potential success of the product.
- **Economist** – determines the correct selling price for the product.
- **Engineer** – works with the technical elements of the project. They may be experts in electronics or material limitations or manufacturing techniques, for example.
- **Ergonomist** – researches human limitations to make the design suitable for use.
- **Manufacturer** – makes the product. They are experts in producing and assembling the parts of the product in the most efficient way.
- **Retailer** – sells the product online or in a store.
- **Senior designer** – manages the design team and communicates with the client.

The retailer, who sells the product online or in a store, can provide input to the design team, such as sales information or by helping to generate demand for a product through store promotion. The consumer, who uses the product, has some links with the design team in that they create the demand for the product, and can provide feedback and useful marketing information through warranties.

Other members of the design team may include materials specialists, packaging specialists, model makers, product testers and environmental specialists.

Make the Link

You will find out more about engineers and manufacturers in the Materials and Manufacturing Unit.

Make the Link

Consumer demand, (see page 35), is created through careful market research.

‘I think it's really important to design things with a kind of personality.’

Marc Newson (inspirational modern product designer of today, 1963)

Activity

The design team placemat

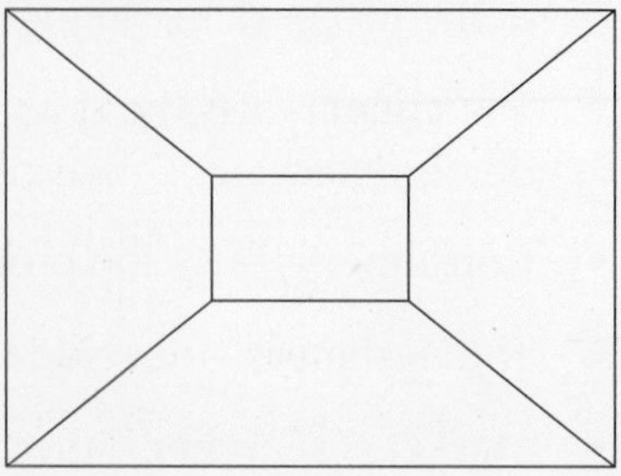

1. Draw the placemat: Divide the paper into segments based on the number of members in the group, leaving a box in the middle. The example shown is for a group of four.
2. As a team, choose one design-team member and write their job title in the middle box of the placemat.
3. **2-minute timed task:** On your own and in your own segment of the placemat, write the skills and qualities which the design-team member must have to complete their job.
4. **6-minute timed task:** Now, as a team, discuss and agree which four main skills and qualities the design-team member must have. Write these in the centre box.
5. **4-minute timed task:** As a group, prepare to feed back your answers.

Design team case study

Real Wood Studios

Graham Murdoch obtained a degree in Product Design at the Robert Gordon University in Aberdeen. He then attended the City of Glasgow College to study Furniture Making, while also working part-time in a furniture-making workshop. He set up business at Real Wood Studios, a cooperatively-owned workshop based in the Scottish Borders, in September 2004. He produces a vast range of wooden products; from jewellery boxes to reception desks.

Graham is responsible for designing and manufacturing his furniture, while also meeting with his clients, and acting as the economist and ergonomist for each project. He also conducts his own market research, along with many other tasks which arise each day.

'Commissioning bespoke furniture involves many key stages, from discussing the initial brief with a client and generating the first draft of a design, to selecting the right timber for each component. These stages are just as important as the construction of the piece itself.'

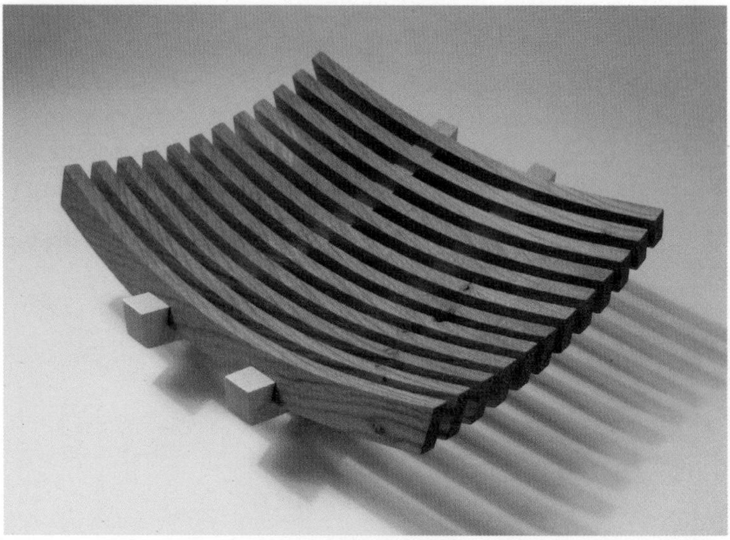

Graham's designs consist of simple forms using clean lines and sweeping curves and often combine two contrasting timbers.

Activity

Understanding the design team

Let's consider the Isle of Skye Soap Company. They design and make their own range of soaps with natural Scottish ingredients. They have been asked to design a range of soap for a five-star Scottish hotel chain. There is a gift shop in each hotel where they would like to sell a soap gift box.

Imagine that you and your classmates work for the Isle of Skye Soap Company.

1. Discuss the task and elect a Senior Designer to chair the meeting.
2. The Senior Designer will allocate everyone a role: designer, market researcher, accountant, manufacturer and economist.
3. **2-minute timed task:** Considering your own role
   On your own, brainstorm your role in the project.
4. **3-minute timed task:** Explaining your role
   You have 30 seconds each to explain your role to the project team.
5. **2-minute timed task:** Helping others
   Now that you have heard your team members speak about their roles in the project, try to add to their responses.
6. **2-minute timed task:** Helping yourself
   Find someone with a similar role from another team and share your answers.
7. Consider the individual team members. Which team member will have a lot to do at the start? Who has the most responsibility? Will the team need any other roles to work on this project?

'Less is more.'

Ludwig Mies Van Der Rohe (German-born architect, designer and teacher with great ideas for society, 1886–1969)

Make the Link

The products we use every day satisfy either our *wants* or our *needs* (see pages 17–18 and 83).

Commercial products

Commercial products are those products which are sold to make a profit for an organisation. They are items which we use in all aspects of daily life, such as trainers, watches, coffee machines, bike locks, bins, fruit bowls, chairs, folders, showers, shelves, radios and so on.

Activity

Commercial Products

1. On your own, think of your daily routine. In your head, take yourself through your day so far. Visualise the rooms that you were in this morning: bedroom ... bathroom ... kitchen ... Consider your journey to school. Did you stop anywhere on the way?
2. Now consider the commercial products you used along this journey. Share your answers with the class.

Hint

Use the answers from this activity to provide a range of interesting products for future class discussions.

Brand names

Some commercial products are so successful that the brand name has taken over the functional name of the product. For example, a vacuum cleaner is often referred to as a Hoover, even if the vacuum cleaner is not manufactured by Hoover. Our use of brand names extends even further into our language as we adapt them to suit our vocabulary, such as 'doing the hoovering'. Other brand names we have adopted into our language are Tannoy, Aspirin, Astro Turf, Hi-lighter, Post-it, Escalator and Sellotape.

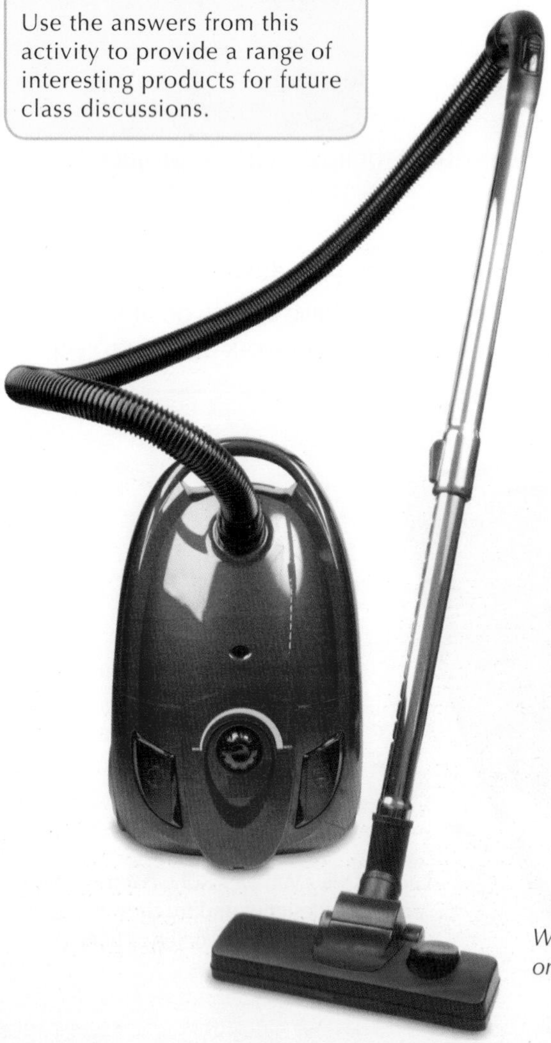

Would you refer to this as a Hoover or a vacuum cleaner?

‘I would think twice about designing stuff for which there was no need and which didn't endure.’

Robin Day (British designer famous for inventing mass manufactured chairs, 1915–2010)

Needs and wants

There are products we **need** and products we **want**.

Products we *need* are those which fulfil our basic needs as human beings. There are products we need to survive, such as food and water, and products we need to keep us safe, such as smoke alarms. Products that satisfy our needs include products that:

- give us shelter
- provide warmth
- protect us from harm
- encourage hygiene
- make us feel valued and appreciated.

A tent is an ideal way of providing shelter, warmth and protection. Tents are a main residence for many people across the world and are often provided as shelter after natural disasters.

Products we *want* are those which fulfil our desires as human beings. Products we want to enrich our lives include TVs and roller blades; products we want to make our lives easier include food blenders and smartphones. Products that satisfy our wants include products that:

- make us feel socially accepted
- enhance our comfort
- keep us up to date or informed
- make us fashionable
- improve our health and wellbeing
- make us happy.

*We may **want** to own a TV, but we don't **need** to.*

Check your progress

I can:	HELP NEEDED	GETTING THERE	CONFIDENT
• describe the overview of design activities	⬭	⬭	⬭
• describe the members of a design team and their roles	⬭	⬭	⬭
• explain the term 'commercial products'	⬭	⬭	⬭
• explain the difference between needs and wants.	⬭	⬭	⬭

2 The factors that influence design

By the end of this chapter you should be able to:

- describe the functional factors that influence design of products
- describe the performance factors that influence design of products
- describe the marketing factors that influence design of products
- describe the aesthetic factors that influence design of products
- describe the ergonomic factors that influence design of products
- explain the ways in which sustainability influences design decisions.

The factors that influence design

There are many different factors that a designer must consider to ensure the final product is a success. The designer has to balance these factors carefully, so that the design proposal meets the design brief and specification, while showing creativity. As a designer, you must both understand and be able to work with a range of factors.

Prioritising factors

These design factors can be broken down into five main categories:

- **Function**
- **Performance**
- **Market**
- **Aesthetics**
- **Ergonomics**

No particular factor is the most important or least important. However, each product has certain factors which are crucial to their success. Each individual product has its own design priorities. An example of this is a tin opener, where *function* is the most important factor as it must open tins. Other key factors include the *performance* of the tin opener as it must be reliable and *ergonomics* as the tin opener must be comfortable and safe to use. Understanding the importance of these factors will help a designer to ensure that products are successful.

Make the Link

Sustainability is covered on page 55.

Design and sustainability

Designers also have a responsibility to ensure that their products are **sustainable**. This is not a single design factor, but an issue that impacts and influences design decisions regarding all five factors.

Function

Function is the purpose of a product; or, to put this simply, function is the job the product is designed to do. A lawnmower cuts grass, a washing machine washes clothes and a pen writes on paper. These are all functions.

The term '**fitness for purpose**' is often used to describe how well a product fulfils its intended function.

A salt grinder is the correct size for an average adult hand, is able to store a reasonable volume of salt, can be taken apart with ease for refilling and cleaning. It also has a grinding mechanism which is made from a material that is not corroded by salt. The salt grinder is, therefore, demonstrating *fitness for purpose*.

Primary function

The **primary function** is the most important function of the product. If a product does not fulfil the purpose for which it is intended, its primary function, then it is useless. Imagine a shoe rack that is not big enough to fit any shoes on it, not even enough space for a flip flop! The shoe rack would not fulfil its primary function, which is to hold shoes.

Simple products like toothpaste tubes can cause frustration if they are not fit for purpose.

Secondary function

The design must fulfil its primary function. However, many products have extra functions. These **secondary functions** are additional features or ways in which the product can be used and so they make the product more attractive to consumers. Imagine the shoe rack again. This time it cannot only hold shoes but it also has hooks on it for hanging jewellery or belts. It has one primary function, which is to store shoes, but the secondary storage function may add some appeal for consumers.

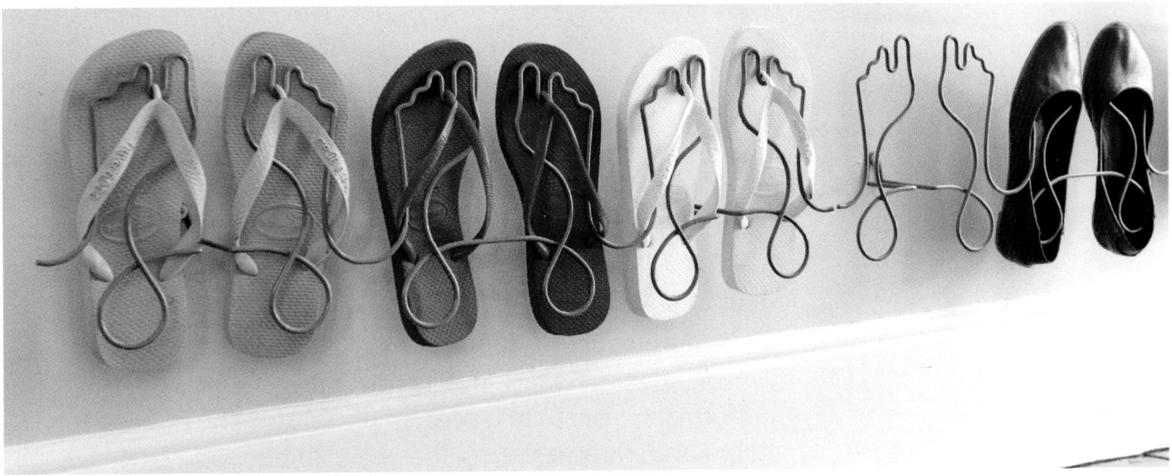

Test your knowledge

Link to suggested answers
www.leckieandleckie.co.uk/tykanswers

Primary and secondary functions

1. Explain the meaning of the term 'primary function'.
2. Describe the primary function of a:
   a) sink
   b) whisk.
3. Explain the meaning of the term 'secondary function'.
4. Describe a secondary function of a:
   a) TV cabinet
   b) toothbrush holder.

A dining table is shown on the right.

5. State the primary function of the dining table.
6. Describe a secondary function of the dining table.
7. Explain the difference between primary function and secondary function.

Performance

The **performance** of a product is how well a product works. For example, you would expect a disposable razor to shave, but not to a high quality for a long period of time. Neither would it be too surprising if it cut you, whereas an electric razor would shave to a higher quality, would be easy to use, comfortable against your skin and you would be very surprised if it cut you. Both products perform the same function but to a different degree of success *or* level of performance.

The performance of a product can depend on external conditions. Lack of power, the level of light, the wrong temperature and the frequency of use are just some of these conditions. For example, a solar-powered garden light gains power from the Sun and so, in this case, the level of light it receives influences its performance. On a cloudy day, the garden light may produce very little light at all.

In extremely cold temperatures, some electrical products do not work at all. LCD (Liquid Crystal Display) screens on smartphones struggle to function below –14°C as the reaction time of the sensors decreases as the temperature decreases. This poor performance is due to a very simple reason: the LCD screen is a liquid and it freezes.

Ease of maintenance

Products are **maintained** to keep them in safe working order and to mend them if they are broken. Of course, this should be *easy*, otherwise the product will be thrown away when consumers are persuaded to replace their broken products with new ones.

Some products last for years before they require any maintenance and others may only last a few uses. Products need to be repaired for many reasons:

- Parts wear away and need to be replaced.
- Materials become damaged and need to be replaced or repaired.
- Joints, screws or fixings become loose and need to be tightened, replaced or re-glued.
- Electrical components fail and need to be replaced.
- Paint, varnish or other finishes wear away and need to be reapplied.
- Mechanical parts need to be serviced, oiled or cleaned to operate.

Some ski and snowboard goggles have an interchangeable lens design that lets you change the lens for different snow conditions or in the event of damage. Other types of goggles have only one lens which cannot be replaced.

Make the Link

Design for disassembly is a key part of the cradle-to-cradle concept, which promotes durability and availability of replacement parts (see page 56).

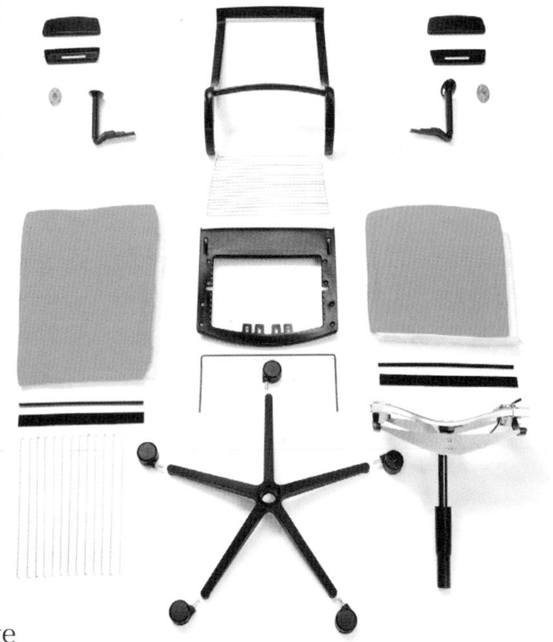

If the quality of construction/manufacture is not good enough, a product can fall apart quickly. Many badly built flat-pack furniture products fall apart quickly as the average consumer doesn't necessarily have the skills or equipment to construct furniture to a high standard. Some product repairs may require a specialist spare part or repairperson, which may only be available directly from the manufacturer. This adds to the overall price of the product. There are some product repairs which require specialist skills and are best left to the experts, such as car repairs.

Consumers should consider their purchase decisions before they invest in a product which may end up in a landfill or have a negative impact on the environment. Products that cannot be repaired create waste when they or their components are thrown away and are not reused or recycled.

Designers, therefore, have a responsibility to design products that can be repaired easily or that can be taken apart for ease of reusing or recycling the component parts. The Think Chair by Steelcase (left) was one of the first products to qualify for **Cradle-to-Cradle certification** as it can be disassembled in 5 minutes with common tools, allowing for parts to be easily replaced if necessary.

Hint

Durability means that a product has a **dur**able **ability**.

The rubber stoppers on the end of the metal legs provide extra durability for the chair.

Durability

The **durability** of a product is its ability to withstand wear and tear. Consumers trust products to be durable. Ideally, we would like all the products we buy to be durable, to work well every time and to last for a long period of time without becoming weak and breaking. Realistically, this is very difficult.

Creating a durable product involves:

- Selecting hard-wearing materials and using resilient manufacturing processes.
- Using robust assembly techniques.
- Understanding how the product is used.
- Considering the conditions of use (hot, cold, indoors, outdoors, etc.).
- Knowing how the target market (the user) will treat the product.

Metal and wood may require a finish or treatment to make them durable in certain conditions. For example, a pine bird table can be varnished, which will protect the pine from being damaged by the weather. Plastic does not require a finish as it is waterproof and is, therefore, resistant to most weather conditions.

Different groups of people treat and use products in different ways. If the target market consists of toddlers, products will be thrown, bashed, grabbed and chewed, so any products designed for this group should be very durable. Other target markets have their own durability needs for their products. For example, chefs require their knives to be durable, cyclists require their tyres to be hardwearing and tourists require their suitcases to be tough.

Therefore, durable products can be described as:

- waterproof
- shatterproof
- heat resistant
- shock absorbant
- sharp
- hard wearing
- strong
- long lasting
- tough
- sturdy
- robust.

Ease of use

The ease of use of a product is how *simple* it is to operate. Products should not be overly complex or difficult to understand. They should not be awkwardly shaped or exhausting to use. When a product is difficult to use, we can feel frustrated, confused, angry and even defeated.

Products should always be designed with ease of use in mind, by making them as user friendly as possible. It is the designer's job to understand the user and their limitations, such as their age, gender, physical ability and if they have any disabilities. Every person is unique and will react differently to products. Designers must consider the needs of the individual in order for the product to be easy to use.

A common product that can be difficult to use is scissors. There are many different types of scissors which are designed for different groups of people or different *markets*. For example, children have their own small blunted scissors, left-handed people have left-handed scissors with the blade reversed so they can see the cutting line, and there are specialist spring-loaded scissors that ease the workload on the fingers of arthritis sufferers.

Make the Link

Varnish, wax, oil, paint and plastic dip-coating are material finishes which can prolong the life of a material.

Hint

Solve bad design by thinking about products which are not easy to use. Consider the frustrations you have with them and then think about what would make them easier to use.

Make the Link

A market refers to the different groups of people who use a specific product.

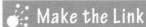

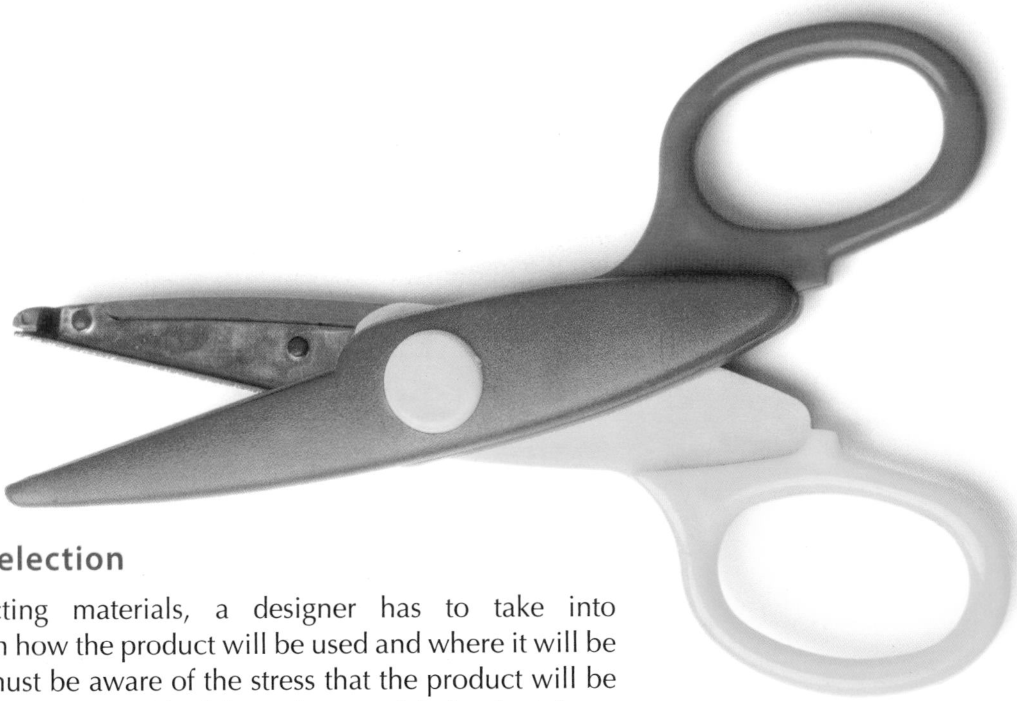

Material selection

When selecting materials, a designer has to take into consideration how the product will be used and where it will be used. They must be aware of the stress that the product will be under when it is in use to find the right materials for the job.

When designers select a material they think about the material's **properties**. These are the unique characteristics of a material. A teak garden chair, for example, will last longer than a pine garden chair, due to its high natural oil content.

Hint

When selecting materials for a product think of their properties as a menu – a list of possible choices. Ask yourself how much material you need, what properties you need and how much money you have to spend.

Make the Link

For enhanced performance, material properties should be matched to the needs of the product. Chapter 5 gives an introduction to materials and their properties.

The challenge is to match the properties of the material to the product, so that the product can perform to its best potential.

Materials are selected based on their:

- **Aesthetics** – how the material looks and feels; its surface finish, colour, texture, etc.
- **Workability** – how easy the material is to work with; cut, shape, form, etc.
- **Practicability** – how practical and sensible the material is; locally sourced, cost, sustainability, ease of maintenance, etc.
- **Function** – how the properties match the purpose; waterproof, shatterproof, etc.
- **Performance** – how the properties match the function and use; lightweight, buoyant, flexible, etc.

The lifespan of the material will have an impact on the lifespan of the product. Some products are designed to be used just once, such as a bottle of water.

Filling up the bottle and reusing it is great for the environment but eventually, through constant use, the thin plastic walls will start to weaken with repeated squashing and squeezing, and will eventually tear.

A more durable and sustainable option is a metal water bottle, which is designed for constant reuse, resisting wear and being able to withstand greater impact than a plastic bottle. The metal water bottle is made from aluminium as it is extremely lightweight but very strong. Therefore, the water bottle can be lifted, carried and refilled easily and it can take the impact of blows which a plastic bottle cannot.

Materials can become damaged with constant use or misuse. Plastic parts can snap, crack or become scratched. Sometimes, they are damaged by weather conditions, such as a wooden shed rotting away.

Hint

Try to use lots of different materials throughout the course to develop your knowledge of different materials.

Make the Link

Disposable plastic products can be bad for the environment.

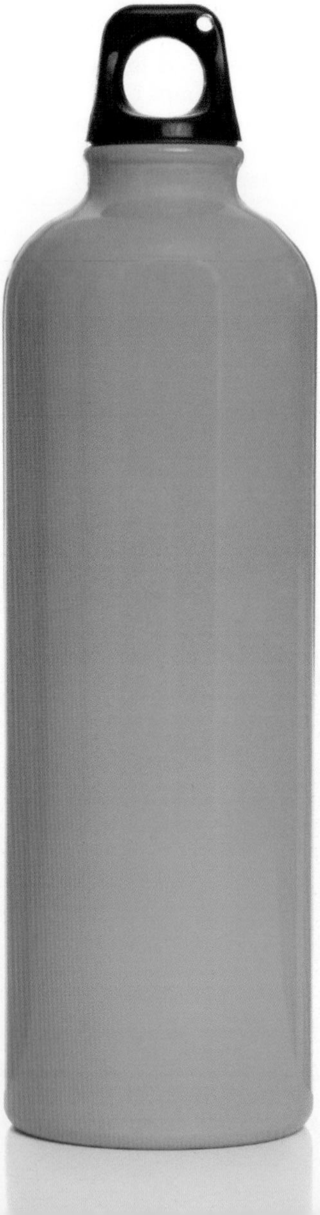

This aluminium alloy water bottle is extremely lightweight, yet very strong.

Construction and manufacture

The way that a product is built will impact on how well it performs. If it is built using manufacture methods that make it strong and durable, then it will have a longer lifespan and will be able to endure more rigorous use. Non-permanent fixings, such as screws, can influence the performance of a product as they can become loose or rust. This may result in the product becoming weaker or even falling apart.

There may be more than one way to construct a product. Some manufacturing methods cost more than others, and so choice of construction method may depend on budget. Some methods may result in a product that is less durable.

Sometimes, choosing a construction method depends on the volume, or quantity, to be manufactured. For example, injection moulding in plastic is fast and precise. However, it is expensive to set up and so only cost effective in mass manufacturing, when thousands of products or components are produced.

When a product is made from more than one component, it must be assembled in a way which allows for the components to join neatly and accurately. Consumers will notice if the product is not assembled well and this will have a negative impact on their confidence in the product when using it. A poorly built product will probably not function efficiently and may even cause injury to the user if components break off or if fittings protrude.

Make the Link

Commercial manufacturing is examined in Chapter 7.

Size

The size of a product impacts on the performance, whether large or small. Products which get smaller and slimmer are said to miniaturise. This is to make products lighter and generally more comfortable to use. Smaller microchips have allowed technology to shrink and this gives designers more flexibility in sizing some products.

Making products smaller, however, can have a negative impact on their performance. For example, a small, lightweight chain lock for a bike might seem like a good solution to the problem of carrying a big, heavy lock around. However, the smaller version may be easily cut off and so offers less security.

Designers no longer create large, boxy electronics like this 1970s TV. Developments in electronics now allow smaller component parts to be used.

Make the Link

Deciding on a product's size requires ergonomic data. Designers must consider human limitations when designing.

Similarly, some electronic products have reduced so much in size that the buttons have become too small for fingers to operate them. The size of a successful product, therefore, requires consideration of ergonomics and function.

Test your knowledge

Link to suggested answers
www.leckieandleckie.co.uk/tykanswers

Ease of use

Battery-powered milk frothers have become a popular way to have a frothy coffee in the comfort of your own home.

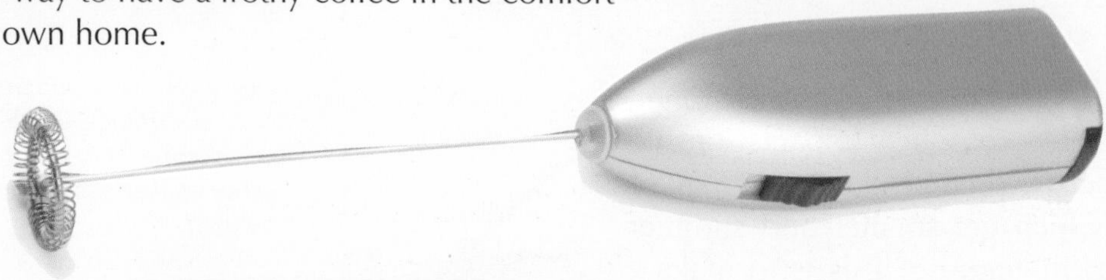

1. Explain the meaning of the term 'ease of use'.
2. With reference to the milk frother, explain its ease of use.
3. Explain the meaning of the term 'durability'.
4. The conditions of use will affect the durability of the milk frother. Explain one method of maintaining the milk frother.
5. Explain **two** additional durability issues relating to the milk frother.
6. Explain the meaning of the term 'ease of maintenance'.
7. Describe **one** reason why the milk frother is easy to maintain in terms of:
   a) materials
   b) joining methods.

Marketing

Marketing is the business of promoting and selling products.

Target market

The **target market** is the group of people who will eventually use the product. The target market can be defined by age, gender, interests, lifestyle and location, along with many, many other categories.

The target market for a product may be broad and general; a pair of mid-priced women's gym trainers is aimed at women who exercise but who don't spend a lot on their gym wear.

The target market for a product may be very specific and select; a pair of high-priced, super lightweight, women's spiked running shoes is aimed at a professional athlete who depends on the product to perform.

Market segments

Different **market segments** can be created by splitting up the market into age, income, lifestyle, location or culture to give distinct groups of consumers and users.

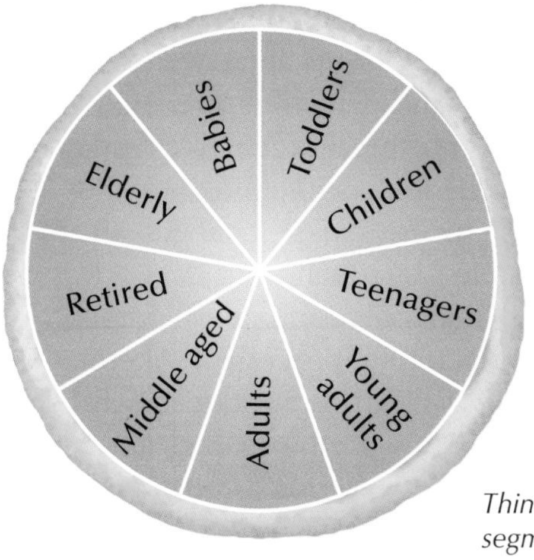

Think of the segments of an orange. Every segment is unique, yet they all have similarities.

A market can be split by cost into low-, mid-, high-priced and luxury. Consumers on a tight budget, for example, would be more likely to purchase low-cost products.

Introduction of new products

New products are introduced to the market when new technology emerges. When older technology is replaced by new technology, which is faster, smaller and easier to use, this is called **product evolution**. Usually, the function of the product is updated or improved, and the aesthetic may be modernised. An example of this is seen in the way we watch movies: DVD players replaced VHS video players in the late 1990s; but before VHS players, there were Beetamax players and Cinefilm predated those. Each time the product was updated, it evolved into something smaller and easier to use. These changes are made possible by technological advances, new materials and developments in manufacturing processes. Alternatively, products can be introduced which are entirely new to the market and do not replace a previous product, such as satellite navigation products.

Social expectations

Today, people in the developed world expect the next 'big thing', life-changing products and the future to be brighter. Products are advertised as the solution to many 'problems' in everyday life, but good quality design can improve the quality of all our lives.

The main **social expectations** from a new product are:

- It has new or better features.
- The style and look are improved.
- It is better value for money.
- There are more options or choices.
- It is more sustainable or environmentally friendly.

A good designer will do their research to find out what consumers want or what issues need to be addressed. This might involve carrying out market research, such as focus groups, consumer reviews and user trials. The designer can then take this information 'back to the drawing board' to make a product which consumers will want.

Here a focus group gives feedback on tropical fruit-scented shampoo. The designer is asking the group some questions to investigate creative ideas for bottle shapes.

Social expectations continually change, and new technology and new inventions emerge constantly. For example, we saw the laptop shrink in size to become a netbook. Then it lost its keyboard and became a tablet. We expect it will shrink a little more, improve its features, improve its quality and change its style.

Designers push the boundaries to create new products that will appeal to consumers. Eventually these products become the norm; they become what the consumer expects.

Niche marketing

When clients, manufacturers and designers see an opportunity whereby a product will sell well, or if they see a market which they can design a new product for, they will work towards making a profit from it, maximising its potential. This type of market is called a **market niche**. Clients target these carefully selected market niches to make their products successful. The product features will be aimed at meeting this market's needs, price range, quality and durability.

The target market for a one-cup espresso machine, such as the one below, is the 'home-brewer' market. It is aimed at the consumer who wants to make a good quality cup of coffee in their own home. The espresso machine may also be sold to small offices, small retailers and cafes, but it has been designed with home brewers' needs in mind.

Products can also be aimed at a wide market. This is simply called the **mainstream market** and these products are in high demand by consumers. Typically, these mainstream products are those that we use every day, such as a hairbrush or shoes, but also include the products which every household owns, such as a washing machine or sofa.

Test your knowledge

Link to suggested answers
www.leckieandleckie.co.uk/tykanswers

Marketing

The Julian chair, designed by Javier Mariscal, is:

- made from plastic
- available in red, green, yellow and white finishes
- suitable for outdoor use
- costs £80·00.

1. Explain the meaning of the term 'target market'.
2. Describe the main target market for this product.
3. With reference to the Julian chair, explain the meaning of the term 'market segment'.

The marketing mix

There is normally a **marketing strategy** for every commercial product. This is a plan which is written to define the marketing aim for the product; where it will be sold, who it is intended for and why it should make a profit. It is useful for the designer to know about this strategy as it will give them a deeper understanding of the product.

The **Four Ps** of marketing are product, price, place and promotion. This is called the **marketing mix**. Making the right choices in each of these categories is the basis for success.

- **Product** – the item for sale. The product must satisfy a *want* or *need* if it is to be successful. The product will be defined by its features and extra benefits to give it a unique selling point (USP) and to make it interesting to consumers. It must have a place within current product ranges or fit into a gap in the market, selling among other brands.

- **Price** – the selling price of the product. The impression the price gives is important. While it must make a profit, the price can make a statement about the product. Expensive products can appeal to consumers as they are regarded as luxury items. The price must set a tone and make the right impression to attract the target market.

- **Place** – where the product is available to the consumer. The buying experience itself is important, from the store location to the 'welcome' from the staff. When online shopping, ease of use and ability to seek assistance are vital to the buying experience. The place makes a statement about the consumer's social status. Place also means where the product is advertised to the consumer, perhaps on specific TV channels, via the internet, pop-up shops, or at specific times of the day on the radio.

- **Promotion** – advertising and informing consumers. Keeping consumers informed and up to date with new products makes them aware of their choices. Clever advertising will push products onto unsuspecting consumers. Other consumers are harder to win over as they rely on details and demonstrations before they make a trusted purchase.

Marketing mix
Product ✓
Price ✓
Place ✓
Promotion ✓

🔍 **Hint**

An effective marketing strategy will combine all of the Four Ps in the marketing mix.

Branding

A **brand** is a product or company identity. It is how we recognise commercial products instantly with our senses, through colours, textures, sounds, smells or tastes. A brand is not a logo; it is a psychological link between you and the product. Brands play an important role in marketing as they make a link between the product and the person.

People actually build relationships with brands. They *love* brands. They are *protective* of their favoured brands. They *trust* brands.

In some products, the brand can be quite discreet. However, in others you will notice the brand instantly. The matt black texture and gold ceramic plates on GHD hair straighteners or the curvy and compact shape of the Volkswagen Beetle make the brand instantly recognisable without the need for any logo.

Actually, there really is no need for a logo on a product. However, it is usually added to keep the company or product name in your head, reminding you of the brand and enhancing your loyalty to it. Placing a logo on a product is also a way to advertise the brand.

Hint

Think about the last time you visited a fast-food outlet. Think about the overall quality of the experience. What words come to mind? Compare that to the last time you visited a restaurant. What words would you use to describe this experience? These words help you to form a mental image of the company. This is the brand.

Make the Link

The types of commercial manufacturing methods explained in Chapter 7 are employed depending on the different levels of consumer demand for the product.

Consumer demand

'**Consumer demand**' is a term used to describe the popularity of a product. Products with a high consumer demand are sought after; perhaps due to fashion, new technology, new design or basic necessity. Products such as toothpaste, water bottles and shoes have high consumer demand as they wear away or run out and are needed by millions of people on a daily basis.

Consumers often feel loyal to particular brands as they have bought reliable and quality products from them previously. This is a way of ensuring that consumer demand for products can be maintained. Products which are in high demand are mass manufactured to ensure that demand can be met. Common products, such as plastic water bottles, can be produced continually, 24 hours a day, seven days a week, to ensure that consumer demand is met.

Amazon has maintained consumer demand through successful branding, teamed with good value and good quality, while the newest Kindle models have improvements which appeal to its network of consumers.

Rise of consumerism

We are increasingly buying products to improve our lives and the societies we live in. This is called **consumerism**. Often we demand affordable products, sometimes without any consideration of how our decisions impact the environment.

For every product we buy, we should be asking ourselves:

- Who has manufactured the product? What age were they? Were they paid fairly? Were the work conditions acceptable? How long were the working hours? Were the terms of employment fair?
- What product is this one replacing? Can the old product be repaired or maintained? Is the old product recyclable? Is the old product a potential pollutant? Is it really worth replacing?
- Where did the materials come from? Were they locally sourced? Were they transported in an environmentally friendly way? Were they replaced or are they a finite resource? What was the impact on the local environment caused by removing these materials?
- When will the next version or upgrade be available? How long will you use the product? Is it a worthwhile purchase considering its potential lifespan?
- Why do you want or need the product? Is it a necessary purchase? How quickly will it go to waste?
- How do I dispose of the product when I no longer want or need it?

As consumers we have a responsibility to reduce the amount of waste we produce and to reduce the number of products we buy. It is also obvious that we should recycle products and their packaging.

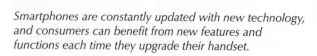

Smartphones are constantly updated with new technology, and consumers can benefit from new features and functions each time they upgrade their handset.

Technology push

'**Technology push**' is a term used to describe how a product comes to market, based on new technologies, new materials and new manufacturing methods, rather than in response to consumer demand based on function. When a new product becomes available to buy, a strong advertising campaign is needed to create consumer demand. To launch a new product is a great risk as the client will lose money if the product doesn't sell.

In the past 50 years the world has evolved into a fast-paced, highly technical and technological place. We constantly experience new technology which is smaller, faster, smoother, quieter, stronger and generally more capable. Technology push may involve an improvement on current technology or simply something totally new.

When a product with new technology is launched, there is huge hype around it. For example, when the Nintendo Wii was launched in 2006, the advertising campaign was so strong that the demand was extremely high and it was almost impossible to find anywhere to buy one. Shops had month-long waiting lists of hundreds of people and it was equally impossible to buy the product online. Nintendo was very successful in creating a buzz around what was, at the time, amazing new wireless-control technology for a games console. However, their technology push was too strong as their manufacturers couldn't keep up with demand.

Market pull

Market pull means there is a demand for a *product* and so a product is designed to fill that need. When bagless vacuum cleaners went on sale they were very expensive and not all households could afford one. A gap in the market opened up for more affordable bagless vacuum cleaners and so the market became wider and more affordable. This is market pull.

Hint

'Market pull' means the market is pulling the designers and manufacturers towards designing a product for them.

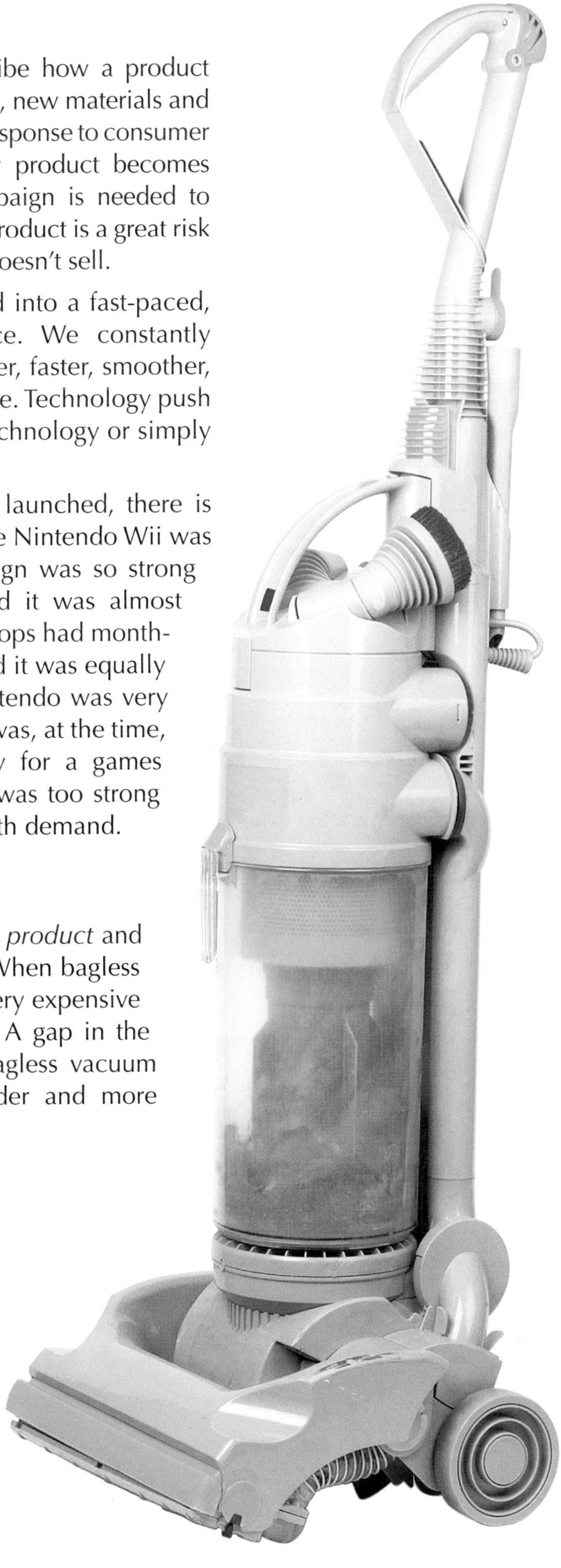

The large range of bagless vacuums on offer these days is a result of market pull.

Activity

Marketing and branding teamwork

The time for each task is **four minutes**. Form small groups with up to four members. Before you begin you must understand what good teamwork is:

- **T**urn to face each team member; don't have your back to anyone.
- **E**nsure all group members are involved; prompt someone quiet to get involved by asking them for their opinion.
- **A**ttentively listen to every comment; try not to interrupt anyone.
- **M**anage the team; elect a team leader and assume roles such as time keeper, reader and scribe.

1. List as many *brand names* as you can.
2. Discuss the meaning of the term 'product branding' and then write the definition.
3. List as many examples of products with a high consumer demand as you can.
4. Discuss the meaning of the term 'consumer demand' and then write the definition.
5. List as many products with *market pull* as you can.
6. Discuss the meaning of the term 'technology push' and then write the definition.

Market research

When consumer demand is high, a product is more likely to succeed. **Market research** can be carried out to investigate whether or not consumers want or need a product. It is a method of gathering information and is the starting point for millions of successful products. Modern market research is evolving into a very complex business with many different areas and it employs many people in different specialist areas.

Modern market research is sneaky and people, perhaps, don't even realise they have provided any information. Surveys are hidden in customer comment cards, in the 'few things to let us know' as you send away for your product guarantee and in the online feedback questions you complete. Store loyalty cards are gathering information about you and your buying habits with the enticement of bonus points and prize draws – if you don't mind just completing a few questions. With a supermarket 'loyalty' scheme there really is no hiding your addiction to bacon-flavour crisps!

To spend time and money designing and manufacturing a product without researching if there is a demand for the product is risky. For example, an LED light for a tent may not sell because an experienced camper, who would be most likely to buy this product, would probably wear a headtorch.

Make the Link

Surveys are also used as a product evaluation method (page 71).

This is a popular market research method.

Hint

Words to avoid using are **cool**, **nice**, **good**, **bad** and **OK**. These words are simply not creative enough. A professional designer would not give a presentation about a 'nice' product.

Aesthetics

Aesthetics is the way a product is perceived by our senses; its look, taste, smell, tactile quality (feel) and sound.

'Aesthetically pleasing' is a term used to describe an attractive appearance; for example, 'the contrast of the crisp, white lamp shade against the polished chrome stand of the floor lamp is aesthetically pleasing'.

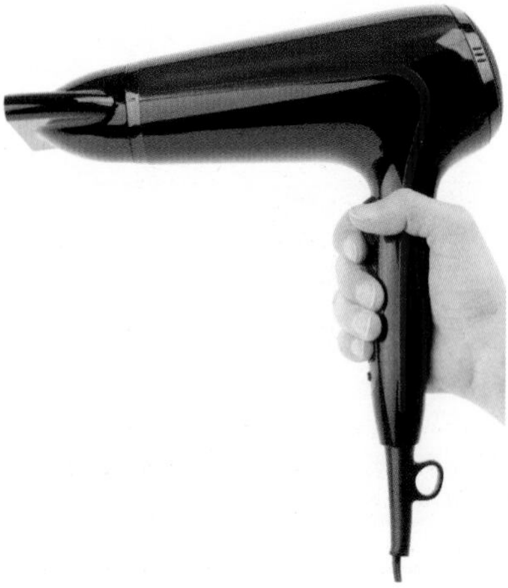

Shape

The shape of a product must be attractive to the eye, while also being functional and ergonomical. For example, a hairdryer has a stereotypical shape, which is composed of a comfortably shaped handle, a cylindrical housing for the motor/fan and a tapered section for the heating element.

The shape of each element of the hairdryer (e.g. buttons, nozzle and handle) must work in harmony with all the other aspects to give a product that is aesthetically pleasing overall. However, each element has its own shape requirements. For instance, when designing the handle, the designer must apply anthropometric data to ensure that the product will fit comfortably into the hand, and that the user can reach to adjust the buttons with ease. When considering ease of use, the designer might choose textured materials for the grip or incorporate colour-coded buttons to make the product easier to understand.

Colour

Colour is usually the first detail that the eye notices. Colour choice is a very personal preference and particular colours can affect people in different ways. To appeal to a wider market, some products are available in a variety of colours and product colours can be updated frequently in line with fashion trends.

Colour, used correctly in product design, can help to bring a product to life, help us understand how it works (such as in colour coding; a green button for 'on') or even evoke an emotional response.

Colour theory is important in product design. We automatically respond to colours on an almost subliminal level, learning the meaning of colours without even realising it. For example, we interpret a red flashing light on a product as a warning light or low-battery signal, without even looking at a manual or the instructions. This strong psychological link between colours and emotions means that designers can use colour purposefully.

To encourage an emotional connection to the product, these aspects of colour theory are used in design:

- **Black** is the colour of authority and power (also of death in most cultures). It is stylish and timeless, always in fashion.
- **White** is the colour of innocence and purity. It reflects light and is also considered to be timeless. It works well with every other colour. It is said to be neutral, blank and plain. White is often used in design, however it shows dirt and is difficult to keep clean.
- **Red** is the colour of love, heat and passion. It is often used in products which are bold, to make a statement. However, it is also the colour of risk and danger, and signifies 'stop', which can bring negative associations.
- **Pink** is a romantic color, which creates a sense of calm and serenity. It is feminine and youthful, with a sense of softness and delicacy.
- **Blue** represents open space, sea, air and sky, bringing peace and tranquility. But blue can also be sad and cold. Darker tones of blue are stronger; they represent trust, and signify loyalty and security. Navy blue represents rules and regulations.
- **Green** symbolises nature, safety and hygiene. It is the colour that is easiest on the eye. Hospitals often use green because it is a calming colour. Green is often positive; it is the colour of 'go' and 'on', but is can also represent jealousy.
- **Yellow** is an attention grabber that lifts moods, encourages focus and promotes positivity. Used correctly, it is uplifting and happy; however, bright yellow products can cause tempers to flare and babies to cry! Writing pads come in yellow as the colour can increase creative thought, but is the most difficult colour for the eye.
- **Purple** is the colour of royalty, luxury, wealth, and sophistication. It is soothing and calming, which boosts imagination and creativity. It can be both hot and cold.
- **Brown** is the color of earth and is abundant in nature. It is a natural colour, which represents simplicity and dependability. Brown products seem organic and wholesome, creating stability and grounding.
- **Orange** is the colour of energy, warmth and flamboyance. Its association with citrus fruit makes links with health and wellbeing. It has strength, but is also fun.

Red is a colour associated with love but it can also be associated with danger.

This coat rack uses colour to brighten the product. The flip-out hooks are painted in a rainbow of colours to bring a childish tone to the aesthetic, while the white panel helps to balance the variety of colours.

Material

All materials have unique characteristics of colour, texture, pattern, form and quality. Walnut, for example, is an expensive hardwood with a very complex wood grain and is sometimes used in car dashboards to give a luxurious finish. It can be varnished or lacquered to make it glossy and shiny, to match the interior of the car.

This stainless-steel worktop has a hard and sterile appearance, but is shiny and hygienic. This makes it functional in a professional kitchen.

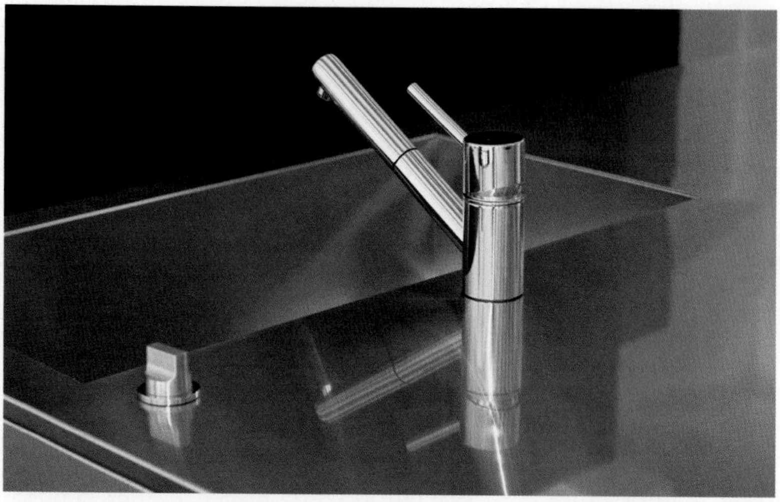

Make the Link

Select a material which is both fit for purpose and aesthetically suited to the design by researching material properties in Chapter 7.

Varnishing is a functional way of showing the natural grain of wood and protecting the material from wear. Without a suitable finish, most materials change appearance and can decay over time. It is, therefore, important to consider whether a finish, such as wax, paint, varnish or oil in the case of wood, is necessary to prolong or enhance the aesthetic qualities of the material.

Texture

The **texture** of a product describes the surface qualities of a material, which we experience through touch and sight. We may be drawn towards products with particular textures. As with colour, our preference for texture is a personal choice. Some people may prefer a soft, upholstered fabric armchair, while others prefer the smooth, shiny surface of leather.

Texture is used to ensure the comfort of the user, to enhance the aesthetics of the product or to assist the user in its operation. Sections of a product may have contrasting textures – to highlight operating controls, for example. In the case of the oven shown below, the ridged texture of the controls contrasts against the smooth shiny metal, making the buttons stand out.

Modern manufacturing methods can achieve such a high level of intricate detail that it is possible for a texture to be imprinted onto products or components during the manufacturing process. Products may have raised patterns, shapes or a company's logo imprinted on them.

Make the Link

Materials must be matched to manufacturing methods. Bear in mind that it may be difficult to achieve intricate shapes or details with some materials.

Make the Link

When considering ergonomics, designers often use texture to enhance grip. The designer should also consider the appearance of the texture to ensure it is styled to match the product.

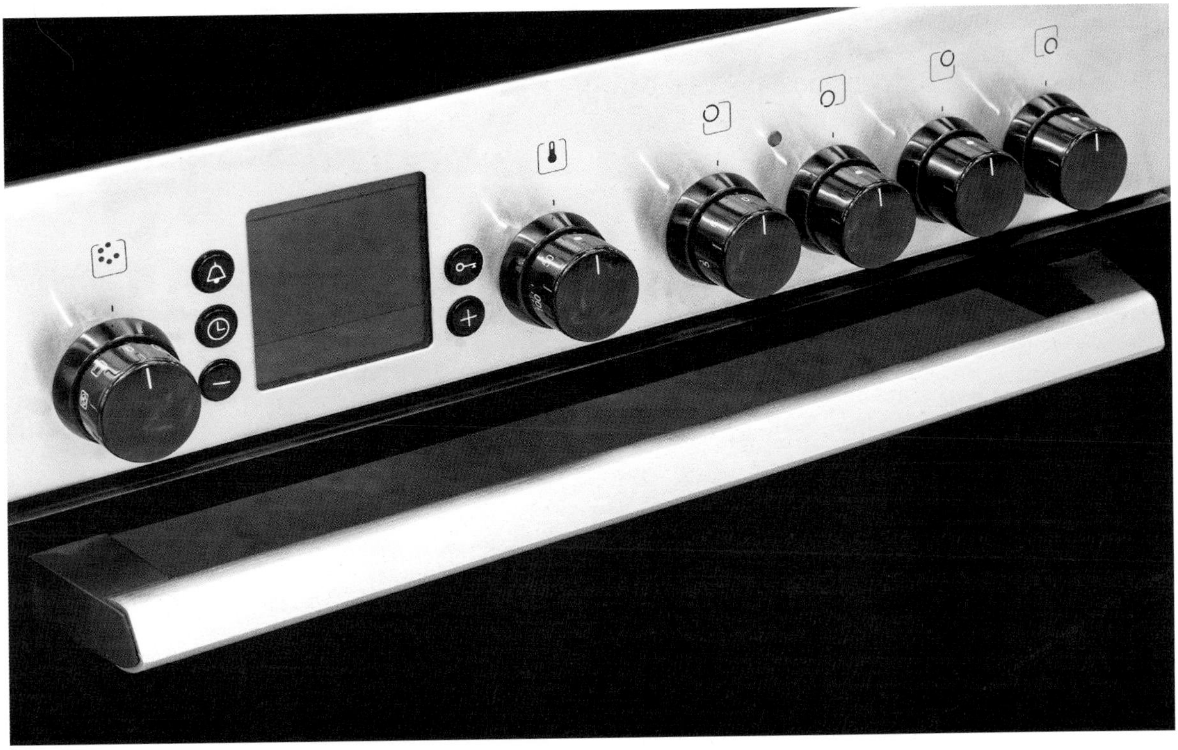

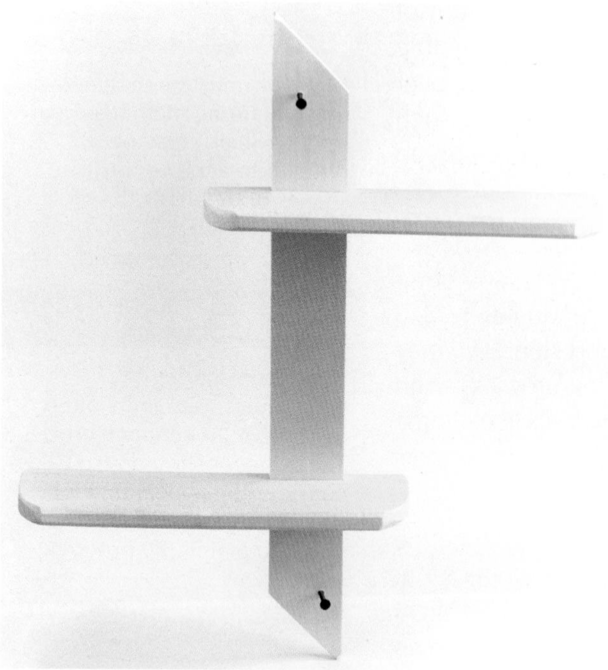

Proportion

The proportion of a product is the scale and size of the product, or the relative sizes and placement of the product parts. When all parts are in harmony with each other, they create unity in the aesthetic of the product.

In this asymmetric wall shelf, the proportion is well balanced: both of the shelves are the same length, and the width and thickness of the wood is the same throughout. The holes for the wall fixings are offset, but – as they are the same distance from the edges of the material – they are well placed proportionally. This wall shelf shows that design does not need to be symmetrical to be proportional.

Test your knowledge

Link to suggested answers
www.leckieandleckie.co.uk/tykanswers

Aesthetics

The pencil sharpener desk tidy shown on the right is designed to hold pens and pencils, while keeping your desk looking organised.

1. Describe the aesthetic qualities of the pencil sharpener desk tidy in terms of:

a) shape

b) proportion.

2. Describe **two** ways in which colour could improve the aesthetic of the pencil sharpener desk tidy.

3. Describe **two** ways in which the materials enhance the aesthetic of the pencil sharpener desk tidy.

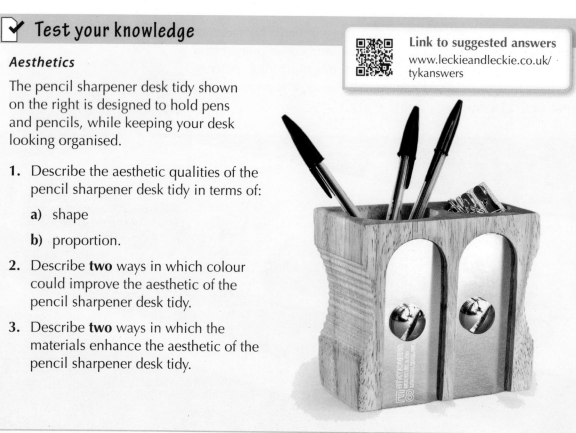

Harmony and contrast

A harmonious product is one that is well balanced and gives a calm feeling. It has soothing textures, proportions, materials or colours and a neutral aesthetic. Products made from one material and in one all-over colour can also create this sense of calm and comfort.

A product which has contrast is one which involves opposite textures, materials or colours. It is designed to draw your attention to a particular part of the product or to make the design stand out.

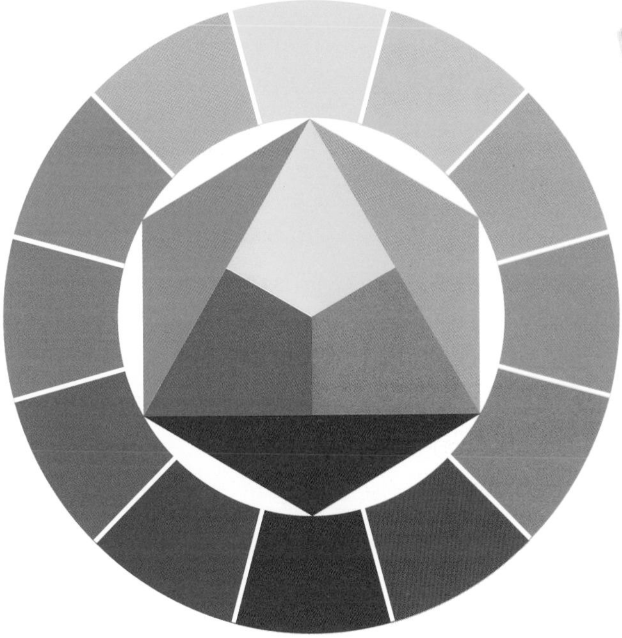

The colour wheel can be used to select harmonising colours. These are the colours which are directly beside each other. It can also be used to select contrasting colours. These are the colours which are directly opposite each other.

This chair uses contrasting shapes and materials, which give it a unique style.

This sofa, in shades of green, has a sense of harmony in its colour scheme.

Hint

To find out which products are currently fashionable, look at home-decoration magazines, store catalogues and in stores.

Fashion

Fashion changes over time and describes, at a particular moment, the current styles, colours, shapes, textures and technologies in our clothes, products, homes, and in many other areas of our lives. Fashion is popular, up to date, fresh and original. It can signify culture, gender, age and values. To many people, it is a way of communicating the essence of their personality. Fashion is a way of stating a social identity and being fashionable meets the basic human need to belong.

It is easy to associate fashion with clothes. However, the products we use go through different fashion trends too. The world of furniture design, for example, has its own fashion shows, called trade shows, where high-street homeware brands snoop to quickly copy high-end designs at a lower cost, much as high-street clothes brands do.

Ergonomics

Ergonomics is about the way that humans interact with products. An ergonomic product will be comfortable to use and will not cause you any injuries or strain when using it. Also, it will not be too loud or make you feel upset.

An ergonomic product is:

- comfortable during use
- easy to use
  - simple to understand
  - easy to lift, twist, push, pull, etc.
  - easy to grip or hold onto
  - straightforward to maintain or repair
- safe to use.

The most obvious ergonomically designed products are adjustable chairs, any product with buttons or controls and anything with a handle shaped to fit fingers. However, most products have been designed with some ergonomic consideration.

A basic pen has many obvious ergonomic design factors. It is long enough to fit your hand width, the diameter of the pen makes it easy to hold, there may be a texture or shape that makes it easy to grip, and the lid probably has a different texture or design feature that makes it easy to feel the difference between the two parts and remove the lid without too much concentration.

A stepladder has a number of ergonomic considerations which make it accessible for a wide range of people.

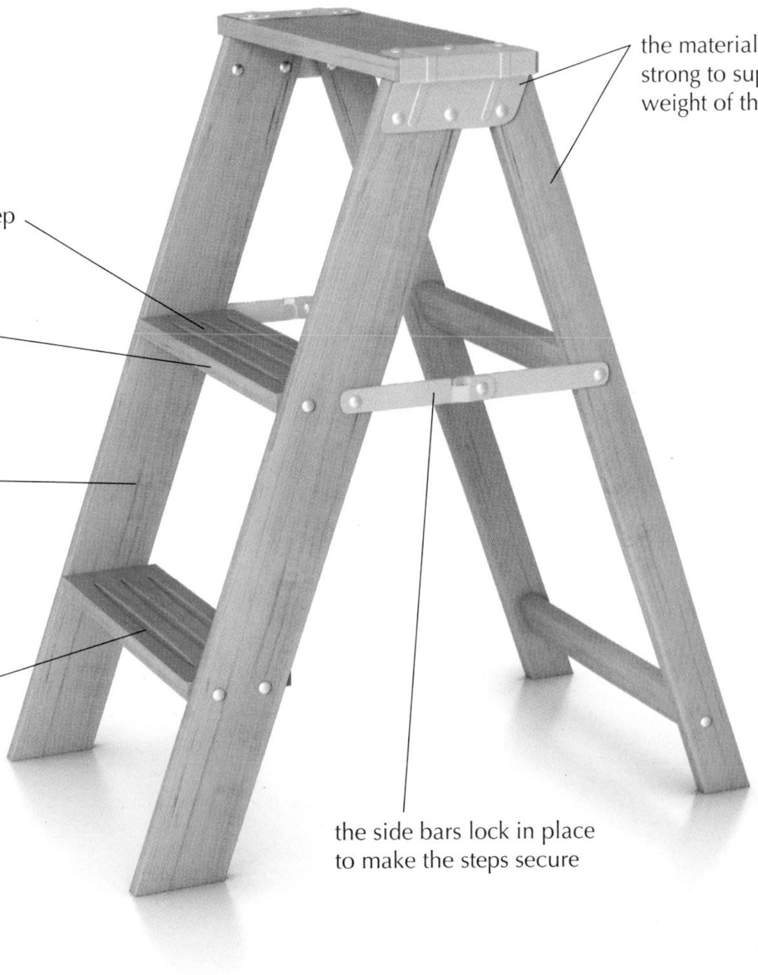
the materials used are strong to support the weight of the user
the width of each step is sized for two feet
the depth of each step is sized to fit the ball of the foot
the distance between the steps is spaced for easy climbing
the surface of the steps are grooved to provide extra grip
the side bars lock in place to make the steps secure

Ergonomic designs can sometimes be quite ugly but are usually very comfortable to use. Computer chairs, for example, have lots of adjustment levers, plastic casing and padding which don't always look aesthetically pleasing. However, they are far more comfortable to use for long periods of time than a basic plastic chair.

Understanding how humans interact with products

Looking at the way in which a product will be used can help you to understand which sizes are important for its design. When designing a kettle, hand size data will be useful to size the handle.

Anthropometric data changes over time as human behaviour changes. The foods we eat, how healthy we are, our level of physical activity and the physical challenges we face each day have changed greatly compared to 100 years ago.

The culture or race of a person can influence anthropometrics. For example, Japanese people are smaller in height. This difference in human sizes means international companies must develop adjustable products or, perhaps, even manufacture an alternative size for a foreign market.

Colour is also important in ergonomics. Products can be colour coded to influence users or communicate something in a split second, perhaps even without the user realising it.

Age and ability can also influence anthropometrics. Big button phones are designed for elderly, disabled and visually impaired people to make calls more easily, as they have extra large, high-visibility buttons that are comfortable to use.

Anthropometrics

To design a product which is comfortable to use, human sizes such as height, arm length, thumb size, etc. need to be researched. The study of human measurements is called **anthropometrics**.

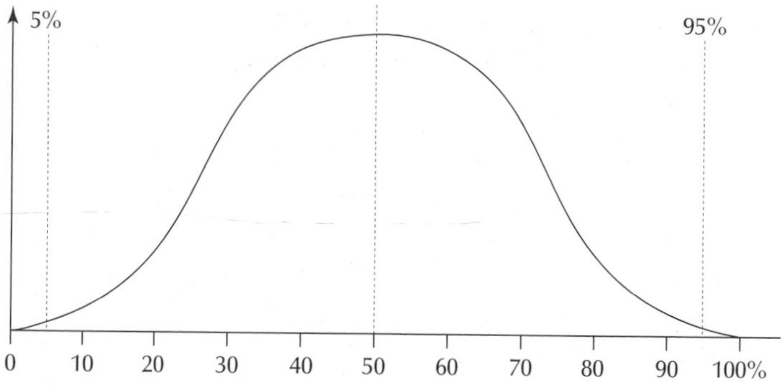

Measurements of human dimensions can be presented in a graph. This graph is called the **normal distribution curve**, or simply the **bell curve**. In the very centre of the graph is the 50th percentile, which is the most common size. This may be the average hand span, the average hip width or even the average size of a big toe.

The 0 to 5th and 95th to 100th **percentiles** are the less common and most extreme human sizes. Below the 5th percentile are the extremely small human dimensions, while above the 95th percentile are the extremely large human dimensions. Generally, designers do not design products for these extreme human dimensions, as there are very few people in this range. Accounting for these dimensions can make products too big and uncomfortable for the majority of users.

So, designers usually design products that suit 90% of the population. This is cost effective as it means products will meet the needs of the majority of people. The remaining 10% of the population may require to make adjustments and adaptations to the product, or may even require a specialist product. Designing to incorporate the needs of this group adds unnecessary cost for a limited return in sales.

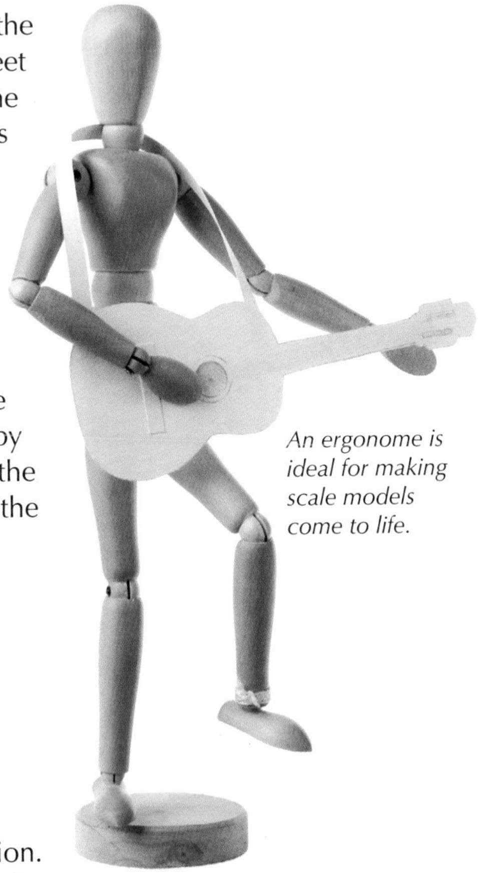

An ergonome is ideal for making scale models come to life.

Ergonome

An **ergonome** is a small, scaled-down human model which is used with scale models to test the size of products. If the ergonome is 1:10 then the model dimensions are divided by 10 to make a model which suits the ergonome. Then the ergonome can be placed next to or on the model to test the dimensions of the product.

Make the Link

Use ergonomes to communicate your designs in 3D.

Establishing critical sizes

Products should be able to be used by 90% of the population. When selecting the best sizes it is wrong to always design for the 50th percentile.

For example, designing a door for the 50th percentile would mean that 50% of the population could not use the door with ease, as they would be too tall. The same door, designed for the 100th percentile (the whole population), would mean that buildings would have to be much taller. This would have an impact on the overall cost of building.

To establish the most important sizes for the product you are designing, you should consider:

- the target market
- the function
- safety
- comfort
- ease of use.

Hint

Consider the length, breadth, thickness and weight of all the component parts of your design to make the product a suitable size.

Test your knowledge

Link to suggested answers
www.leckieandleckie.co.uk/tykanswers

Anthropometrics

Games controllers are designed with human sizes in mind.

1. State the meaning of the term 'anthropometric data'.
2. Explain how the following anthropometric data has been applied to make the design of the games controller comfortable to use:
   a) thumb length
   b) hand length.
3. State and justify the percentile range which would be used when selecting anthropometric data for the games controller.

Hint

Human physiology determines the key physical movements that are studied in ergonomics: pushing, pulling, twisting, turning, lifting, grabbing, gripping, holding, pressing, squeezing, etc.

Physiology

Products must meet the capabilities of the human body and so designers must understand physical ability as we all have limitations when it comes to pushing, pulling, twisting, turning and lifting. This is called **physiology**. Take a sports drinking bottle for example. It should be designed in such a way that any person can easily twist the top to open it. Everyone has a different set of hands but the bottle should be easy for any shape and size of hand to grip and lift it.

Repetitive actions, such as pressing the button on a power drill many times, can cause muscle fatigue in your hands and fingers. Ideally, use of products should not cause muscle strain or mental tiredness, which is known to reduce reaction/response times.

Psychology

Psychology is the study of the human mind and behaviour. Designers must understand human behaviour to design appropriate products. For example, we are naturally sensitive to noise, temperature and light. Extremes of any of these aspects could make a product uncomfortable, difficult or even impossible to use.

Product psychology can also influence our use of a product – it can help us to understand how the product operates. Successful products are usually straightforward, as users understand them and are confident in their use. Clever design can help the user to trust products, by making them look strong, durable or sturdy. For example, the wheels on a skateboard are chunky and, therefore, look robust.

We interact with colour coding of products every day. We know that the blue tap is cold and the red button is off. The human brain is trained subconsciously over time to automatically recognise colours. Use of a contrasting colour can be used to indicate a different feature or function of a product.

While many products can make you feel happy or make tasks easier, overly complicated products are frustrating. Understanding how to operate a new product can be confusing, especially when it comes to technology. Complicated products can also be intimidating, making the user feel nervous about using them. For a product to be successful, it must be simple to use.

Hint

Designers must consider how the product will make the user *feel*.

Make the Link

Adding **texture** to a product can make it more appealing to the human eye. Sometimes it makes us want to reach out to touch products. It can also give a sense of reassurance. Textured bike handles give a feeling of added security through their grip. A textured surface can also send a subconscious signal to your brain to interact with a product, such as indentations on a button for pressing, knurling on a handle for gripping or ridges on a plastic bottle top for twisting it off.

If a first aid box was pink, would it feel reliable? If a vitamin C packet was grey, would it look as if it were good for you? Would you eat this blue apple?

Activity

Product psychology and physiology

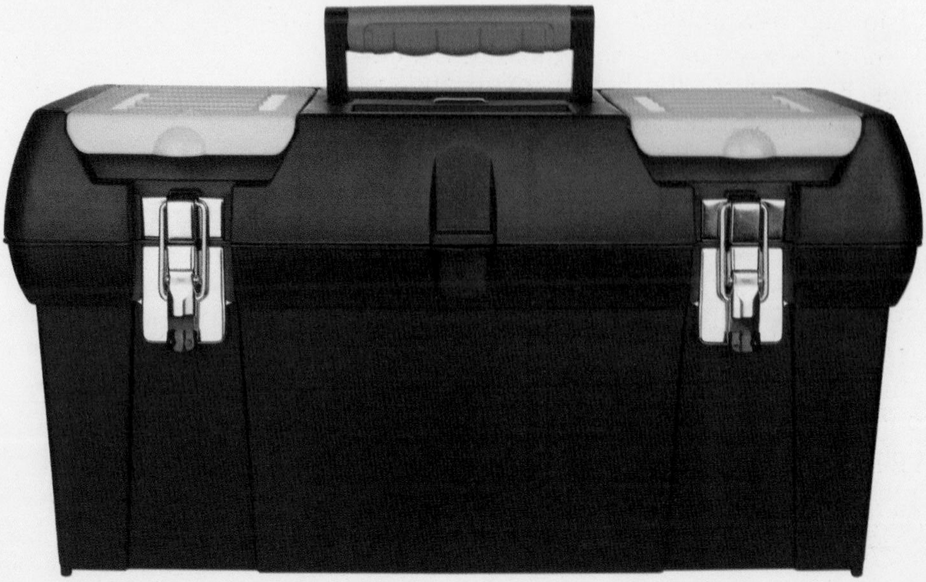

1. Describe how psychology has influenced the design of the tool box in terms of:
   a) function
   b) colour
   c) texture.
2. Describe how physiology has influenced the design of the tool box in terms of:
   a) opening
   b) closing
   c) lifting.

Health and safety

All designers have a responsibility to design products that are safe. Designers, engineers and manufacturers work with regulations which are laid down by law to ensure that we are not injured or even killed by the products we use.

Manufacturers declare that their products are safe and meet the required **standards and regulations** by labeling their products with the BSI (British Standards Institution), ISO (International Standards Organisation) and CE (Conformité Européenne or European Conformity) logos.

Products are tested to make sure that they meet the required standards. For example, a child's remote controlled helicopter must not have any mechanical or physical hazards.

The three main categories of safety breaches are strains, injuries and death.

- **Strains** – usually caused by overuse of a badly designed product. This is called a repetitive strain injury (RSI). Occasionally, new products can cause instant strain, and these must be 'worn in' to make them comfortable. Careful ergonomic consideration during designing should prevent strains. However, even the most ergonomically designed products can cause strains if they are overused, such as bike handles causing strains on long cycle journeys.
- **Injuries** – can mean a hospital visit for a plaster cast, stitches or even surgery. Products which cause injuries are recalled to avoid further injury or legal action. Poor material choices, badly assembled components or loose fixings can cause products to fail, resulting in an injury to the user. Not all products are to blame for injuries. A deliberately misused product can easily cause an injury, such as an adult falling off a child's swing.
- **Death** – products which contain chemicals, have blades or electrical parts are most likely to cause death. Some people may have life-threatening allergies to commonly occurring chemicals.

Safety design considerations

When designing, avoid:

- Small removable parts, which children can swallow
- Any sharp blades, jaggy edges or spikes
- Finishes which are poisonous, such as toxic paint
- Traps where your fingers can get stuck
- Exposed electronic components or wires
- Your discomfort; using the product should not cause you any strain

These logos act as a reassurance to consumers and allow companies to sell their products in Europe.

Activity

Prioritising design factors

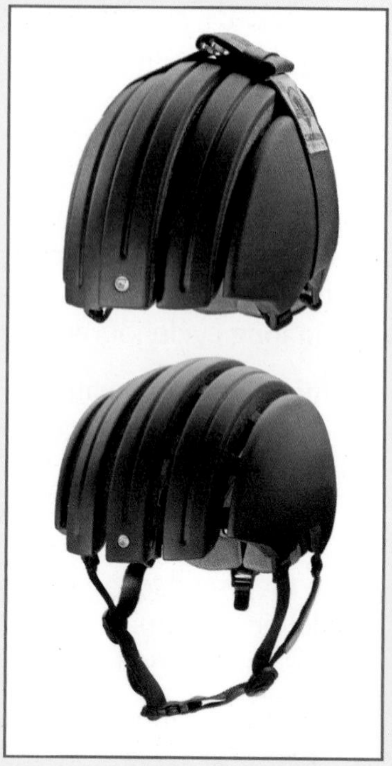

1. Research folding helmets online.
2. State the benefits which folding helmets have over standard helmets.
3. Explain how the following design factors have influenced the design of the folding helmet in terms of:
   - function
   - performance
   - market
   - aesthetics
   - ergonomics.
4. Copy and complete the diagram below. Rank the factors in order of importance, in your opinion, from the top down to the least important factor at the bottom.

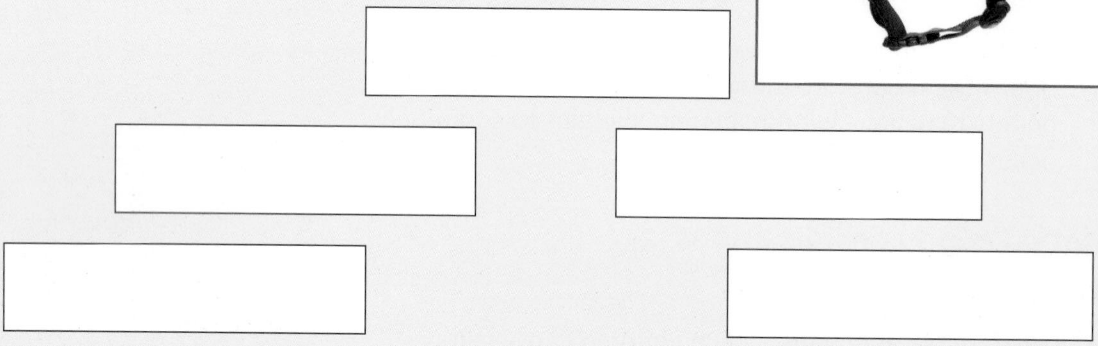

Make the Link

One design factor can have more importance than the others, depending on the product.

Hint

To sustain something is to make it last as long as it possibly can. Sustainability is considering the Earth, and all its natural resources, as the most important thing to sustain.

Environmental considerations in design

Alongside the five factors which influence design, designers must also consider the environmental impact of design and how it influences society.

As designers shape our world and influence our lifestyles, they are environmentally responsible for the products they design. They must ensure that products either work in harmony with our environment or positively add to it in their use and in their disposal.

Sustainability

A sustainable product is one which is designed to have minimal negative impact on the environment; it does not use finite resources, cause pollution or damage the Earth. Its manufacture takes account of the social aspects of production in that it does not damage the natural habitat to source the materials and it is not produced by people working in exploitative conditions.

Make the Link

Sustainable manufacturing and sustainable materials.

Hint

A sustainable product supports the world's sensitive natural ecosystem.

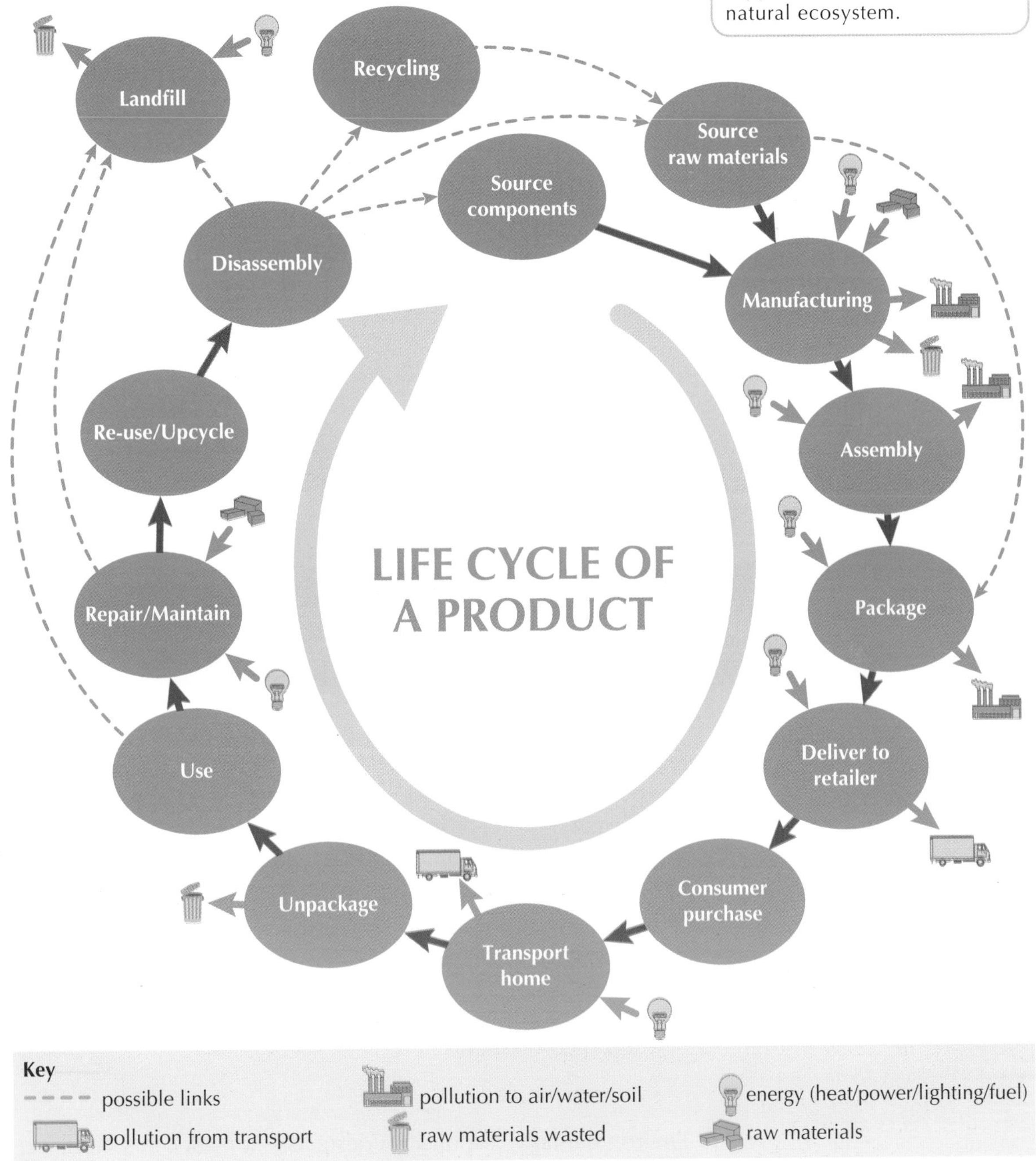

There are many stages in the life cycle of a product which can impact on the environment, from the pollution caused by the transportation of the materials to the factory, to the packaging of the product that is disposed of in landfill.

While it is difficult to ensure that a product is made from sustainable materials, is sustainably manufactured, is sustainably packaged, is sustainably transported and is subject to sustainable disposal, efforts must be made to try to reduce the environmental impact of the product.

Make the Link

Clean manufacturing, explained in Chapter 7, requires a sustainable approach to manufacturing and the use of sustainable materials.

Hint

To sustain something is to make it last as long as it possibly can. Sustainability is considering the Earth and all its natural resources, so that these resources last for future generations.

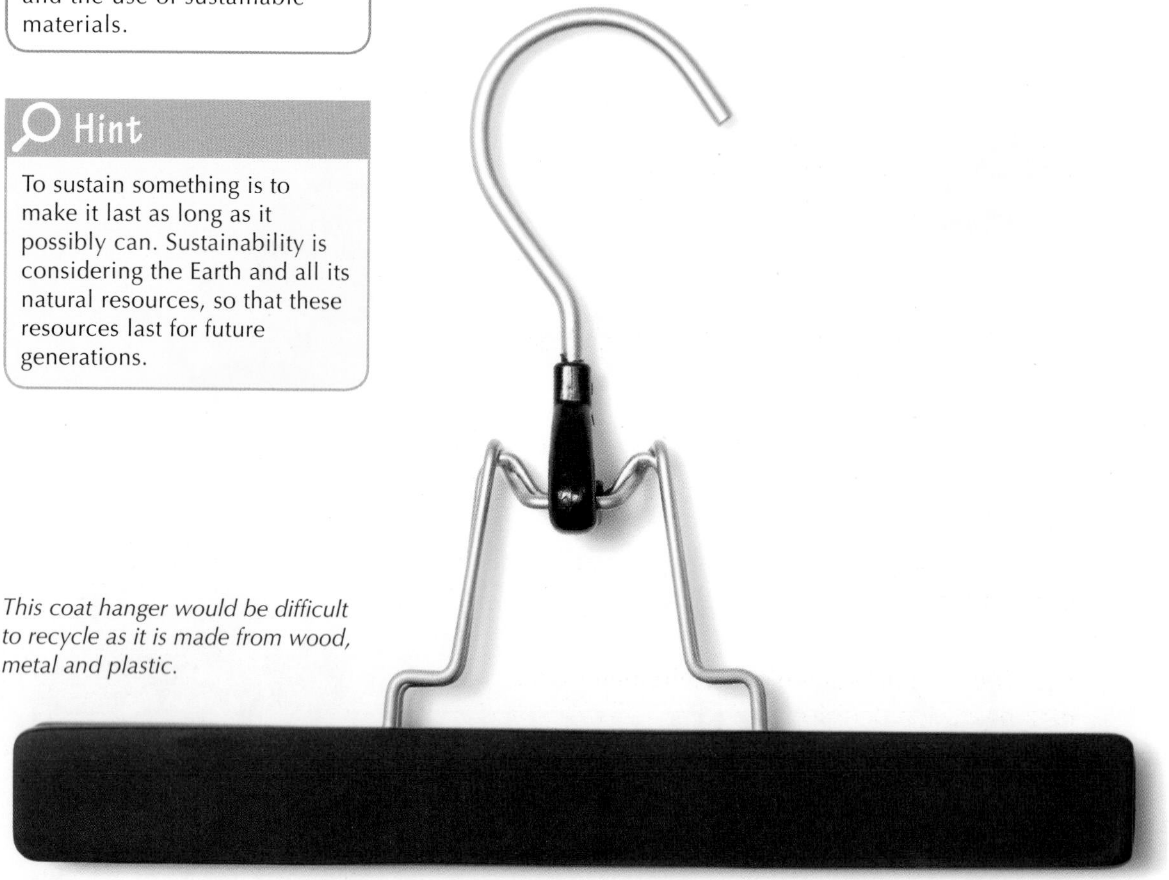

This coat hanger would be difficult to recycle as it is made from wood, metal and plastic.

Cradle-to-cradle design

At the end of a product's life, the sustainable approach is to recycle the product or its components. However, many products are difficult to take apart and some materials cannot be recycled. **Cradle-to-cradle design** means that products are designed to be:

- easily maintained and repaired
- made from recyclable or reusable materials and components
- disassembled.

Environmentally responsible designers consider this cradle-to-crade approach during the development of the design and products can receive certification if they meet these standards.

Check your progress

I can:	HELP NEEDED	GETTING THERE	CONFIDENT
• describe design activities	⬭	⬭	⬭
• explain the ways in which the function of a product influences its design	⬭	⬭	⬭
• explain the ways in which the performance of a product influences its design	⬭	⬭	⬭
• explain the ways in which the marketing of a product influences its design	⬭	⬭	⬭
• explain the ways in which the aesthetic of a product influences its design	⬭	⬭	⬭
• explain the ways in which the ergonomics of a product influences its design	⬭	⬭	⬭
• describe the importance of sustainability when making design decisions.	⬭	⬭	⬭

3 Evaluating products

By the end of this chapter you should be able to:

- state what makes products suitable for evaluation
- explain different evaluation methods
- state suitable evaluation methods for evaluating a product
- explain the purpose of creating a strategy for evaluation
- describe the results of the evaluation
- state the purpose of the conclusion.

Product evaluation

A **product evaluation** is carried out to gain a deeper understanding of a product. Through evaluation, a designer can obtain valuable information about a product, which they can then apply when designing to bring an improved product to the market. For example, a designer may wish to find out more about folding bicycles before they begin to design one. They would find out how to operate folding bicycles, which parts wear out first, what safety risks they have, what styles or colours are popular, what size it should fold down to, etc.

Evaluation approach

Throughout the product evaluation, you must collect evidence of your evaluation work and the results that you found, even if your results were inconclusive. Your research should be real and you must have evidence to prove that it was carried out, such as photographs, a video, a written record, copies of questionnaires etc. When completing your evaluation, your research must be meaningful. Before you start, decide the purpose of each evaluation method, think about what you want to find out. To ensure that your research is valid follow the flow-of-work approach shown below.

Flow of work

The flow of a good product evaluation should be clear.

Select: Firstly you must select a product to evaluate. You may require some help to choose one.

↓

Plan: Plan the strategy for your evaluation – identify your design factors, methods of evaluation and evaluation aims. State what your research aims to find out.

↓

Evaluate: Complete your evaluation of the product.

↓

Present: Gather the information and present it in a way that makes it easy for someone else to understand your evaluation.

↓

Conclude: Reflect on the project and outline the findings to sum up your evaluation.

Make the Link

English – Writing a report.

Science – Completing an experiment and writing up the results.

Art – Evaluating the work of designers and artists.

Selecting a product to evaluate

There are some important considerations when planning a product evaluation, such as equipment and test subjects. For example, if you plan to evaluate a bicycle pump, you will also need a bicycle tyre; if you plan to evaluate a child's toy you will need to get parental permission for a child to help you. Some questions to ask yourself are:

- Who is the target market? Can someone from the target market help me test the product?
- What is the price of the product (cheap, mid or high priced)?
- Is the product available to me? Where can I get the product from?
- When is the product used? What type of environment it is used in?
- Does it need particular working conditions (dark, cold)?
- Why do people use it? Is the function of the product easy to understand? Do I know how to use it?

Consider these thoughts when you choose a product:

Simple yet interesting products

It is important that you select a product which you will be interested in for the duration of the project. A good product to evaluate has many design features. Small but detailed products can be just as interesting as large products.

Products which have few design features are difficult and boring to evaluate, such as certain electronic devices with one button. They offer less scope for your project and do not provide much opportunity to demonstrate your evaluation skills. Talk to your teacher to check that your product is not too simple for this project.

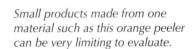

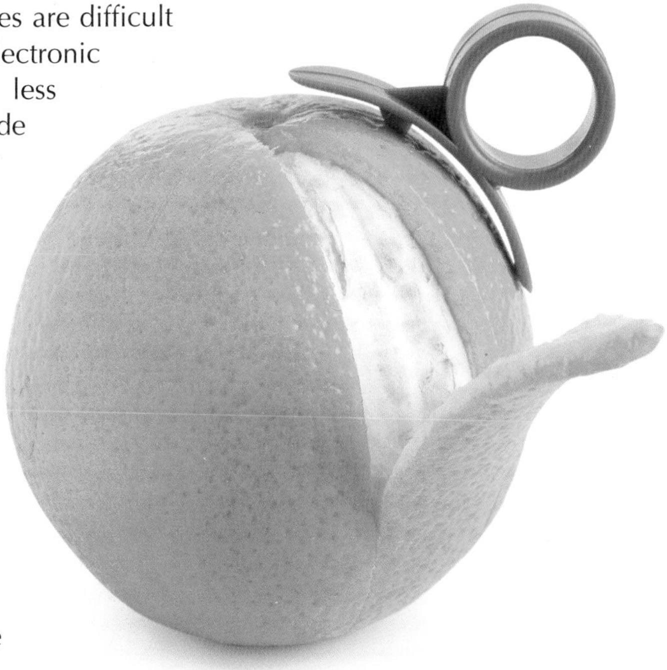

Small products made from one material such as this orange peeler can be very limiting to evaluate.

Collecting evidence

To carry out a realistic evaluation and collect evidence, you must have the product to hand. Useful things to gather include:

- the **receipt** – to remember the price and where you bought it
- the **packaging** – as it may include important information
- **instructions** – for assembly or use
- additional **resources** – for example cheese to evaluate a cheese grater
- **power sources** – batteries, cables, etc
- any other things that are needed to operate the product and clean up after use.

It is also useful to write down any first impressions you have about the product. The first impression a product gives is important but it can be easy to forget.

How to present the product evaluation

The product evaluation includes a range of information and evidence. There may be written, oral, graphic and practical work, such as:

- a written report with images, diagrams and other information
- a prepared presentation with a slideshow
- a digital story
- a recorded presentation
- a blog recording the evaluation activities
- sketches and annotated diagrams
- tables, graphs and charts of information.

Strategy for evaluation

A strategy is a **plan of action** which is made *before* the evaluation activities take place. Having a strategy gives a clear framework for your evaluation project and helps others understand your work.

A strategy for evaluation should include:

- the factors to be evaluated
- the specific questions/statements that will be evaluated within each factor (these are the evaluation aims, page 64)
- the evaluation methods that will be used.

Link to example Strategy for evaluation
www.leckieandleckie.co.uk/evaluationstrategy

Design factor	Evaluation aims	Evaluation method	Presentation method
Performance	Is the screen durable enough to withstand constant use? Is the casing durable enough to withstand being dropped? How long does the battery charge last?	Consumer reviews	Screen shots of consumer reviews
Ergonomics	Can it be used with one hand? Are the buttons a suitable size for pressing? Is it easy to understand how to use it? Does the touch screen require a lot of pressure to operate it?	Observation	Storyboard of photographs
Function	How many songs can it hold? How is it recharged? Can it link to a cloud to backup files? Does it have Bluetooth?	Comparison to specifications and standards Using the internet to research facts	Screen shots of internet pages and scanned text/images from product leaflet
Market	Does the colour appeal to a teenage/young adult target market? Is the MP3 player priced for the target market to afford it? What features of the MP3 player appeal most to the target market? What features of the MP3 player do the target market not use?	Survey	Questions with responses shown in graphs

STRATEGY FOR EVALUATION

More than one evaluation method can be used for each design factor, as shown here. In this strategy for evaluation a pupil plans to evaluate the function of an MP3 player using a 'Comparison to Specifications and Standards' *while also* 'using the internet to research facts'.

Depending on the product, you may find that there are some evaluation methods which do not work with certain evaluation factors. It takes careful consideration to match the method to the factor.

At the point of planning, you should consider evaluating production methods, materials and sustainability in relation to your product. However, you may unexpectedly discover information relating to these aspects during the evaluation and this information can be included if it supports the evaluation aims.

Hint

Keep it simple by using just one or two methods per factor.

Evaluating with the factors which influence design

Once you have chosen a product to evaluate, the next step in planning is to identify the factors which influence its design. This can be done by examining the features of your product – work out the purpose of each feature and think about what design factors relate to that feature.

Orla Kiely is an Irish textile designer. Her distinctive retro and geometrical patterns are popular around the world.

Features	Consideration	Evaluation factor
Lid	Water and tea bag must go in	Function
Spout	Tea must come out	Function
Container	Must hold tea	Function
Handle	Hand must fit	Ergonomics
Balance	Must be easy to pour	Ergonomics
Retro pattern	Interesting style	Aesthetics
Ceramic	Must be strong	Materials
Microwave / dishwasher safe	Heat-resistant material	Performance

Whether you use this method or have another approach, take some time to decide which factors to include in your product evaluation. Try to ensure that your evaluation can investigate a breadth of different design factors with a good depth of investigation in each area.

This toothbrush holder is an excellent product for an evaluation. However, some factors would be difficult to evaluate. For example, as the user interacts mostly with the *toothbrush* (not the *holder*), ergonomics, specifically anthropometrics, could not be evaluated in great depth.

Tips for selecting evaluation factors:

- Make sure that the factors are distinctly different from each other.
- Work on your own (your classmates probably don't have the same product as you).
- Consider your own experience of using the product.
- Look at all the features of the product.
- Find out the unique selling points of the product compared to other similar products.

Evaluation aims

The next step is to make a list of evaluation aims to explore for each design factor. This is a way of showing that the correct design factors and evaluation aims have been selected, and of justifying the selection.

- The evaluation aims may be a **list of questions** to be answered such as: *'Does the red button stand out on the product?'* The research could then investigate whether differently coloured buttons would stand out more.
- Alternatively, the evaluation aims may be given as a **set of statements** to be qualified such as: *The red button stands out*. The research could then be conducted to prove that the point is correct.

Either way the research has a purpose!

Hint

If you have spent a lot of time on one factor and are still finding the evaluation very difficult, perhaps you have selected the wrong factor to use in your evaluation.

When evaluating a garlic press, an obvious factor to select is ergonomics. The key evaluation aims for the ergonomics of a garlic press are shown below.

Ergonomics of the garlic press

- Does the thickness of the handle fit an average hand?
- Is the shape of the handle comfortable for the average person's hand to hold?
- Can the garlic press be easily closed to crush the garlic?
- Is the garlic press easily opened for cleaning?
- Does the garlic press have any texture on it to offer more grip?
- Is it clear where to put the garlic and how to use the product?

When presenting your work, you may wish to group your research points by design factor, as shown in the example below.

Link to example Evalution by design factor
www.leckieandleckie.co.uk/designfactor

Evaluation strategy

To evaluate the potato peeler, I have considered the **aesthetic, functional, safety** and **ergonomic** features. I will research the following statements in my product evaluation:

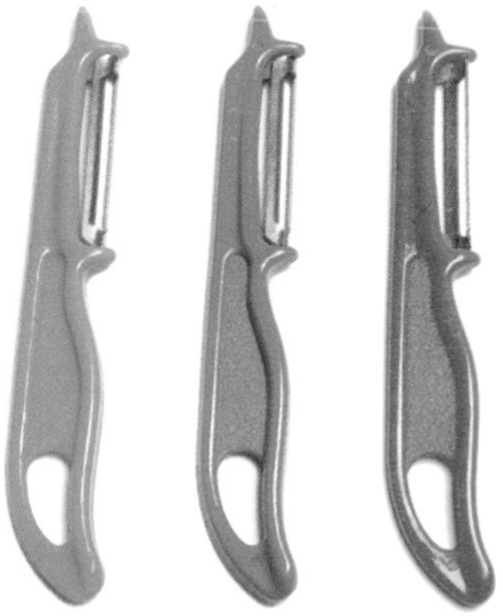

Aesthetics – consumer reviews

- The style of the potato peeler is suitable for a wide target market.
- It is available in a variety of colours.
- The quality of the materials used for the blade and handle look appealing to the target market.

Function – user trial

- The product peels potatoes.
- The product can be used to peel other vegetables.
- The tip of the blade can be used to remove potato eyes and sprouts.
- There is little or no maintenance required to keep this product working.
- The quality of the assembly allows the product to function without falling apart.

Performance – product testing /user trial

- The blade of the potato peeler does not become blunt with frequent use.
- The blade of the potato peeler does not rust with frequent cleaning.
- The material used for the handle is waterproof.
- The blade is assembled securely to the handle and will not fall out.

Ergonomics – survey

- Length of the handle fits the 95th percentile to suit the hand sizes of the target market.
- Shape of the handle is comfortable to hold by the target market.
- Weight of the potato peeler is easy to control.
- The potato peeler looks reliable and safe.
- The potato peeler is easy to twist to remove potato eyes and sprouts.

In this evaluation strategy a pupil has identified the evaluation aims for aesthetics, function, performance and ergonomics.

GO! Activity

Selecting evaluation factors for products

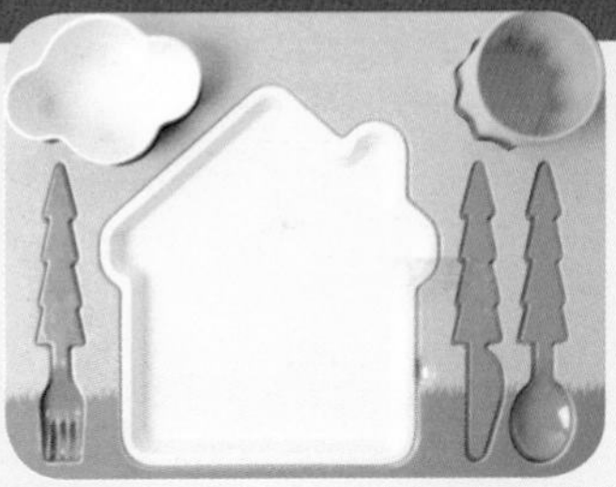

The Landscape Dinner Set takes inspiration from a child's drawing. It is made from melamine plastic, which is food and drink safe. It is aimed at children aged 12 months and over.

1. Copy and complete the table below.

Features	Consideration	Evaluation factor
		Market
Bright colours and shapes		
		Function
	Must be easy to clean	

2. Make a large copy of the diagram below. Complete the diagram using the design factors from the table in Question 1. Write **four** evaluation aims for each design factor.

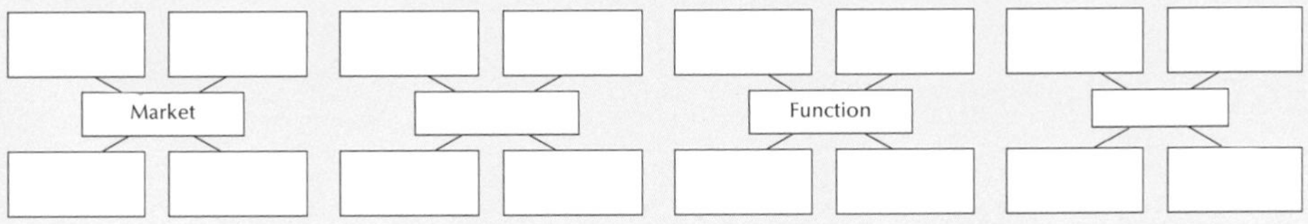

Methods of evaluation

There are certain ways to complete a thorough evaluation of a product. We call these **evaluation methods**.

The methods used are:

- Comparison to specifications and standards
- Consumer reviews
- User trial
- Survey
- Product testing
- Measuring and recording
- Using the internet to research facts

Try to use a broad range of these methods to gain firsthand experience of each evaluation method. This will help to strengthen your knowledge and understanding of each method.

> **Hint**
> Support your classmates by participating in their evaluations and gain skills in evaluation methods you may not be using yourself.

Comparison to specifications and standards

Comparing your product to a specification (sometimes found on the packaging or online) or comparing the standard of your product to other similar products will give you a better understanding of it. This method is ideal for evaluating economics or aesthetics. However, depending on your product choice, there are other factors which could be evaluated using this method.

> **Make the Link**
> Researching products when developing design concepts.

To carry out a comparison with other products, first find out the information for your own selected product. Then gather the same information about other similar products. When the comparision is finished, it should answer all the evaluation aims outlined in your evaluation strategy and it may also identify some other findings which will support your evaluation.

> **Hint**
> Use the internet, catalogues or, if you can, visit a shop to view similar products.

The 'Comparison to specifications and standards' can be presented as a collection of images with notes, a list of facts, a video diary or perhaps as a labelled drawing. It is important not to simply present a collection of images; remember to explain what the images prove.

Evaluating the function

Evaluation questions

1. Performance: is the cooking time quick compared to other products?
2. Durability: are the plates non-stick to allow continual use of the cupcake maker?
3. Ease of use: is a power/ready light a standard feature on cupcake makers?
4. Size: how many cupcakes can be made in the cupcake maker compared to similar products?

I am evaluating cupcake maker A. Three other cupcake makers were compared to A:

	Cupcake maker A	Cupcake maker B	Cupcake maker C	Cupcake maker D
Cost	£19.99	£17.50	£49.99	£59.99
Cooking time	7 minutes	3 minutes	12 minutes	10 minutes
Cooking capacity	6	7 (mini)	6	6
Power/ready lights	Yes	Yes	Yes	Yes
Non-stick plates	Yes	Yes	Yes	Yes

Evaluation results

1. **Performance**: the cooking time is quick compared to other products as it takes 7 minutes to cook a batch of products, whereas the more expensive products take up to 12 minutes.
2. **Durability**: the plates on all the cupcake makers are non-stick, which could potentially allow continual use of the cupcake maker as there would be no need to scrub off cake mixture.
3. **Ease of use:** the power/ready light is a standard feature on the cupcake makers I researched.
4. **Size:** my cupcake maker can make six cupcakes, which is the same amount as the two most expensive products I researched.

Consumer reviews

Consumer reviews are a written evaluation of a product, made by people who have used the product. Magazines often feature such reviews, of washing machines for example, to allow consumers to make informed choices regarding their purchases. These reviews may use star ratings, consumer comments and marks out of 10.

Consumer reviews are ideal for evaluating a variety of different aspects of a product. You can source your reviews from product-review websites or consumer magazines. Always give the name and date of the publication, or the web address and date of accessing the website, where your found the review. This is called the source.

Remember to explain what the consumer reviews prove – do they answer the evaluation aims which you set? Don't just present a page of reviews; include your own summary of the facts to show that you understand the information and that the reviews are relevant to your product evaluation.

Link to example Evaluation by function

www.leckieandleckie.co.uk/function

Hint

It is a good idea to use *italics* and "quotation marks" to show the reviews are not your own writing.

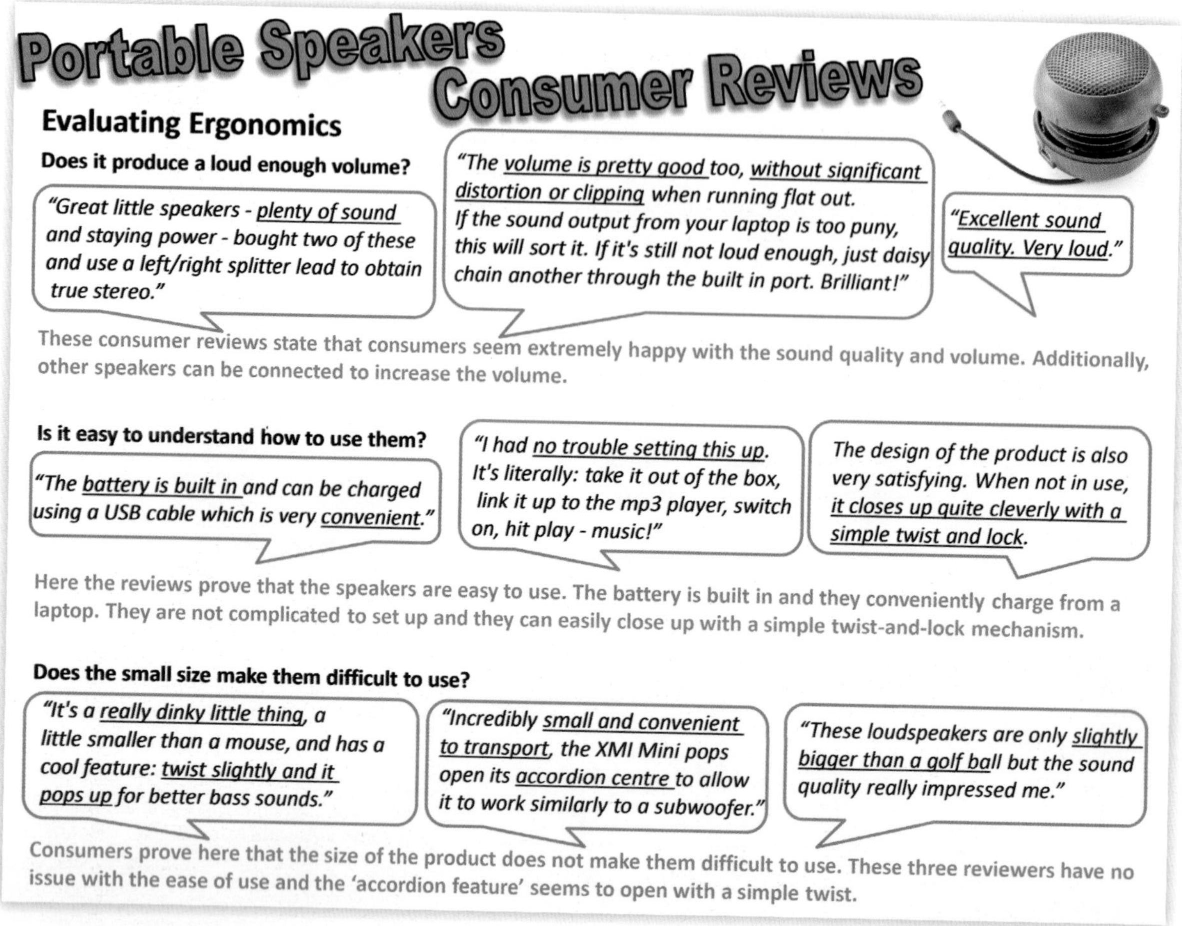

Portable Speakers Consumer Reviews

Evaluating Ergonomics

Does it produce a loud enough volume?

"Great little speakers - plenty of sound and staying power - bought two of these and use a left/right splitter lead to obtain true stereo."

"The volume is pretty good too, without significant distortion or clipping when running flat out. If the sound output from your laptop is too puny, this will sort it. If it's still not loud enough, just daisy chain another through the built in port. Brilliant!"

"Excellent sound quality. Very loud."

These consumer reviews state that consumers seem extremely happy with the sound quality and volume. Additionally, other speakers can be connected to increase the volume.

Is it easy to understand how to use them?

"The battery is built in and can be charged using a USB cable which is very convenient."

"I had no trouble setting this up. It's literally: take it out of the box, link it up to the mp3 player, switch on, hit play - music!"

The design of the product is also very satisfying. When not in use, it closes up quite cleverly with a simple twist and lock.

Here the reviews prove that the speakers are easy to use. The battery is built in and they conveniently charge from a laptop. They are not complicated to set up and they can easily close up with a simple twist-and-lock mechanism.

Does the small size make them difficult to use?

"It's a really dinky little thing, a little smaller than a mouse, and has a cool feature: twist slightly and it pops up for better bass sounds."

"Incredibly small and convenient to transport, the XMI Mini pops open its accordion centre to allow it to work similarly to a subwoofer."

"These loudspeakers are only slightly bigger than a golf ball but the sound quality really impressed me."

Consumers prove here that the size of the product does not make them difficult to use. These three reviewers have no issue with the ease of use and the 'accordion feature' seems to open with a simple twist.

Link to example Evaluation by consumer review

www.leckieandleckie.co.uk/consumerreview

User trial

A user trial can find out information about the way the product works and how the user interacts with it. A user trial is ideal for evaluating function, performance and ergonomics. There are also other factors which could be evaluated; again, this depends on the product.

Every time we use a product we subconsciously carry out a user trial. For example, when wearing a pair of earphones that keep falling out, we evaluate that *ergonomically* they are unsuitable and *economically* they were not worth the money. This is a basic user trial; to carry out a user trial in more depth requires planning and thought. A user trial can be used to investigate the product function in depth. For example, the suitability of the material in relation to the function can be researched and the physiological demands on the user could be researched in relation to ergonomics.

When evaluating the ergonomics of an upright vacuum cleaner, the user trial could investigate the physiological demands of pushing/pulling the product over different floor surfaces.

It could also test the user's ability to manoeuvre the vacuum cleaner around tight corners or to access difficult areas. Further tests could be carried out to investigate whether there are any finger traps or safety hazards on the vacuum cleaner. Your plan for the user trial could look something like this.

Ergonomics user-trial plan

- Easy to push/pull: try the product on vinyl, tiles and carpet, and report on ease of use with respect to pushing/pulling the vacuum cleaner.
- Easy to move: is it easy to move about? Is it heavy? Is there any grip or a textured surface to help me hold it?
- Comfortable for me to use: is it shaped to be able to access difficult areas? Is the nozzle long enough?
- Safe: can the user use it without getting their fingers trapped? Are there any small parts that could break off? Are the wires and electrical components totally covered?
- Easy to adapt: does the user need to change the attachments to carry out different tasks? Are the attachments easy to change?

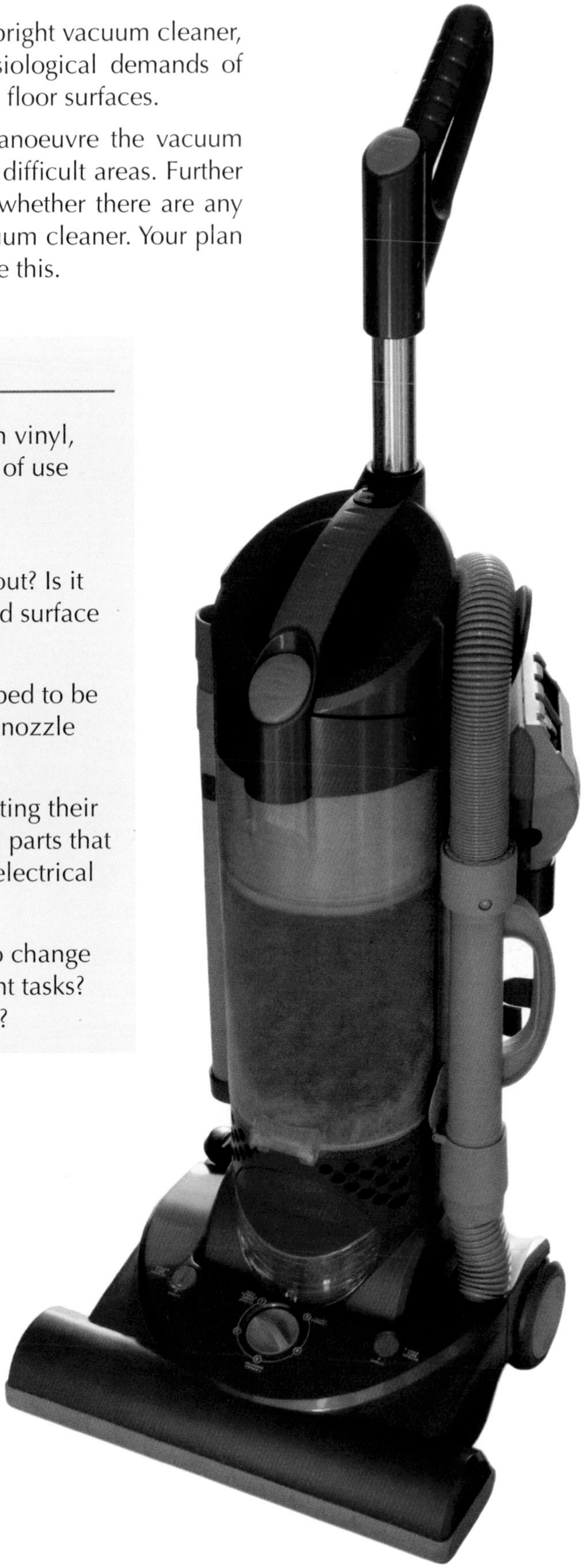

Make the Link

Market research can involve people carrying out user trials of products under a variety of different conditions in a testing centre.

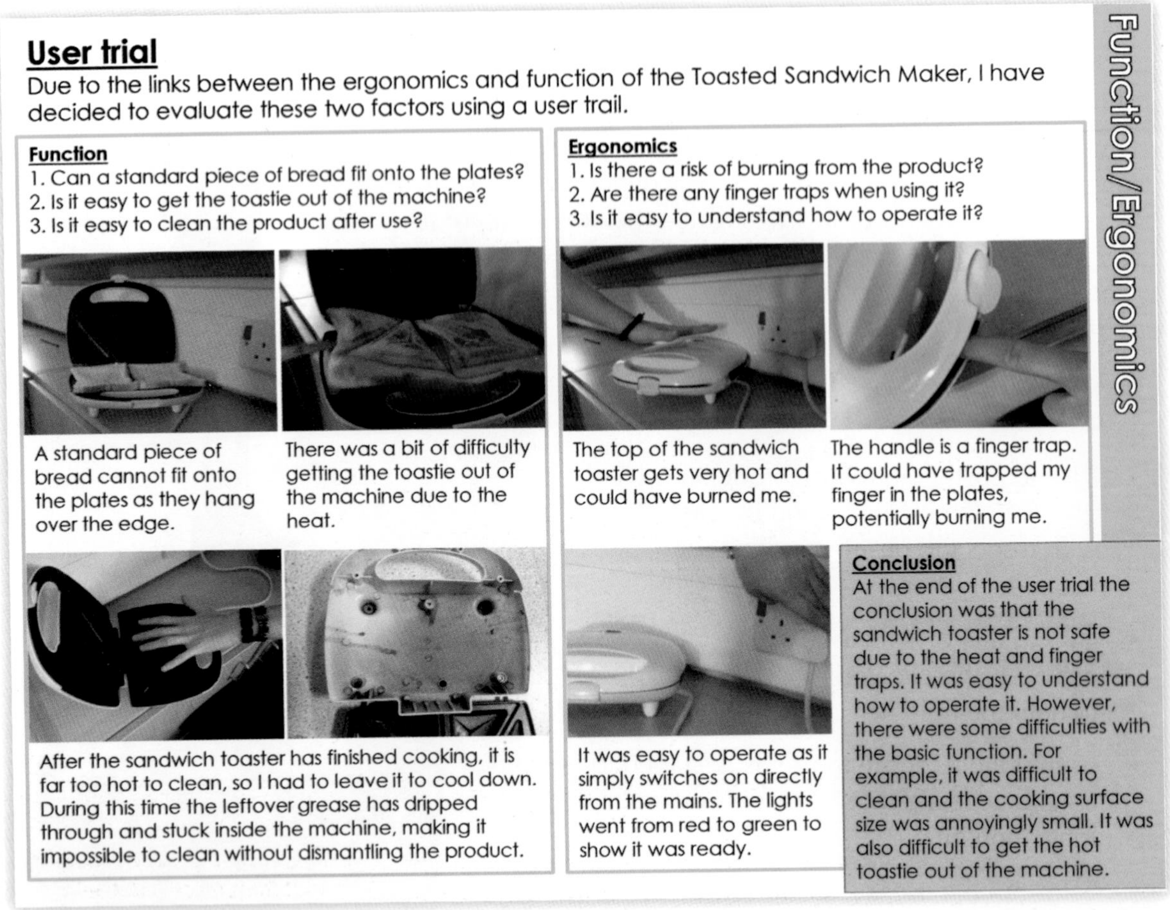
Function/Ergonomics

User trial

Due to the links between the ergonomics and function of the Toasted Sandwich Maker, I have decided to evaluate these two factors using a user trail.

Function
1. Can a standard piece of bread fit onto the plates?
2. Is it easy to get the toastie out of the machine?
3. Is it easy to clean the product after use?

A standard piece of bread cannot fit onto the plates as they hang over the edge.

There was a bit of difficulty getting the toastie out of the machine due to the heat.

After the sandwich toaster has finished cooking, it is far too hot to clean, so I had to leave it to cool down. During this time the leftover grease has dripped through and stuck inside the machine, making it impossible to clean without dismantling the product.

Ergonomics
1. Is there a risk of burning from the product?
2. Are there any finger traps when using it?
3. Is it easy to understand how to operate it?

The top of the sandwich toaster gets very hot and could have burned me.

The handle is a finger trap. It could have trapped my finger in the plates, potentially burning me.

It was easy to operate as it simply switches on directly from the mains. The lights went from red to green to show it was ready.

Conclusion

At the end of the user trial the conclusion was that the sandwich toaster is not safe due to the heat and finger traps. It was easy to understand how to operate it. However, there were some difficulties with the basic function. For example, it was difficult to clean and the cooking surface size was annoyingly small. It was also difficult to get the hot toastie out of the machine.

A user trial is used to evaluate both the function and ergonomics of a toasted sandwich maker.

Link to example Evaluation by user trial

www.leckieandleckie.co.uk/usertrial

When completing a user trial, remember organisation and observation. Consider evaluating an electric toothbrush:

- **Prepare** – first you must prepare the product for use. Remove it from the packaging (if new), assemble it and charge it up.
- **Place** – you must consider the place where the product is normally used. Simulating real conditions of use is important as this will help you gather information which is relevant and true. A toothbrush is normally used at a sink with water; if no water is used, the trial may give false information. When wet, the toothbrush may be more difficult to control, the grip may be ineffective or the on button could be difficult to push.
- **User** – select a user to complete the trial. An adult cannot test a child's toy properly as they have larger hands, more strength and better fine motor skills.
- **Resources** – collect together all the necessary materials, equipment and any accompanying products that are needed. A user trial is not a pretend test – to gain accurate results, toothpaste must be used when testing an electric toothbrush!

When planning, use these questions to make sure your user trial is a true test of the product under real conditions of use:

- Who is trialling the product? Select an appropriate person for the user trial. Consider age, size, physical ability, etc.
- What will be involved in the trial? Ensure the product is ready to be used and prepare any resources before you begin.
- Where will the trial be carried out? Trial the product in an environment where it is normally used.
- When will the trial take place? Plan the best time to carry out the user trial. Does it need to be done in bright light? Is it a night-time product? Will the trial need to be completed in several stages over a long period of time?
- Why is the trial being carried out? Consider what you want to find out about the product before you begin.

Survey

A survey is ideal for collecting lots of opinions about a product and for evaluating a variety of evaluation factors, depending on the product. However, some factors are difficult to evaluate through a survey. Durability, for example, cannot be easily evaluated in a survey.

Tips for a good survey:

- Mix up the types of questions so that a range of answers is required: for example, yes/no, on a scale of 1 to 10. Ask 'why?' for further evidence in support of the response.
- Avoid too many open questions as results can be time consuming and difficult to analyse.
- Check your survey is clear before you use it by asking another person to read it over and try the questions.
- Give out, for example, 10 or 20 questionnaires to make it easier to present results: 8/10 people agree that the product is easy to use.
- Make sure the person answering the survey has access to the product to get valid results.

Hint

Conducting a survey that asks if a kitchen mop is durable enough to last 10 years, for example, would take a very long time.

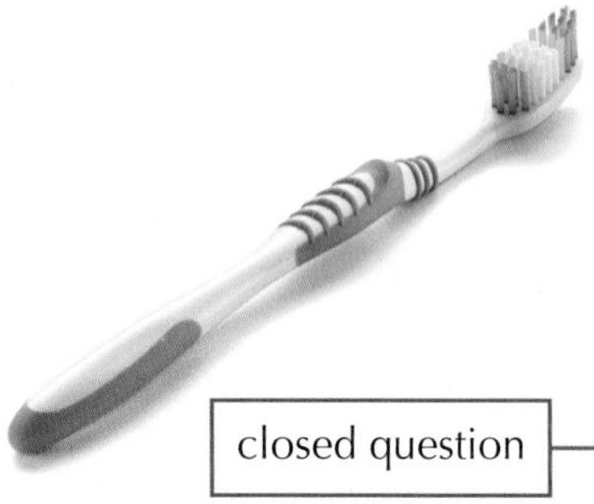

To compile a survey, use a set of **closed questions** with answer options provided. You might then follow this up with an **open question**. The benefit of using a supplementary open question following a closed question is that it can provide reasons for the results and can help to justify the response.

Survey question examples

closed question → Does the textured handle make the toothbrush easier to grip?

Yes [ ]   No [ ]

Response: 95% said yes, 5% said no

open question → Please explain the reason for your response:

____

____

Response: 30% of the responses stated that the grip benefited the user as, without it, the toothbrush would have been difficult to handle when it was wet. 60% of the responses stated that the texture allowed the thumb to grip the toothbrush. One response also stated that the height of the textured ridges made it easier to grip, compared to other toothbrushes with shallower textures.

Link to example Evaluation by survey

www.leckieandleckie.co.uk/survey

Pictorial representations, like graphs and pie charts, are great ways to display data. But presenting written statistics can also work well.

Survey to evaluate marketing for a games console

A range of males and females of different ages were surveyed for question 1. Question 2 was then asked to those within the age bracket identified from question 1. The survey encouraged people to write additional comments, so that I could understand their responses and also to help me to justify the results.

1. What age range is the product aimed at?

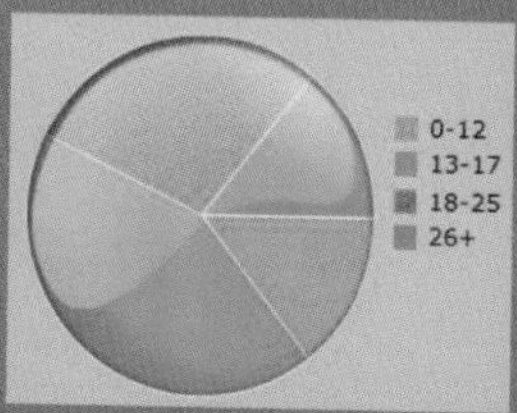

- *"I wouldn't buy it, I'm not interested in gaming, its more for teenagers." female 38*
- *"I think teenager and young adults would mostly be interested in this. I'm torn between choosing 13-17 or 18-25. Its such a popular thing." male 43*
- *"I love gaming, its definitely for teenagers!" male 14*
- *"My 14-year-old grandson plays this all the time." female 63*
- These results show that of the people surveyed they mostly felt that the product was aimed at age 13-17. The age bracket of 18-25 was also selected a lot and together these two age brackets made up 75%. It is fair to say that the age bracket this product is aimed at is 13 to 25.

2. Is the price of the product (£149.99) reasonable compared to similar products?
(a collection of five other similar products with pricing was shown)

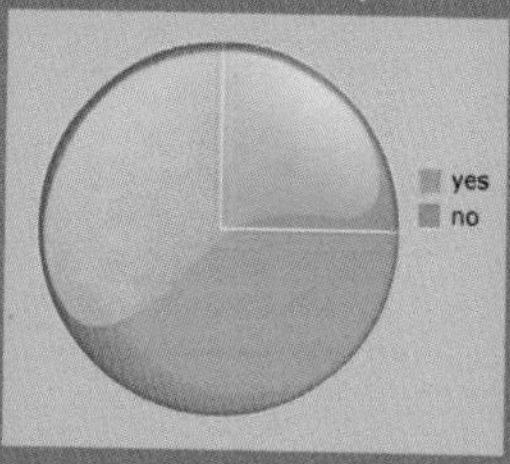

- *"I think that's a fair price to pay." male 23*
- *"I wouldn't pay much more but that's an ok price." female 21*
- *"Looking at the other products he showed me I think its quite a good price, some of them were much more expensive." male 16*
- When shown the higher prices of other similar products, most people surveyed agreed with the pricing, 75% saying they would pay £149.99 for it. Only 25% disagreed.

Presenting a variety of different question types will keep the person interested in the survey, so try to avoid lots of yes or no questions and mix in a range of different response options.

Try including a question with a scale of 1–10 as the answer, such as:

On a scale of 1–10, how would you rate the overall performance of the product?

1	2	3	4	5	6	7	8	9	10
Poor				Acceptable					Excellent

Another survey method is to write a statement and offer possible responses, such as:

The red colour makes the product look modern.

Agree strongly	Agree	Neither agree nor disagree	Disagree	Disagree strongly

Simplify tricky questions by giving four options as choices, such as:

The apple slicer blades are:

a) Too sharp
b) Just sharp enough
c) Not sharp enough
d) Blunt

The results of a survey can be recorded either by writing the data and information in a report or by making a presentation with a slideshow. Remember to answer the research points you set out to examine and evaluate.

Product testing

Product testing is another way to find out information about the way a product works. The product is put through a series of intense tests to evaluate the key facts for the relevant design factor. This can reveal how the product performs with frequent use and is, therefore, ideal for testing function and fitness for purpose.

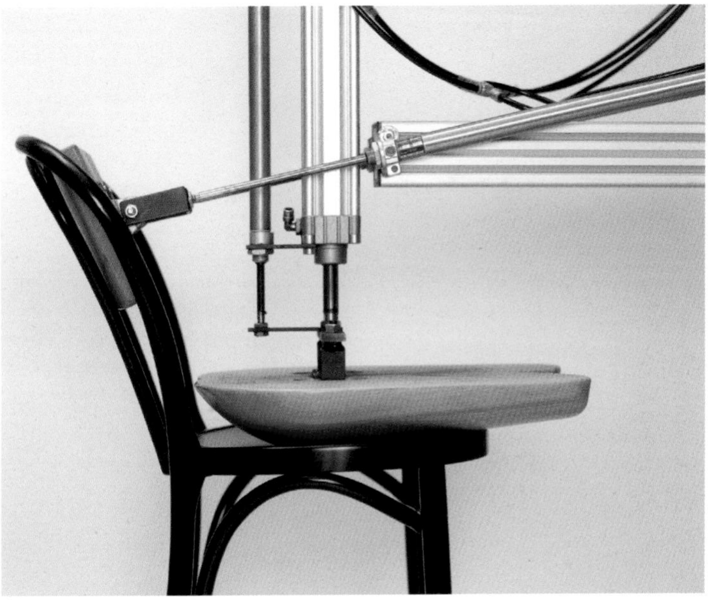

Here the durability of a chair is being tested in a test rig, set up to measure the force the frame can withstand before breaking.

A common method that companies use is to set up controlled experiments called **rigs** to check the product's performance with controlled testing. A variety of investigations are carried out on the product, such as repetitively tumbling the product in a box to test its durability. Each test is measured in terms of weight, applied force or time. The results are then compared to the typical use of a consumer. Product testing is ideal for evaluating performance and function. There are, of course, other factors which could be evaluated; again, this depends on the product being evaluated.

Link to example Product test

www.leckieandleckie.co.uk/producttest

Product testing: function

Can I saw through the padlock?

I chose a range of metal workshop saws capable of cutting through metal.

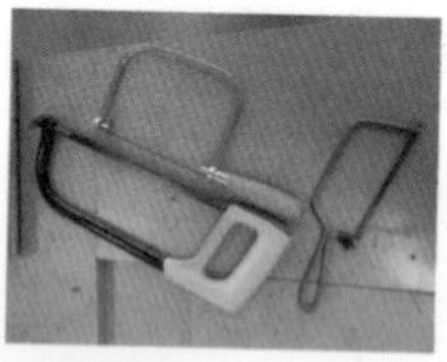

I started with the hacksaw as it was the smallest.

It took about 30 seconds to cut through. I, therefore, did not test the other saws.

Can the padlock be forced open?

I used some pliers to try to force open the padlock, which was held in a vice.

I bent it backwards really easily with leverage against the padlock.

It popped open within about 15 seconds with hardly any force required.

Summary

The saws I chose could all cut through metal (the coping saw needed a special blade attached to it). But this would be difficult when the padlock was attached to a suitcase.

The hacksaw would be difficult to use if the padlock was not clamped in the vice and was attached to a suitcase.

The other saws could probably cut the padlock open but were not tested as the junior hacksaw proved it was possible.

The pliers would also be difficult to use if the padlock was not clamped in the vice and was attached to a suitcase. However, they would be easier to use than a junior hacksaw.

The leverage against the padlock helped to burst it open. The padlock is, therefore, not very reliable.

Hint

Product testing is best left as the last evaluation method as a broken or damaged product can pose difficulties for other evaluation methods.

To record this evaluation method you can create a drawing, a storyboard of events, take photographs or make a video diary. You should also include a description of the test, the number of times it was carried out, the result of the test(s) and some notes or comments about the key facts under investigation.

Measuring and recording

Measuring is a way to find out numerical facts about a product. Measuring requires some form of apparatus, perhaps to measure sound, weight or sizes. Careful planning of resources and equipment may be required to carry out the test. For example, to test an apple corer you would need a range of different types and sizes of apples. You would need to measure the different apple parameters.

Measuring and recording is useful for evaluating function, performance and ergonomics. There are also other factors which could be evaluated by measuring, depending on the product being evaluated.

As a simple example, measuring could be used to evaluate a CD rack: measure the rack and the CD to check that the CD can be stored.

A more advanced example is to measure the power in a wind-up torch. A timer could be used record how long the torch takes to power down from 20 seconds of winding, compared to 30 seconds of winding, 40 seconds of winding and so on.

Link to example Evaluation by measuring

www.leckieandleckie.co.uk/measuring

PERFORMANCE MEASURING AND RECORDING

Water boiled at 100°C	1 minute	5 minutes	10 minutes
Observations	No change	Plastic became very warm	Plastic was extremely hot
Results	No change	Plastic held its shape	Plastic held its shape

Is the plastic affected by boiling hot water?
The plastic was boiled in a pot to 100°C for varying times. It was not affected during the tests and so it would be suitable to use with hot water.

Does the submarine tea infuser fit the diameter of a standard sized mug?
Figure 1 shows that the length of the product is smaller than the diameter of a standard sized mug therefore it can fit inside the mug comfortably.

Will the tea infuser hold one teaspoon of loose leaf tea?
Figure 2 shows that product can easily hold a teaspoon full of loose leaf tea. This shows that the tea can be fitted into the tea infuser.

Will the tea leaves fall through the tea infuser?
Figure 3 shows that the small holes on the side of the tea infuser are less than 0.5mm in diameter. I researched the size of loose tea leaves and found out that they are between 1 to 3mm long by 1mm thick. The grade of tea used in tea bags is however smaller at less than 1mm. Therefore if proper loose tea leaves are used they will not fall through the holes.

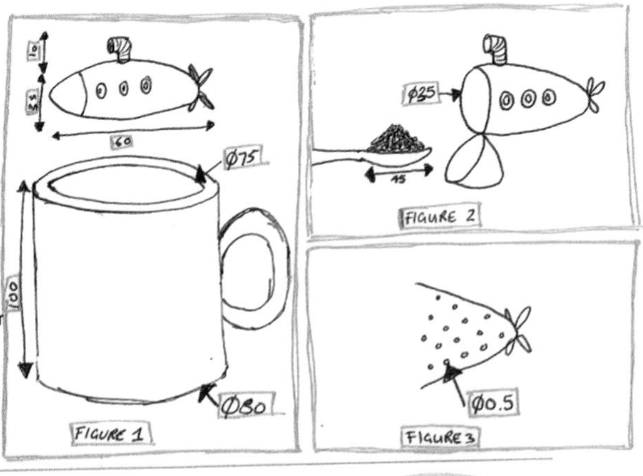

THE SUBMARINE TEA INFUSER EVALUATION

Using the internet to find out facts

The internet is a great tool to find out information. However, there is also a lot of false information on the internet and many personal opinions.

When using the internet, follow these guidelines:

1. **Search widely and wisely for information**

   Use different search criteria to locate the facts such as: *Dustbuster value for money, handheld vacuum cleaner reviews,* etc.

2. **Record your sources as you go**

   Record the websites you use as you go. Keep a note of them in a jotter or sketchbook, add them to your favourites or use a pinboard-style website which allows you to access this information from different computers.

3. **Use more than one source to validate a fact**

   While one person may rate a product as very poor, five other people may rate it very highly. Consider that every person is an individual with different likes, dislikes and interests. Work out the average opinion from a range of opinions.

Test your knowledge

Link to suggested answers
www.leckieandleckie.co.uk/tykanswers

Evaluating products

1. State the name of a suitable evaluation factor to use when employing consumer reviews as the evaluation method.
2. A user trial was used to evaluate ergonomics of a rocking horse. Explain the user-trial activity which would show:
   a) the suitability of the hand bar size
   b) the suitability of the size of the seat.

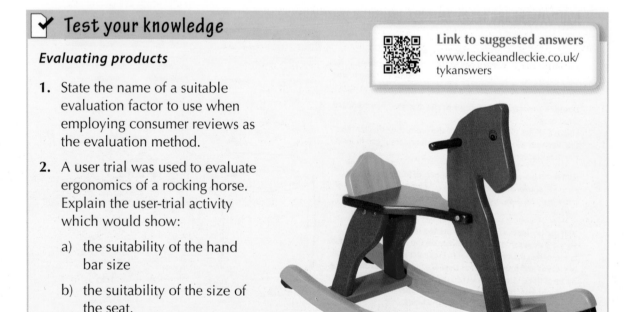

3. State **two** questions which would be given in a survey about aesthetics for the rocking horse.
4. To test performance, a test rig was set up. Describe the term 'test rig'.

Evidence of results

When it comes to gathering evidence and recording your results, it is important to obtain all the facts and to clearly display the evidence. Use your evaluation strategy as your plan and *follow it*.

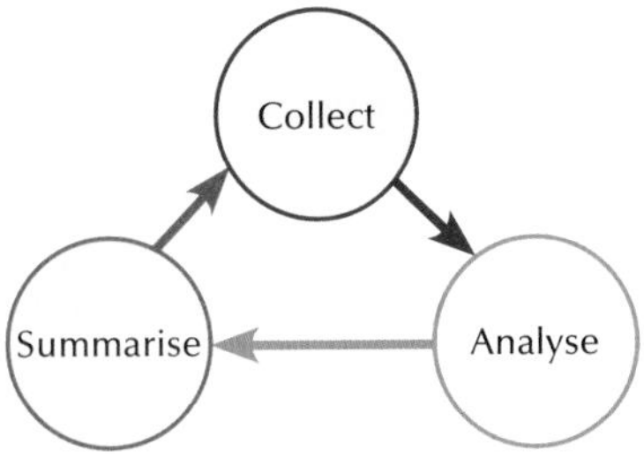

Get into the habit of following this process to avoid missing anything out.

Hint

Ensure that the evaluation aims identified in the evaluation strategy are met.

Make the Link

English – Using "quotation marks" when quoting from literature, a website or from someone's responses.

Evidence

The evidence is the foundation of any product evaluation. Whatever evaluation method is used, the evidence must be concrete, solid, substantial and with no cracks in it. Without good evidence, the project will crumble.

Different evaluation methods give different types of evidence, as explained in the methods of evaluation section (see pages 66–76).

When using images from the internet, use good quality images that are not pixelated and that don't have watermarks (words) over them. If you are taking your own photographs, try to take them with a plain background and avoid having people in the scene (unless necessary) so that others don't spoil your picture. Corridors, the corner of a classroom or meeting rooms are ideal locations.

Sources

When including any factual information or pictures, the source must be included as evidence of where the information was found. The source is the place the information came from, such as the website URL (http//:www ...) or the book name and author.

In research, it is important to record the source of all the facts found on the internet, in magazines or in books as it allows a project manager or client to gain an overall view of the research. They also have the option to look themselves at the sources to check information or to analyse in more depth.

Sources reassure clients that the research is useful and reliable. Research without sources could be false and should not be considered trustworthy. A client will not invest in a product based on unreliable research.

Tips for adding a source:

- Copy the website URL from the internet browser bar and state the date that you accessed the website.
- Write the title of the book, the author and publication date.
- Write the magazine name, date of publication and page number.
- Perhaps add a bibliography, if lots of books and magazines are used.

Make the Link

It is important to refer to the source to identify the origin of any information, as explained here and in the section on Consumer reviews (page 67).

> **Make the Link**
>
> The methods of evaluation explained in this chapter suggest certain presentation methods.

> **Hint**
>
> Along with the evidence of your evaluation, a record of your strategy for evaluation is also necessary.

Presenting your work

The presentation of a product evaluation must include information on what was evaluated, should explain the results and draw relevant conclusions.

For each evaluation aim you could use this format:

✓ Heading	Evaluation factor *and* evaluation method
✓ Sub heading	Evaluation aim being researched
✓ Evidence	Such as graphics, photographs, survey responses, statistics, consumer reviews, etc.
✓ Source	If you have taken information from elsewhere, you must give the source
✓ Result	A summary of the findings in your own words

Different evaluation methods give different types of evidence. Photos of the user interacting with the product can convey useful information about ergonomics, for example.

Of course, you may be submitting your work via a verbal presentation or a video diary. If you use either of these formats, consider submitting a written report or a slideshow to support your work.

> **Hint**
>
> Use flash cards to memorise your presentation. They can be stored as evidence of your hard work.

Presentations

Giving a presentation is a true-to-life method of presenting results. Designers make presentations to clients, manufacturers and investors all the time. To make a professional-looking presentation, prepare a slideshow. Try to keep the writing on the presentation to a minimum. The screen should be used to show images, charts or diagrams.

Reports

To make a professional-looking report, keep it simple. Overcrowding the page layout with unnecessary graphics and big headings will detract from the report itself.

Summarising your findings

When presenting the results, stick to the hard facts, observations and findings. Personal opinions should be avoided. Here are some ways to begin your summary:

- The survey set out to determine ...
- In this part of the evaluation, the aim was to ...
- It is now possible to state that ...
- One of the more significant findings to emerge is ...

- This result proves that ...
- Testing of the product has shown that ...
- The findings of the user trial indicate that ...
- The product was found to be ...
- As expected, the results prove that ...
- Generally, the majority agreed with ...
- The following conclusions can be drawn from this ...
- Without doubt, this confirms that ...
- The most obvious finding to emerge from this evaluation is ...
- Analysing the information revealed ...
- The evidence suggests that ...
- Consumers responded positively, proving that ...
- The results indicate that ...
- When these results were examined they revealed that ...
- This evidence proves that the ...
- The results of this research support the idea that ...

Conclusion

A conclusion is a **summary** of the whole report. It explains what the most interesting findings were and draws a conclusion from the information found for each evaluation factor. In your conclusion, you may wish to further justify your choice of evaluation methods through the strength of your results.

Tips for writing a conclusion:

- List the evaluation factors and use this as a guide to layout.
- Do not write any new information; summarise the information in your work.
- Avoid repeating information word for word from your evaluation. Use a thesaurus to find alternative words.
- Use words which indicate the project is completed.
- Evaluate the success of your strategy for evaluation.
- If appropriate, outline your findings regarding the sustainability and/or environmental impact of the product.

Check your progress

I can:

	HELP NEEDED	GETTING THERE	CONFIDENT
• select a suitable product for evaluation	◯	◯	◯
• select evaluation factors that are relevant to my product	◯	◯	◯
• plan a strategy for evaluation	◯	◯	◯
• evaluate the product and present my results	◯	◯	◯
• justify why the evaluation methods I have chosen are suitable	◯	◯	◯
• conclude my research.	◯	◯	◯

4 Designing

By the end of this chapter you should be able to:

- describe the ways in which designers identify problems
- state the purpose of a design brief
- explain different approaches to analysing a design brief
- describe research techniques
- explain a product specification
- describe the purpose of idea-generation techniques in designing
- explain synthesis when refining ideas for development
- describe the graphic techniques used to communicate and develop ideas in 2D and 3D
- describe the modelling techniques to communicate and develop ideas in 2D and 3D
- explain how to apply research to a design proposal
- explain how to justify design developments using the specification
- state the purpose of planning for manufacture.

The design brief

Designing a new product usually begins with a design brief. The design brief is the first step in a series of design activities called the design process. Designers work from a design brief, whether they are designing a pair of trainers, a computer table, a hairdryer, a vacuum cleaner or a toothbrush.

Make the Link

The design process diagram is on page 9.

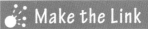

Situation

We are a modern fitness centre in central Edinburgh. The fitness facilities we have are exceptional.
We offer a five-star fitness experience with cutting-edge modern equipment and tailored personal training.
A typical member is a young professional, who is fit and active, with a busy lifestyle.

Design Brief

Design a plastic drinks bottle which new members of Active Edinburgh would receive as a joining gift.

Make the Link

Communication between the client, designer and design team may be via the phone, internet or in person.

Whether the job is an improvement to an existing product or a new invention, a designer needs a design brief to find out the details of the project and to identify any restrictions they will have to consider. The client and the design team will discuss the design brief before designing begins. Communication between the client and the design team throughout the process is the key to success. It is important to make sure there is a shared understanding of the brief.

A designer talks to her client on the phone.

This design brief may be short and to the point, or it may be long and very detailed. Either way, it will state what the product should do or what it should offer.

Identifying a problem

Some design briefs focus on improving current products or fixing existing problems. Potential product improvements may be identified through product evaluation. Many new products are simply evolved versions of products that we use every day, but are bigger, stronger, last longer or are easier to use. Therefore, a design brief is a statement of a problem, of an opportunity for a design development or of an issue which can be resolved through redesigning the product.

In 1974 Art Fry worked for adhesive company 3M and in his spare time he sang in the local church choir. He had a problem, however, with his bookmark falling off his book during choir practice. He solved his problem by designing a product with light yet still quite sticky glue on a little piece of paper and the Post-it note was born.

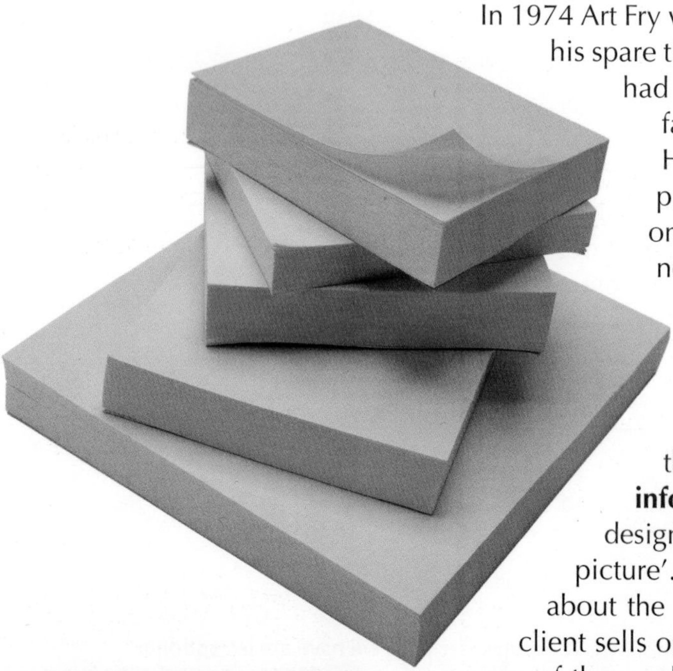

Situation analysis

Sometimes the designer is presented with additional information along with the design brief. This **situational information** is usually provided to give the designer an appreciation of the 'bigger picture'. The extra information may be a story about the client, details of the other products the client sells or even information about the location of use of the product. The designer must read through all the information and select the most important aspects. This information helps designers to understand the market and may stimulate ideas.

Make the Link

A designer can refine a design problem through situation analysis, considering needs and wants, and product evaluation.

Needs and wants

Designers must find out whether the target market needs or wants the product. Some products will always be in high demand as they are constantly required to satisfy basic human needs. For example, Anna *needs* a new toothbrush because her toothbrush is three months old and needs to be replaced. Products we want will only be in high demand if they are fashionable, highly recommended, durable, reliable or appeal to us personally. For example, Paul *wants* a new electric guitar. His current guitar is not as high-tech as he would like and he wants a more stylish guitar to make him stand out on stage.

Hint

To analyse a design brief and any situational information, use a highlighter to identify the key points.

Make the Link

See the section on needs and wants (pages 17–18).

The target market

Designers need the design brief to find out **what** it is they are designing, **who** it is for, **where** it will be used, **when** it will be used and **why** it is needed. A good design brief will outline the **5Ws**, giving the designer a clear picture of the project ahead and helping them to form an idea of who makes up the target market. This information is important as it helps the designer to make design decisions, ensuring that the product is successful in its market.

Test your knowledge

Link to suggested answers
www.leckieandleckie.co.uk/tykanswers

The design brief

1. Explain the meaning of the term 'design brief'.
2. Describe a situation in which a designer has identified a problem and state the product which solved the problem.
3. State **five** products which satisfy human
   a) needs
   b) wants.
4. Explain why good communication is important between the designer and the client when setting a design brief.

Analysing a design brief

Once you receive a design brief it is important to read it more than once. Scribble, sketch and write notes all over it while fresh ideas and questions pop into your head. It is important not to get one idea stuck in your head and to try to let lots of ideas emerge. Quick, colour-coded notes are great to get a wide range of ideas on paper.

Hint

Start by looking for the main design factors.

In this early stage of designing, it is necessary to identify the main **design factors** that will influence the design. The design brief may include details regarding the function, performance, market, aesthetic or ergonomics. Identifying the correct design factors from the design brief helps on the road to a successful design.

For example, using the design brief below, a student has identified the design factors using a mindmap format.

Design brief example

Situation

Kids between 8 and 16 need their own space for homework, computer games and having friends over.

They are finding this space in lofts, garages or spare bedrooms, and furniture retailers are recognising the need to offer unique and specialist furniture solutions for these new living spaces. Modern, stylish products are being produced.

Design brief

Design a gaming chair for a teenager.

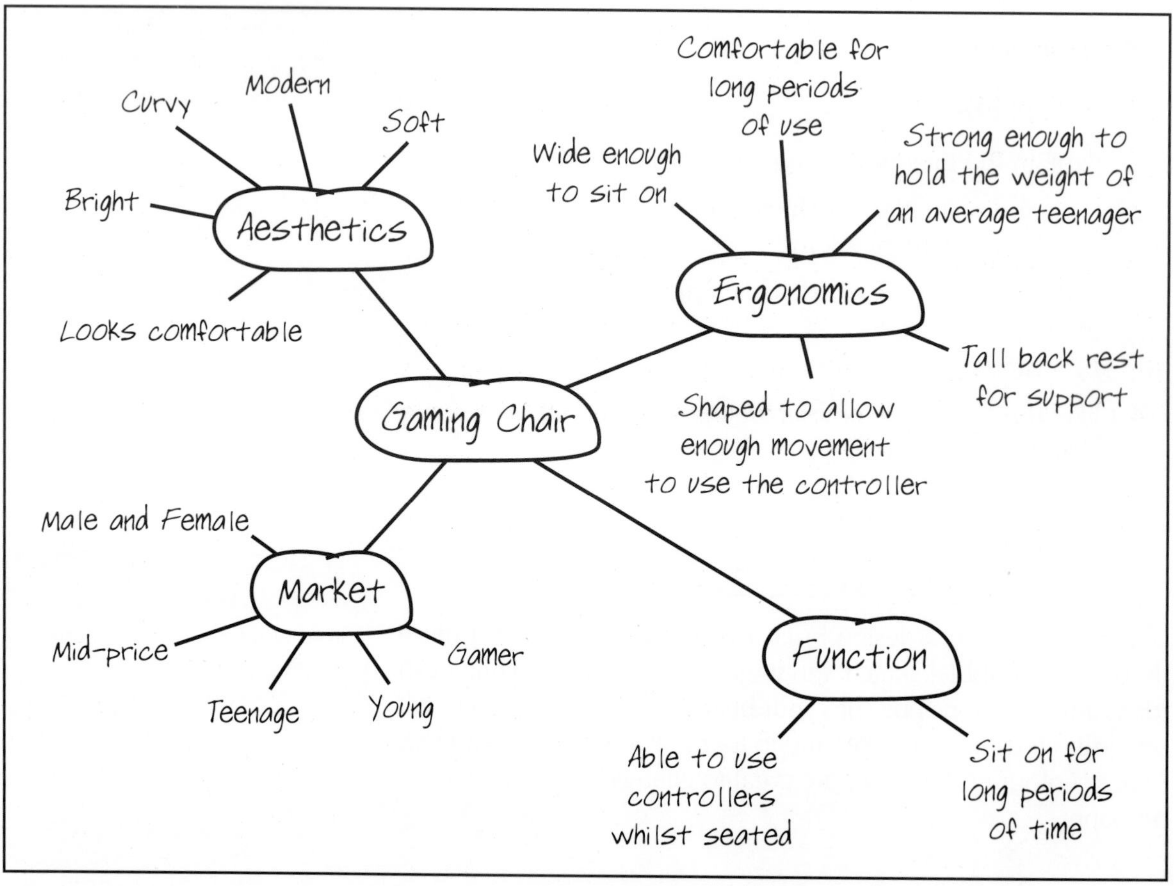

When analysing a design brief, different words and phrases can help you to identify the design factors. There is no set list of words to look for as each design brief is different, but these words and phrases can provide a starting point:

- **Function:** able to hold/store/display, should be able to, must be able to, references to additional functions
- **Performance:** last for, achieve, work, capable of, provide, replace
- **Market:** need, want, suitable for, appeal to, age range, gender, price range
- **Aesthetic:** modern, style, shape, colour, links to market appeal, fashion, contrast, harmony, references to location/environment of product, materials, finish
- **Ergonomics:** suitable for, grip, strong enough to, tall/wide/deep enough for, links to market age/gender.

Remember this list is just a starting point; the brief will contain many more words and phrases that will give you clues about the design factors.

There are various ways to present the analysis of a brief to provide evidence of your work:

- a mindmap
- written lists
- a table of information
- a recording of a discussion
- a meeting with minutes taken to record ideas
- a video conference with minutes taken to record ideas.

The analysis should identify areas to research, and you may wish to compile a list of questions raised by your analysis to use as a basis for this research.

Activity

Analysis task

A design brief for a child's toy is given:

Design a toy for indoor use. The toy must help children under the age of three to develop fine motor skills, such as developing precise movements in their hands. It should bring learning and play together in a colourful and interesting way. The toy must be durable to endure daily use by toddlers. It must be safe to use and comply with all safety guidelines.

1. Copy the design brief and underline the key words and phrases.
2. Research any words and phrases that are unfamiliar to you.
3. Analyse the design brief using the **five** design factors, by either drawing a mindmap or completing a table.
4. State the most important design factors in the design brief.
5. Write a list of questions based on your analysis which could be used to research these factors further.

Research

Research is an important element when designing as it provides the information you need to design a successful product. Research helps designers to make meaningful design decisions.

Although research is especially important at the start of a design project, it should continue all the way through, as and when necessary. For example, while you are developing your ideas, you may find you need to research extra ergonomic considerations that you had not thought about previously.

Make the Link

To get a better understanding of this ongoing approach to research, look back at the diagram of the design process on page 9.

Research techniques

When completing research, any of the methods of evaluation from the previous chapter can be used to gather information.

These methods include:

- Product comparisons
- Consumer reviews
- User trial
- Survey
- Product testing
- Situation analysis
- Measuring and recording
- Using the internet

Research plan

A research plan will help you to organise your work and ensure that you have selected the most relevant design factors. An example research plan is shown below.

Hint

Organise your research by design factors.

Designing a wall-mounted jewellery box for a fashionable woman in her 30s		
Design factors	**Research method**	**Justification**
Ergonomics	Measuring and recording	I need to find out: • What is the size of the lady's hand? • At what height should the box be mounted on the wall?
Function	Using the internet to research facts	I need to find out: • What jewellery will be stored in the box? • How will I make my design easy to open and close?
Aesthetics	Comparison to other products	I need to find out: • What styles, shapes and colours are currently available on the market?

Following completion of the research plan, the designer is ready to begin their research. The questions posed or statements drawn up will help the designer to justify the design factors they have chosen, providing reassurance to the team and the client that they are on the right track. In the jewellery box example above, for 'function' the following statements might be used: jewellery types, jewellery volume, jewellery sizes, hinges and catches, storage features.

Methods for presenting research

When doing research, you will gather a range of evidence. When presenting your research findings, a clear layout is important. This helps to make your work easy to understand and use when you are designing.

Your research evidence may include:

- A collection of images
- Written information
- Annotated sketches
- Labelled diagrams
- Tables of information
- A series of photographs
- Video evidence

> **Hint**
> Remember to include your sources (see page 77).

Your research should provide the answers to the questions or statements you complied for your research plan. You can present your answers by annotating tables, images and diagrams, or by highlighting text. You may also wish to write a summary of the most relevant findings using bullet points.

Some key phrases to use are:

- This would be the best (material, finish, etc.) to select and use because ...
- Analysing all this information reveals ...
- This identifies the most suitable ...
- This can be incorporated in ...
- The range of information here can be applied to ...
- These details would be appropriate for ...
- Although this is useful, it cannot be applied to the design because ...

Product specification

> **Hint**
> A design that does not meet the specification will not meet the brief.

A **specification** is a list of things that the product must do. It gives details about the product with precise information and facts. The specification is written following discussions with the client and analysis of the design brief, and is based on the outcomes of any research.

Designers use specifications as checklists to ensure their designs match the design brief and to avoid designing something unsuitable. The specification should be presented as a list of clearly defined statements that correspond to the research gathered. No information should be added in at this stage, unless it is recorded as part of the research.

When designing, it is a good idea to keep your specification handy. Designing within the specification helps designers to ensure that they do not overlook or forget about any of the main points.

Write the specification points on Post-it notes and stick them next to where you are working.

Presenting the product specification as a list

This first method of presenting a specification requires an opening statement followed by bullet points.

The soap dish must:

- hold a bar of soap with a maximum size of 70 × 50 × 30mm
- have a durable waterproof finish that will not rot in a humid environment
- be available in different finishes or materials to appeal to a wide target market
- be made from a material which will not rot in a damp environment
- be shaped to hold a bar of soap
- be easy to clean with water
- protect the underlying surface from being damaged by soap
- be waterproof
- be easy to assemble
- be designed in a modern style.

Hint

The key word in a specification is 'must'.

Presenting the product specification by design factors

The second method of presenting a specification is to list the points by design factor.

Function

- The soap dish must hold a bar of soap of dimensions 7 × 5 × 3cm.
- It must be shaped to hold a bar of soap.
- The soap dish must protect the underlying surface from being damaged by soap.

Durability

- The soap dish must have a durable waterproof finish or be made from a waterproof material.
- It must be made from a material which is suitable for a damp environment.

Aesthetics

- It must be available in different finishes or materials to appeal to a wide target market.
- It must be designed in a modern style.

Performance

- The soap dish must be easy to clean with water.
- It must be waterproof so it does not come apart when in contact with water.
- The soap dish must be easy to assemble.

Make the Link

Later on in the design process you can revisit your specification to update it. This is explained on page 107.

Activity

Product specification

A designer receives the following design brief for a bookcase:
A school library wishes to display a selection of recommended books which will be updated on a weekly basis. The bookcase should be able to store books of different sizes. The librarian has chosen a central location for the bookcase, intending that it will become a focal point in the library, attracting the attention of lots of pupils. Preferably, the bookcase should be able to be accessed from the front and the back, so it has to be sturdy and free standing. It will be used by a range of pupils aged 11 to 18, as well as adults such as the librarian and teachers.
The library itself is located centrally in the school which is in a new building. It is a bright, modern and spacious place with areas for quiet study and reading.

1. Write a product specification for the bookcase; produce a list with **15** bullet points.
2. Write a product specification for the bookcase by listing the points by design factor, using the following **five** design factors: function, performance, market, aesthetics and ergonomics.
3. State which method you prefer to use when presenting a product specification.
4. Explain why you find this method easier.

Idea-generation techniques

Designers often use idea-generation techniques to stimulate their creative thinking.

There is a range of idea-generation techniques and there is no particular technique to use in any specific situation; the choice of technique simply depends on the client, the project and the design team. Some designers have their own preferences. However, the technique *must* foster new ideas.

When you develop design ideas, you must show how you have used your selected idea-generation technique to find inspiration. You should justify its purpose in your designing. For example, a student might write a simple comment next to one of their sketches which states, *"I used the analogy idea-generation technique – the shape of the spout on this design is inspired by the natural fold of a leaf."*

Make the Link

Look at the spout on the watering can on page 94, which demonstrates the use of analogy in design.

Scamper

SCAMPER is an idea-generation technique which challenges the designer to come up with alternative ideas by changing the design, or aspects of the design, according to these seven considerations:

- Substitute
- Combine
- Adapt
- Modify
- Put to another use
- Eliminate
- Reverse

Link to example SCAMPER

www.leckieandleckie.co.uk/scamper

Six-hat thinking

Some major organisations, such as IBM, Microsoft, British Airways, BP and Polaroid, use this technique when designing and also to help them make important decisions.

There are six different-coloured, imaginary hats. The colour of each hat relates to a way of thinking, and so it encourages participants to adopt new ways of thinking about the task.

Everyone in the group 'wears' the same hat at the same time – so the group focuses on one particular way of thinking, before switching to the next hat.

Link to example Six-hat thinking

www.leckieandleckie.co.uk/sixhat

The six thinking hats are:

- The **white** hat is neutral. When wearing the white hat sensible and functional ideas should be created, giving practical suggestions for construction.
- The **red** hat is passionate. When wearing the red hat emotions and gut reactions are encouraged, giving artistic ideas. These might be quite unusual but they are still worth recording!
- The **black** hat is serious. When wearing the black hat, ideas are cautious and careful, focusing on health and safety.
- The **yellow** hat is happy. When wearing the yellow hat, positive ideas should be created, exploring benefits to the user.
- The **green** hat is creative. When wearing the green hat, imaginative ideas that are considerate of the Earth and the environment should be created.
- The **blue** hat is control. When wearing the blue hat, ideas should be balanced and organised, with consideration of how they might develop and progress.

To help the group focus on one way of thinking at a time, try putting coloured cards in the middle of the table to represent the hat which is being is worn. When designing, the first hat to be worn is usually the blue hat. Then, use the green hat to generate new ideas followed by red, yellow and black. Finish with the white hat to ensure the ideas are functional.

Hint

The word 'lateral' comes from the Latin word for side (*latus*), so lateral thinking is just looking at the problem from a different side.

Lateral thinking

Lateral thinking is to think about the design task from a different point of view or perspective.

The aim of lateral thinking is to come up with a number of new ideas through thinking about alternative ideas; thinking '**outside the box**' as it is sometimes called. As lateral thinking is a way of considering different outcomes, it can be applied to many different idea-generation techniques.

Brainstorming

This technique, also known as a **thought shower**, works best with a group of people as more ideas can be created. However, it can also work with small groups or pairs. Brainstorming is an opportunity for the team to share their ideas and see the project through the eyes of other group members. The team can build on and improve ideas as they are suggested. Brainstorming should have a fast and productive pace.

A team leader records all the responses and manages the group. A good team leader will ensure everyone participates and all the ideas are recorded without editing or question, as long as they relate to the topic. The results can be written as a list, diagrams, written as notes pinned to a notice board or can even be doodles or sketches. A successful brainstorming session will be a supportive teamwork exercise with only positive comments. It will include a range of fun, obvious, unusual, boring, weird and wonderful ideas.

A marketing team brainstorm a marketing strategy to generate new ideas for the colour and style of the product.

Brainwriting

First, the group must decide how many ideas should be written down in the time allocated (five ideas in five minutes for example), then **brainwriting** begins as everyone writes down their thoughts and ideas in silence.

Next, the group share ideas together and add to each other's ideas. This can also be completed in silence. However, the organisation of this part needs to be agreed in advance. For example, after three minutes, pass your notes to the left and spend two minutes adding to this list, then pass the notes on again and again until you get your own notes back. The best ideas are finally agreed and recorded.

It can be embarrassing to put forward an average idea after another group member has just come up with a great idea. This embarrassment is avoided in brainwriting. There are also no distractions that cause you to forget your idea, you are not interrupted by other group members and you don't need to wait for your turn to speak.

Hint

In a 25-minute brainwriting session, a group of four people can come up with 100 ideas, if every group member has one idea every minute.

Analogy

Analogy is used to find a new train of thought by thinking about similar products, comparable circumstances or by looking at nature.

Hint

The word 'analogy' means to compare two things that are similar to help to describe something unfamiliar. An analogy includes the term 'is like'. For example, *'life is like a box of chocolates. You never know what you're gonna get.'*

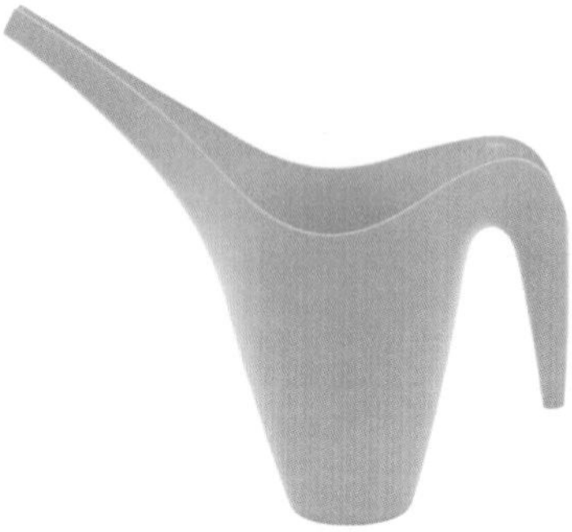

The design team working on this watering can investigated water in nature to discover the ways water flows naturally. Then, when designing the shape of the spout, they shaped it with the idea of water pouring over a folded leaf.

The easiest way to approach an analogy is to write a list of important features of the design and then consider these questions:

- What other products does it remind you of?
- Where have you experienced something similar?
- What is the product like?

Bio-mimicry is a type of analogy that uses nature for inspiration. It can be a powerful and imaginative approach to generate ideas. One example of a product that was designed using bio-mimicry is Velcro. It takes its inspiration from a burdock plant that has burrs (small hooks) on the surface of its seeds. In nature, the hooks are used to disperse seeds as they catch onto an animals' fur or a person's clothing and the seeds fall off in a new location. Velcro uses similar hook technology – these latch onto a softer surface, creating a reusable joining method.

Mood boards

A **mood board** is a collage of images that relate to the project. Designers use mood boards to collect their ideas and to inspire new ideas. Mood boards are popular with graphic designers, product designers, interior designers and architects as they help to create an aesthetic vision for the project ahead. A mood board will investigate the patterns, textures, shapes and colours the product could have.

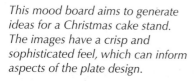

This mood board aims to generate ideas for a Christmas cake stand. The images have a crisp and sophisticated feel, which can inform aspects of the plate design.

Lifestyle boards

Designers use **lifestyle boards** to understand the person who will use the product and, therefore, to gain a deeper understanding of the target market. A lifestyle board looks just like a mood board. However, it has a different content. The images in a lifestyle board represent the lifestyle of the typical person who would use the product.

This technique helps the designer to understand the user by considering where they live, what they eat, what they wear, what hobbies they have, what music they prefer, what pet they have, where they go on holiday, etc.

A lifestyle board for a female consumer in her twenties.

Activity

Mood boards and lifestyle boards

A designer receives a design brief for a set of fridge magnets.

Situation

Chloe owns and works at a busy, modern coffee shop in St Andrews which is popular with students. Chloe has bright red hair, is bold with fashion and is always smiling. Her interests in art and politics make her popular with a variety of customers.

Design brief

After a busy day on her feet, Chloe dreads her cycle home but looks forward to relaxing in the tub with a good book. She loves to travel and is visiting her brother Leo in Finland in March and plans to visit her other brother Croy in Japan next year.

Chloe runs lots of different events in the coffee shop. She would like to display the events on the cafe notice board and needs a set of eight fridge magnets to do so.

1. Make a mood board for the coffee shop.
2. Make a lifestyle board for Chloe.

Hint

The design factors are ideal to use as categories for morphological analysis.

Make the Link

Morphology is also used to analyse plants and organisms in biology, and words and language are analysed using morphology in English.

Link to example Morphological analysis

www.leckieandleckie.co.uk/morphological

Morphological analysis

The term '**morphological analysis**' means to look in detail at the possible form and structure of a product. This is done by 'breaking down' the design project according to different features, aspects, functions or categories, each of which is then analysed in more depth. The technique of morphological analysis, also known as **attribute analysis**, uses the information that you have collated so far (from the design brief and specification for example) to create this set of categories, such as material, colour, style and manufacturing method, and then listing (maybe brainstorming) possible responses for each category.

These categories and lists can then be entered onto a grid (or matrix), so that entries can be combined randomly to create several unique combinations of words that can be used as inspiration for a design idea. The purpose of this technique is to create unusual combinations of attributes which the designer may not have considered previously; aiding their creativity, extending their thoughts into new areas and, therefore, broadening the range of ideas.

One alternative method of creating a morphological analysis is to collate your lists on strips of paper, cut a letter-box style slot in a piece of card and place the strips behind the card. Move the lists up and down to create different word combinations, which are viewed in the slot. Another simple method is to circle randomly one word in each column and then combine these to generate ideas.

Morphological analysis of a lamp

Location	Feature	Market	Style
Dining room	Touch control	Child	Rock and Roll
Bedroom	Uplight	Adult	Circus
Office	Dimmer	Elderly	Seaside
Garage	Adjustable	Baby	Formal
Classroom	Spot	Teenager	Sporty

Technology transfer

Transferring technology from existing products into new design ideas can bring very interesting results. It involves considering the design properties that are top priority and thinking about other products that can meet these priorities. The analysis involves making a list of these priority features and entering against each feature the name of a product that can deliver that feature.

Case study

The Dyson roller ball

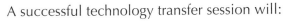

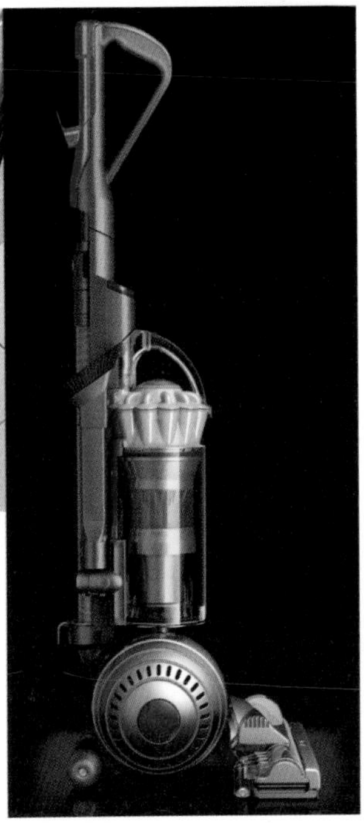

James Dyson designed the Barrowball, a wheelbarrow design with technology transfer. The plastic wheel was designed like a ball; spherical so it was easy to roll, hollow so it was lightweight, and plastic so that it could be used outside. The Ballbarrow was, therefore, easy to manoeuvre on soft ground, thanks to the large surface area of the ball.

In 2005 Dyson then went onto transfer this technology into his design for the ball-based upright vacuum cleaner, which is now a familiar product in homes around the world. Just like the Barrowball, the vacuum cleaner is noted for its excellent manoeuvrability.

A successful technology transfer session will:

- list the features required in the design
- list other products which have these features
- incorporate a method of researching products during the process.

Application of idea-generation techniques

While it is a good idea to use some of these idea-generation techniques before settling into the next stage of the design process, where design concepts are sketched and drawn, this is not the only stage in the design process where they can be used. In fact, designers use these techniques throughout the design process and some ideas might be useful for small details, not an entire design project.

Hint

It is important not to sit looking at blank paper trying to come up with ideas to sketch or draw. During the next few stages of the design process, remember to use idea-generation techniques if you find you have run out of ideas.

Test your knowledge

Idea-generation techniques

> **Link to suggested answers**
> www.leckieandleckie.co.uk/tykanswers

1. Explain the meaning of the term 'lateral thinking'.
2. Explain **one** way in which brainstorming can encourage creative thoughts.
3. Explain why brainwriting can produce more ideas than brainstorming.
4. State the name of the idea-generation technique where the designer looks for a similar occurrence in nature to generate ideas.
5. Describe how morphological analysis could help a designer to improve the breadth of their ideas.

> **Link to example Initial ideas**
> www.leckieandleckie.co.uk/initialideas

> **Hint**
> Don't forget to have the specification next to you as you design. Use it as a checklist to ensure your designs stay on track.

Design ideas

The next stage in the design process is to take all the information you have gathered and begin to create design ideas, or concepts, in 2D and 3D. The idea-generation techniques you have used already will help you to begin to explore ideas through sketching, diagrams, annotations and use of rough or sketch modelling.

The important aspect of this stage is that the ideas in your head are communicated clearly. The design ideas must be different to each other, match the specification and show the scope of your creativity. Creative ideas show imagination, are original and have value.

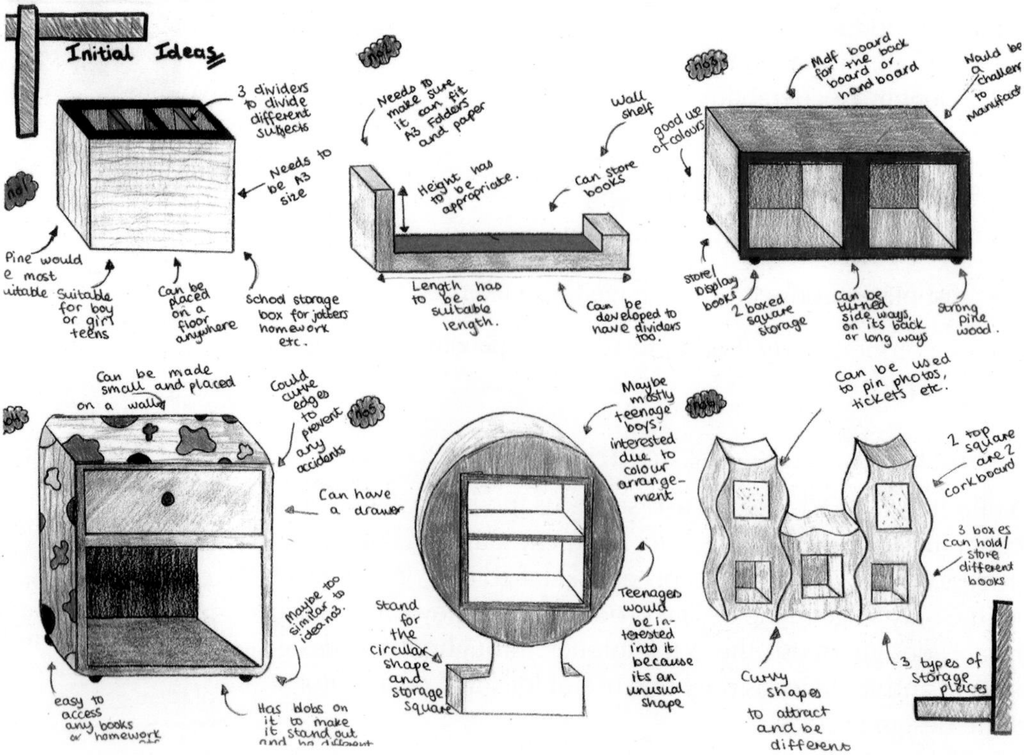

Synthesis of ideas for development

When a number of different design ideas have been produced, designers then **refine** or **synthesise** these ideas to give one design to develop further.

So, **synthesis** is the process of evaluating and judging the design ideas. This can involve morphing some of the best features from a few different designs into one stronger design idea.

During this stage, all the ideas which are considered unsuitable are discarded. The designs which are most feasible and most appealing are developed.

A simple method of synthesis is to compare each of the design ideas to the specification, to check which design is the strongest. By doing this, you will evaluate the designs against the relevant design factors and re-examine all the design decisions that have been made to arrive at this point. The strengths and weakneses of the each design idea will become clear, enabling you to identify the strongest design to develop.

> **Hint**
>
> Synthesis can be approached as a single stand-alone task or can be undertaken as a series of justifications during the development.

> **Hint**
>
> When beginning the development stage, start with a statement that explains which design is to be developed and give reasons why.

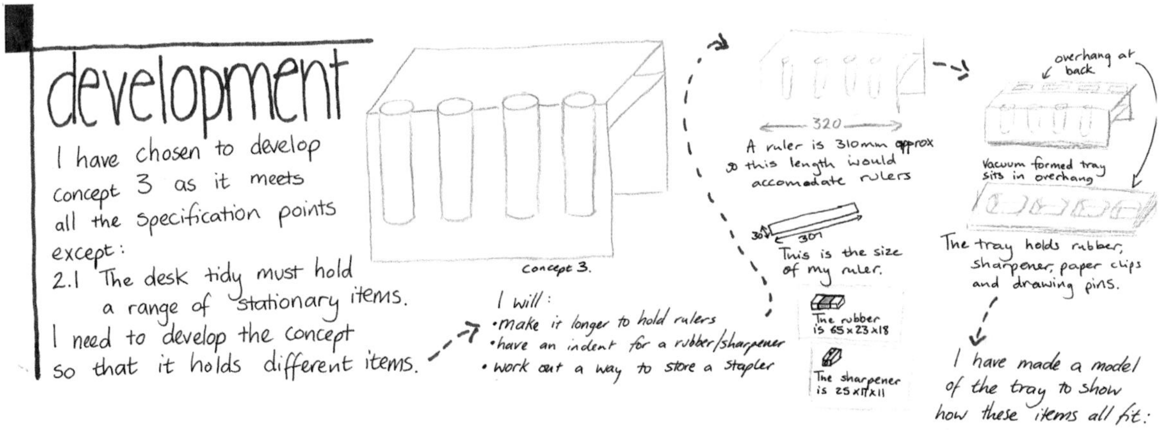

One approach to synthesis is to identify the design ideas which meet the specification, then combine these ideas to create a stronger and more creative design.

> **Link to example Synthesis**
>
> www.leckieandleckie.co.uk/synthesis

Development

The next stage is to **develop** these concepts into potential design ideas.

This will involve:

- producing a range of sketches, drawings and diagrams using different graphic techniques
- writing notes
- annotating your work
- creating a range of models.

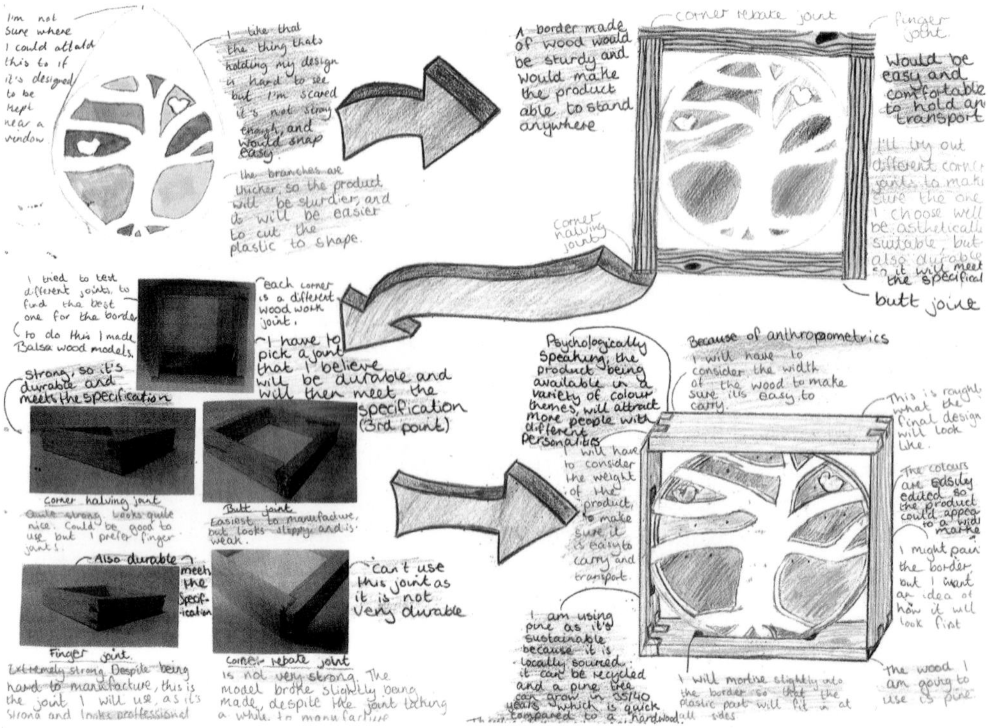

Graphic techniques to use in development

When designing, a range of graphic techniques should be used to communicate ideas in 2D and 3D. These techniques include:

- isometric
- oblique
- perspective
- working drawings
- computer-generated drawings

Link to example Development

www.leckieandleckie.co.uk/development

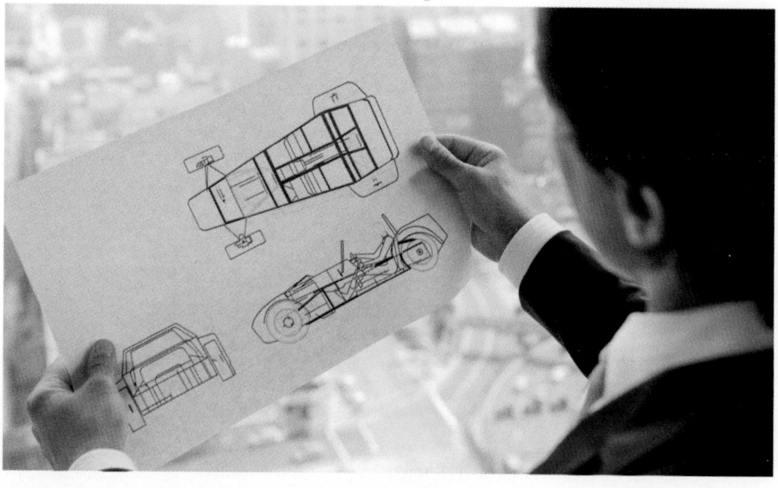

A racing car manufacturer uses a working drawing to visualise the design.

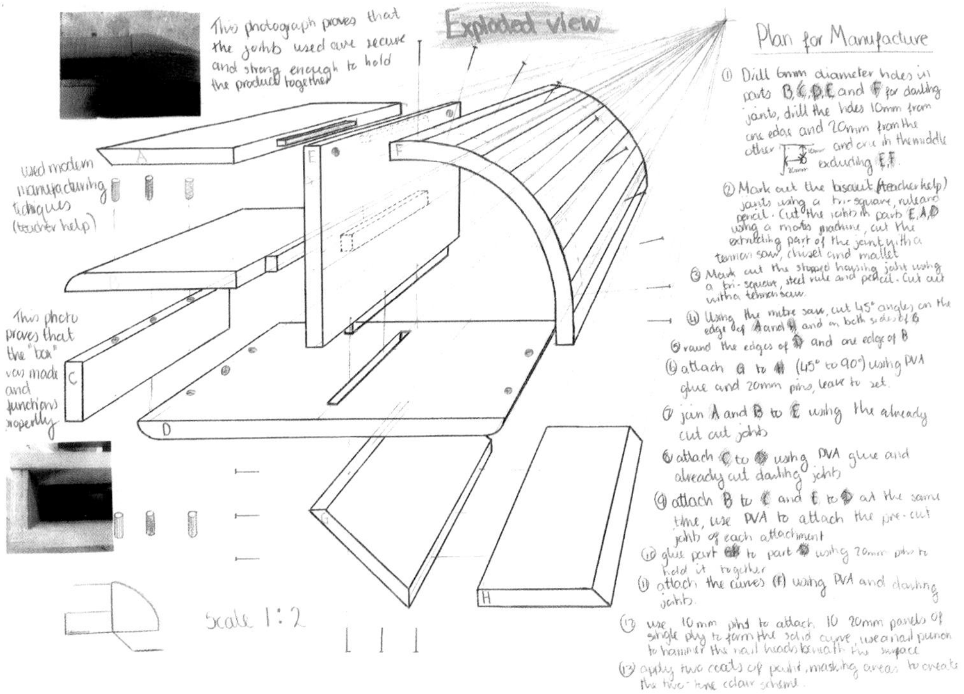

You must consider which graphic technique will be most suitable to communicate your development of ideas. For example, if the drawing is to show how the product is assembled, then an **exploded view** may be the most suitable method of communicating this.

Designers use **scale** to create a true representation of their designs. Drawings appear more realistic if the **proportion** of the design is accurate.

- When drawing and sketching small products (such as kitchen utensils, pencil holders, tealight holders, etc.) it is possible to draw to full-size scale (1:1) on A3 or even A4 paper.
- When drawing and sketching mid-sized products (such as picture frames, key cabinets, magazine racks, etc.), it may be possible to draw to full scale, on A3 paper or to a scale of 1:2. To draw to this scale, divide all the sizes by two. For example, if the height of the product is 240mm then the drawing will be 120mm high.
- When drawing and sketching larger products (such as bookcases, coat racks, bird tables, etc.), a suitable scale may be 1:4 or 1:10. When working with products of this size, consider the scale before putting pencil to paper. To draw to a scale of 1:4, divide all the sizes by four. For example, if the width of the product is 160mm then the drawing will be 40mm wide.

Link to example
Exploded view

www.leckieandleckie.co.uk/explodedview

Hint

To help you visualise large designs, sketch your design full scale either on a large roll of paper, on a whiteboard or onto the ground outside with chalk.

Make the Link

Proportion is also explained in the section on Aesthetics (see page 40).

Hint

Including a familiar object (such as a coin or pencil) in a scale drawing can further communicate the scale in context. The object must also be drawn to scale.

Applying colour and texture **rendering** will bring your ideas to life. This can be done with a range of media:

- pencils (2B–6B are ideal for rendering)
- coloured pencils
- watercolour pencils
- pastels
- marker pens
- CAD rendering

Adding texture will help to communicate the materials and convey the tactile qualities of the design. Good texture rendering will enhance the overall quality of the drawing, making it look more realistic.

Make the Link

Use the Colour theory section on page 41 to help you select colours which suit the product in terms of function, ergonomics and aesthetics.

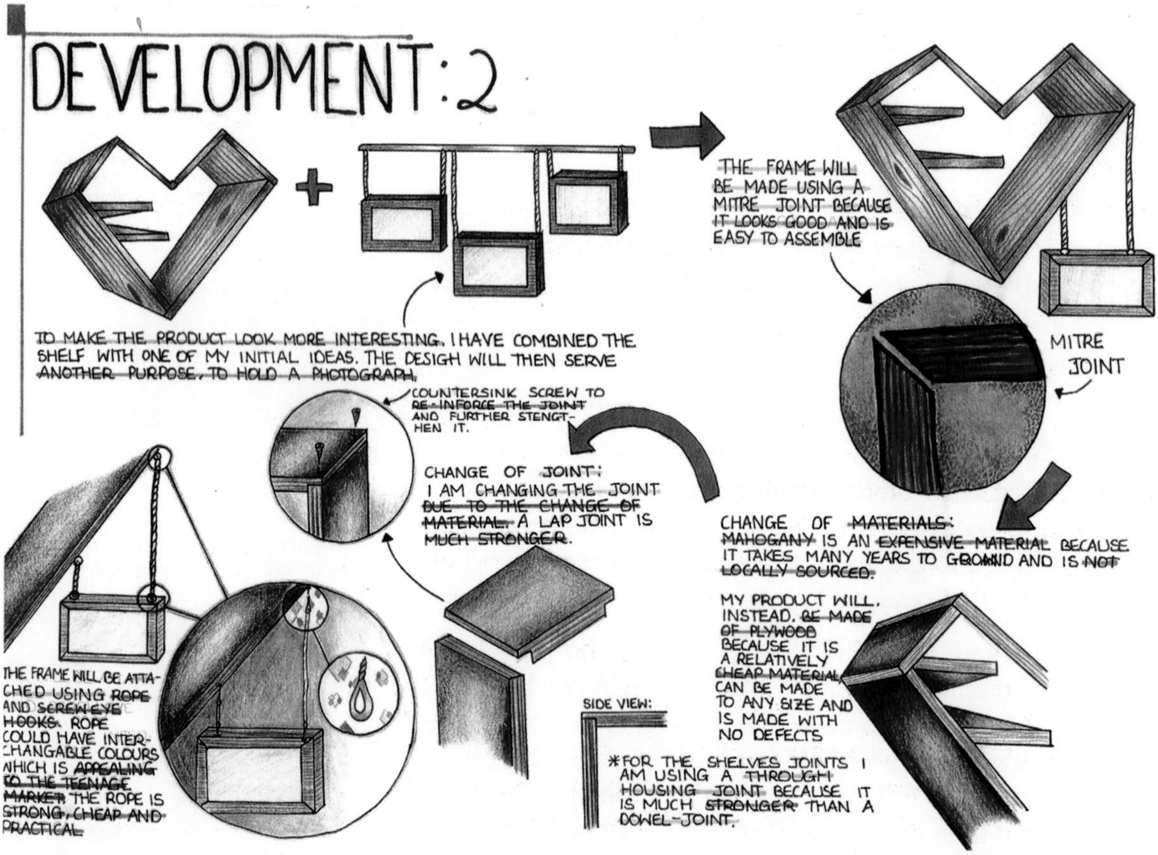

A pupil has used pencils to create a realistic wood effect on their development page.

Link to example Rendering work

www.leckieandleckie.co.uk/rendering

Activity

Texture rendering

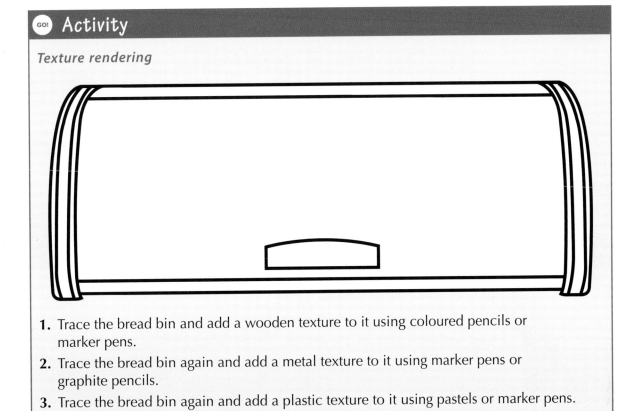

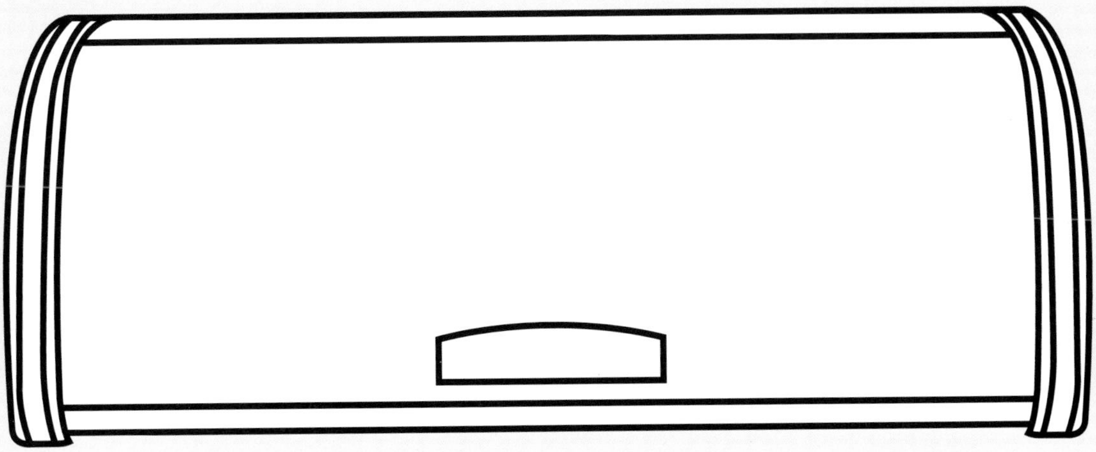

1. Trace the bread bin and add a wooden texture to it using coloured pencils or marker pens.
2. Trace the bread bin again and add a metal texture to it using marker pens or graphite pencils.
3. Trace the bread bin again and add a plastic texture to it using pastels or marker pens.
4. Sketch or draw your own bread bin and render it with a medium of your choice.

Modelling techniques

Models can communicate ideas in 3D, in addition to supplying drawings and sketches or as an *alternative* to drawings and sketches. The purpose of modelling is to help visualise shapes, forms and proportions in three dimensions. The process of creating and refining a 3D model can provide opportunities to generate new ideas and can also be used to solve problems.

Models can be made at any point in the design process; while generating ideas, problem solving or developing designs. It is not essential always to model the entire design – some models may be produced to show specific details, such as a joining method or a component part. Creating models is not just an activity which is used at the end of the design process to show off the final design, but is an approach to visualising design solutions throughout the process.

Make the Link

Models can be used to communicate a final design to a client in a design proposal, but they are also useful in other ways.

The purpose of modelling is to:

- **m**easure and test the success of the design in terms of ergonomics, aesthetics, etc.
- **o**pen a discussion with clients, showing the model to the client for feedback
- **d**etermine how parts fit together
- **e**valuate the design and any problem-solving solutions
- **l**earn about the strengths and weaknesses of a design.

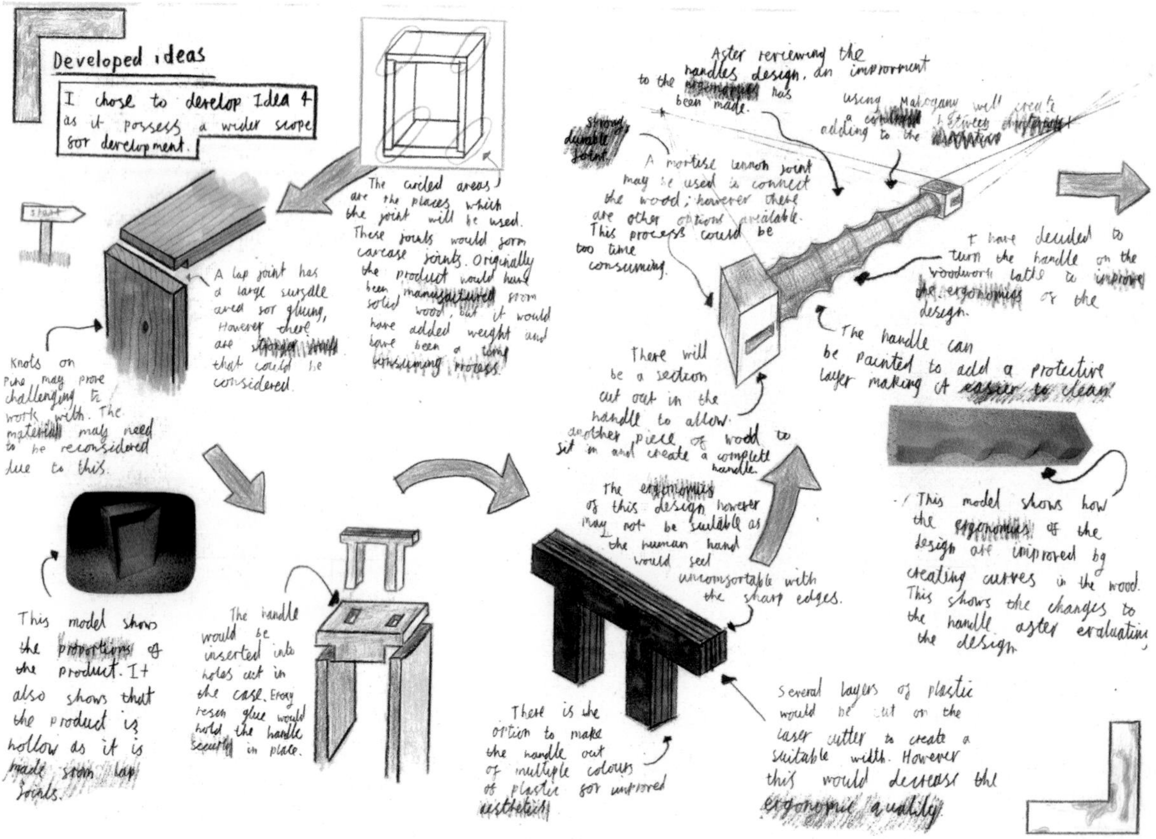

Link to example Modelling work

www.leckieandleckie.co.uk/modelling

There are many different types of models:

- **scale model** – a model made to a scaled size
- **mock up** – a model which helps to realise a shape in 3D; it has to look realistic but does not function as a working product
- fully crafted **prototype** – a full-scale, working model, made from the exact materials allowing tests to be carried out on all aspects of the design
- **computer-generated model** – a virtual model drawn using computer software.

When producing a model, it is important that the type of model used suits the intended purpose. For example, when beginning to develop your ideas, a range of mock-up models could be made from clay to show different shape possibilities in 3D. Then, as development continues, a wood scale model could be used to investigate proportion and size. As the development is refined, a computer-generated model could be produced to explore exact sizes and to show how the component parts fit together. When using models to develop your ideas, you should explain the purpose of the model. A simple annotation to describe the purpose *and* outcome of the modelling process will make the modelling a valuable addition to your work. Try starting your annotations like this:

- This model shows ...
- Through modelling this design I discovered ...
- When I produced this model I decided ...
- This model was used to test ...

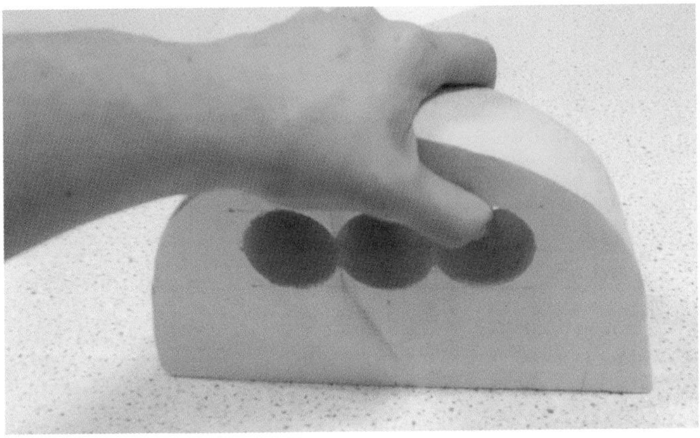

A full-scale model made from modelling foam is used to test ergonomics.

Modelling materials vary from things you find in your recycling bin to specialist modelling materials, such as balsa wood. Some popular modelling materials are:

- paper
- card
- corrugated card
- MDF
- wire
- pipe cleaners
- foam
- clay
- modelling compound
- balsa wood
- expanded foam
- sheet plastic
- construction kit materials
- smart materials.

Hint

Consider the purpose of the model before selecting a type of model.

Test your knowledge

Link to suggested answers
www.leckieandleckie.co.uk/tykanswers

Communicating Ideas in 2D and 3D

While developing a vanity unit, the designer manufactured a scale model from balsa wood.

1. Explain the benefit of a 3D model when showing the vanity unit to the client.
2. State the name of an alternative modelling material for the scale model of the vanity unit.
3. State the name of another model the designer could create and explain its purpose.

The designer used a range of graphic techniques during the design development.

4. State the names of **three** graphic techniques the designer could use to communicate ideas in 3D.
5. State the name of **one** graphic technique the designer could use to communicate ideas in 2D.
6. Describe why texture rendering is important when designing.

Annotations and notes

Designers use annotations and notes to clearly communicate their design decisions

Annotation: a short one- or two-word label which is added to a drawing, usually with an arrow or line pointing out the feature. Use annotations to add information to your diagrams, not to state the obvious. For example, annotating a picture of a cookie cutter with the words 'cuts cookies' adds nothing; annotating the cutting edge with a label that says 'sharp edge' would be much more appropriate.

Note: a sentence which is written next to a drawing, again usually with an arrow or line pointing out the feature. Notes provide more in-depth explanations than annotations and are ideal for justifying design decisions. For example: 'The cookie cutter is made from aluminium, which will not rust'. When writing notes, be careful not to write too much. Consider that small diagrams, models or sketches can explain technical information and take up less space (and time!).

Hint

Continually review your ideas to show an ongoing evaluation of your development.

Justification

During designing, you must be able to **justify** your design decisions, especially when evaluating and developing your design ideas. This requires some designerly thinking: applying all your knowledge gained from the research to develop your ideas to reach a suitable design.

These justifications can be communicated through drawings, sketches, models, annotations or notes.

Justification of your design development will involve:

- incorporating the findings of your research
- referring to your idea-generation techniques
- including references to the design specification
- referring to the design factors
- discussing the suitability of materials and manufacturing techniques
- considering the sustainability of the design and its impact on the environment.

Finalising the development

Once a final design has been reached, it may require some final tweaks, further investigation or detailing to ensure it is the best possible solution. This may involve making and testing a prototype, or creating a computer-generated model to work out the sizes.

Some questions to ask yourself at this stage are:

- Do I know which materials will be used for all the parts?
- Are these the best materials for the job?
- Do I know the method of manufacture for all the parts?
- Have I selected the most suitable manufacturing methods for the materials?
- Do I know how the parts will join together?
- Am I sure there are no better ways to join these parts?
- Have I considered the sizes of all the parts?
- Can I make this design more environmentally friendly?

Hint

A drawing of the design proposal is just one part of the information you need to progress to the next stage.

Updating the product specification

It is possible, at this point, to revisit your specification and to write a more detailed version as further information, research, design details and decisions contribute to a more precise understanding of the product. You may wish to include detailed sizes, manufacturing methods, final material choice, finishes, etc.

Make the Link

Earlier in the design process a basic, less detailed specification was written. Now that you have more facts about the product a more detailed specification can be written.

Development checklist

- Sketches or drawings in 2D and 3D using graphic techniques
- Consideration of scale, proportions and dimensions
- Clear improvements to the design
- Justification of design decisions
- References to the specification, design factors and research
- Notes and annotations
- Colour and texture rendering
- Consideration of manufacturing methods and suitable materials

Make the Link

Just like the product evaluation (pages 58–76), the design proposal involves a range of information and, therefore, the way that it is presented depends entirely on the way that the designer works. It can include a range of oral, graphic and practical work, but you must have something to show at the end of your project which can be kept as evidence that you completed it.

Design proposal

When a final design is reached, this must be presented or proposed to the client. This is an opportunity to explain the design decisions and justify the final design. This may involve:

- a collection of digital images of models and drawings or sketches
- a presentation with a slideshow and a prepared talk
- a digital story about the evolution of the design
- a recorded video presentation.

Presentation of the final design proposal

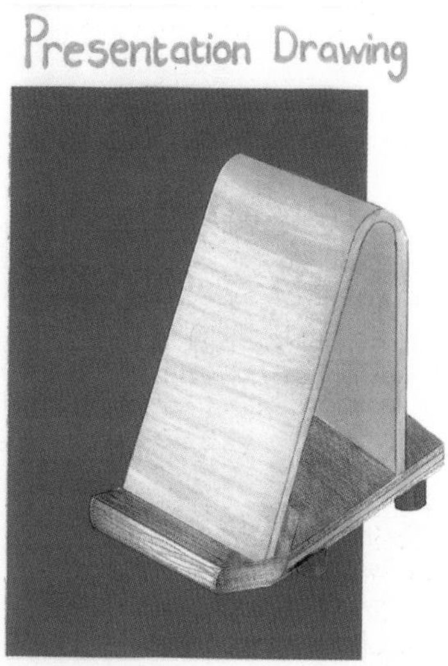

Designers can produce a **presentation drawing** as their main method of communicating the final design proposal. This may be a computer-generated drawing or a manual illustration of the product. It must show the final design proposal in a way which is easy to understand. Another way to communicate a final design proposal may be to make a fully functioning **prototype** and take photographs of the main features of the design. These photographs could be annotated to explain their relevance to the specification and design factors.

Plan for manufacture

This is a set of instructions for how to manufacture the product you have designed. For this you will need knowledge of the materials, tools, machines, joining methods and surface finishes.

A good way to approach the plan for manufacture is to write a list of the manufacturing tasks you will need to carry out. Next, discuss your list with your teacher to check the tasks are in the correct order and you haven't missed any stages. Then produce a more detailed list of instructions for each stage to explain the manufacturing techniques, assembly methods, sizes, tools required, finishing techniques and any other relevant details. This information, together with **cutting lists** and **component part lists**, should explain the manufacture of the product.

Hint

Look ahead to the next chapters for information about materials, tools, machines, joining methods and surface finishes.

Plan for manufacture
Coffee table

1. Check all the wood is cut to the correct size using the cutting list.
2. Mark out the dowel joint on the four rails using a try square, steel rule and pencil.
3. Drill the holes in the rails using a power drill with a 6mm twist drill bit with masking tape on it to set the depth to 20mm.
4. Use the dowel jig and dowel markers to mark out the holes in the legs, numbering each part as they are marked out.
5. Drill the holes in the legs with a pillar drill and the same 6mm drill bit with the depth gauge set to 20mm.
6. Cut 16 dowel pegs to 40mm using a steel rule and pencil to mark them out, and a tenon saw to cut them.
7. Sand all wood smooth with an electric sander.
8. Dry clamp one end (two legs and one rail to make an A-frame) using a piece of scrap wood cut to length to keep the legs evenly spaced. Use a try square to check the angle, and check the wood is free from any marks or pencil marks. Make any necessary adjustments.
9. Glue this A-frame together using sash cramps, scrap wood and PVA glue. Check for squareness and wipe off excess glue with a wet paper towel.
10. Repeat steps 8 and 9 for the other end to make another A-frame. Leave overnight to dry.
11. Dry clamp the two long rails to the two A-frames. Check for squareness.
12. Glue the table together using sash cramps, scrap wood and PVA glue. Check again for squareness and wipe off excess glue with a wet paper towel. Leave overnight to dry.
13. Mark out holes for the knock-down fittings on the inside of the rails, then use a bradawl to make small holes for the screws.
14. Screw the knock-down fittings to the inside of the rails with a screwdriver and 15mm self-tapping screws.
15. Place the table top down and put the table frame upside down on top of it. Carefully g-clamp them together with scrap wood.
16. Attach the table top using the knock-down fittings as in step 13 and 14.
17. Wipe the table clean with a damp cloth and carry out a final check for pencil marks. Use the electric sander again if necessary.
18. Apply an even coat of varnish using a brush. Ensure all surfaces are covered and there are no drips or runs of varnish. Leave overnight to dry.
19. Lightly sand the first coat of varnish with fine grade sand paper.
20. Apply a second coat of varnish. Leave to dry overnight.

A simple list of the stages of manufacture is one method of presenting a plan for manufacture, along with a cutting list and a working drawing.

Hint

Don't underestimate the time it takes to achieve a good finish. Set aside a few hours at the end for finishing and remember that varnish or paint may need more than one coat.

Activity

Plan for manufacture

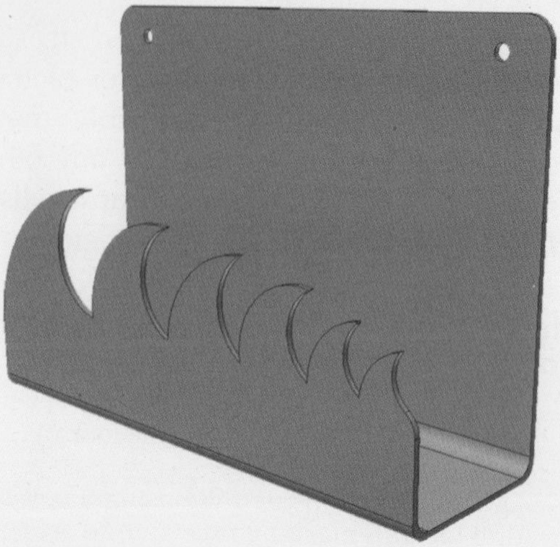

A pupil has designed a letter rack and produced a presentation drawing using CAD.

The steps for the manufacture of the letter rack were written down in the wrong order:

- Mark out the shape on the sheet metal.
- Round the edges of the metal sheet.
- Smooth any rough edges or dribbles of primer with wet-and-dry paper.
- Apply the first coat of paint.
- Drill the holes.
- Apply the second coat of paint.
- File the edges of the metal sheet to create a smooth edge.
- Mark out the holes.
- Form the shape of the metal by bending it using the metal press.
- Use emery paper to finish the edges of the metal.
- Cross file the edges of the metal sheet to remove any bumps.
- Apply the primer using a brush.
- Cut sheet metal to wave shape using a junior hacksaw and an abrafile.
- Smooth any rough edges or dribbles of paint with wet-and-dry paper.

1. Group the tasks into the following **four** headings:
   a) Marking out
   b) Cutting, shaping and drilling
   c) Smoothing the edges of the metal
   d) Finishing
2. Using a flow chart, reorganise all the steps into the correct sequence.

Hint

Use the information on pages 171–184 to help you understand sheet metalwork.

Working drawings

During manufacturing, a **technical drawing** is often required to find sizes, details of parts and joining methods. This is called a working drawing. It usually includes an **orthographic drawing** (manual or computer generated) with dimensions. However, a range of 3D drawings with dimensions can also be used.

To communicate the design in a working drawing, use:

- drawings and diagrams to show all the essential information and details
- British standards for dimensioning (BS 8888)
- 3rd angle projection layout (plan is directly above the elevation, end elevation is directly in line with the elevation)
- an appropriate scale.

In industry, working drawings are very detailed, with many drawings produced for each product. These drawings are given to all the production workers and they must be accurate to avoid any mistakes. Incorrect working drawings can cost the factory time and money.

Hint

Use a working drawing when you are in the workshop.

Make the Link

See sections on Drawing types and proportion used when developing a design (page 100), Drawing to scale (page 101), Standards for orthographic drawings (page 149).

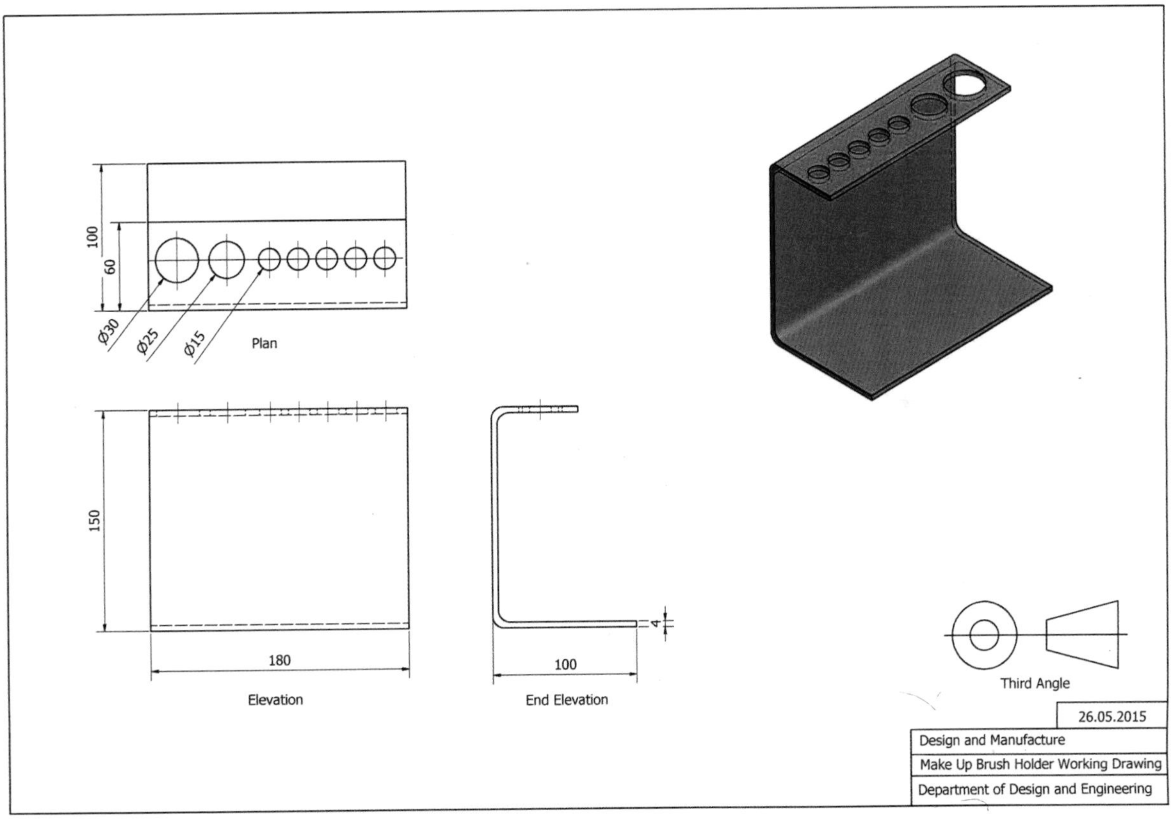

Cutting list

The cutting list is part of the plan for manufacture. It is a table of information which contains the materials and parts required for the product. Manufacturers use cutting lists to order materials before the manufacturing begins and they refer to it during manufacturing to check sizes.

Link to example Working drawing

www.leckieandleckie.co.uk/workingdrawing

A good cutting list will include:

- part names – keep them simple (left side, base, etc.)
- length – the length of the material
- breadth – the breadth of the material
- thickness – the thickness of the material
- sizes in millimetres
- quantity – number of parts required.

Cutting list

Part	Material	Length	Breadth	Thickness	Quantity
Bottom	Pine	500	300	16	1
Top	Pine	350	300	16	1
Back	Pine	648	300	16	1
Feet	Pine	45	45	20	4
Support	Plastic rod - red	648	20∅	-	2
Support	Plastic rod - orange	648	20∅	-	2
Support	Plastic rod - green	648	20∅	-	1

Preparing for manufacture

At this point in the design process, the product should be ready for manufacture.

Check that you have:

- a plan for manufacture
- a working drawing
- a cutting list.

You can now prepare for manufacture by cutting materials to size, checking there is enough paint, screws, adhesive, etc. and buying any additional parts you need. Consider where your project will be stored while you are working on it. Photocopying your working drawing, cutting list and plan for manufacture is a good idea, so you have a spare, clean copy. Even displaying these pages on the workshop wall can help keep them in good condition.

Hint

Use your working drawing to work out sizes.

Activity

Cutting list

Part name	Material	Length	Breadth	Thickness	Quantity
Base					
Top					
Side					
Bar					

1. Copy the cutting-list table above.
2. Complete the cutting list for the bedside table using the information from the working drawing below.

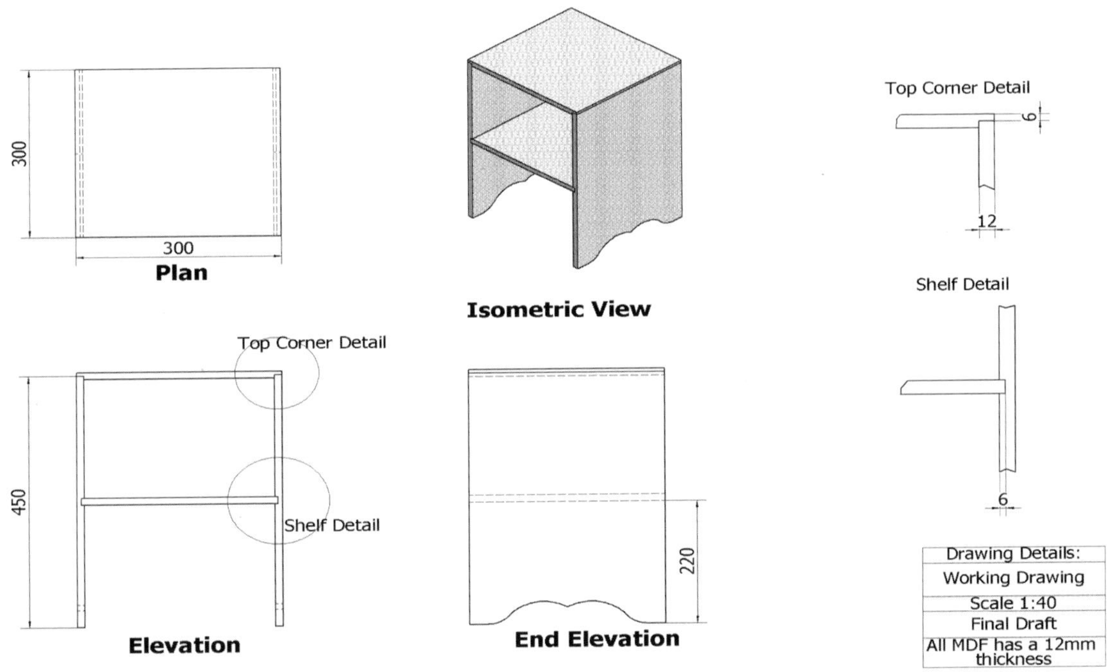

Evaluation

Prepare yourself for writing a basic evaluation by making some notes and listing the information that will go into the evaluation. Some reading and reflection is required at this point. Look back at the design brief and the specification. Compile your notes with references to the design factors and the specification. Consider the success of the final product in terms of its functionality and fitness for purpose. When you have enough notes, you can put your evaluation together.

The evaluation can be:

- written paragraphs
- detailed bullet points
- a presentation
- an annotated drawing or image
- a series of photographs with a talk or text to explain the evaluation points.

Additionally, the evaluation methods from the previous chapter can also be used to evaluate your product. These include:

- comparison to the specification
- user trial
- survey
- product testing.

Link to example Product evaluation

www.leckieandleckie.co.uk/productevaluation

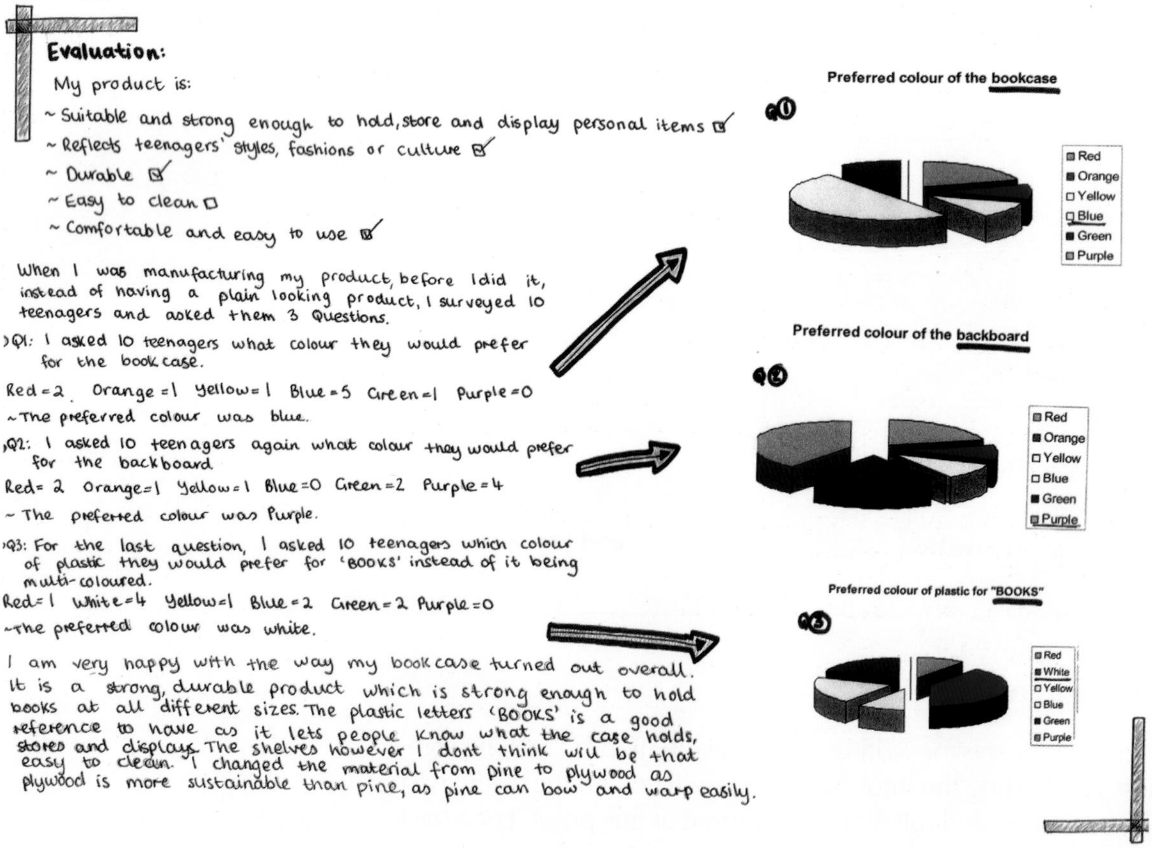
Evaluation:

My product is:

~ Suitable and strong enough to hold, store and display personal items ☑

~ Reflects teenagers' styles, fashions or culture ☑

~ Durable ☑

~ Easy to clean ☐

~ Comfortable and easy to use ☑

When I was manufacturing my product, before I did it, instead of having a plain looking product, I surveyed 10 teenagers and asked them 3 Questions.

Q1: I asked 10 teenagers what colour they would prefer for the book case.

Red = 2 Orange = 1 Yellow = 1 Blue = 5 Green = 1 Purple = 0

~ The preferred colour was blue.

Q2: I asked 10 teenagers again what colour they would prefer for the backboard

Red = 2 Orange = 1 Yellow = 1 Blue = 0 Green = 2 Purple = 4

~ The preferred colour was Purple.

Q3: For the last question, I asked 10 teenagers which colour of plastic they would prefer for 'BOOKS' instead of it being multi-coloured.

Red = 1 White = 4 Yellow = 1 Blue = 2 Green = 2 Purple = 0

~ The preferred colour was white.

I am very happy with the way my bookcase turned out overall. It is a strong, durable product which is strong enough to hold books at all different sizes. The plastic letters 'BOOKS' is a good reference to have as it lets people know what the case holds, stores and displays. The shelves however I dont think will be that easy to clean. I changed the material from pine to plywood as plywood is more sustainable than pine, as pine can bow and warp easily.

Check your progress

I can:	HELP NEEDED	GETTING THERE	CONFIDENT
• describe the ways in which designers identify a problem			
• state the purpose of a design brief			
• explain different approaches to analysing a design brief			
• describe research techniques			
• explain a product specification			
• describe the purpose of idea-generation techniques in designing			
• explain synthesis when refining ideas for development			
• describe the graphic techniques used to communicate and develop ideas in 2D and 3D			
• describe the modelling techniques used to communicate and develop ideas in 2D and 3D			
• explain how to apply research to a design proposal			
• explain how to justify design developments using the specification			
• state the purpose of planning for manufacture.			

CONTENTS

MATERIALS AND MANUFACTURING SECTION OVERVIEW

The second section of this book will provide you with the knowledge and understanding for **Unit 2, Materials and manufacturing**. It will also help you to complete your course assignment. Combined with your classwork, workshop experience and the guidance of your teacher, these chapters will help you to develop the knowledge and understanding required to manufacture your own prototype. At the end of this section, there are also some examples of the types of questions you might meet in the National 5 question paper.

Chapter 5, **An introduction to materials**, contains useful information on different materials, their unique properties, identifying features and uses. Sustainability issues associated with materials throughout the life cycle of a product are described. The aim is to make you aware of your responsibility as a designer to use materials wisely. Also in this chapter, you will learn how to test materials in order to find the most suitable materials for a component or product, and how to justify why a particular material is appropriate for a manufacturing task.

Chapter 6, **Manufacturing in the workshop**, explains common manufacturing methods used in a school workshop. The tools, machinery and equipment used to manufacture with metal, plastic, wood and manufactured boards are listed. This chapter aims to help you to select suitable manufacturing methods for a component or product. The information in this chapter will be useful to your study for Section A of the National 5 question paper. It will also be useful for the course assignment.

Chapter 7, **Commercial manufacture**, explains the methods by which commercial products are manufactured in factories. Computer aided manufacture features in this chapter and the commercial manufacturing processes for wood, metal and plastic products are described. The drawbacks and benefits of these processes are explained. You will gain an insight into the global impact of commercial manufacture and the associated sustainability issues. This is all essential knowledge and understanding for Section B of the National 5 question paper.

SECTION 2

Materials and manufacturing

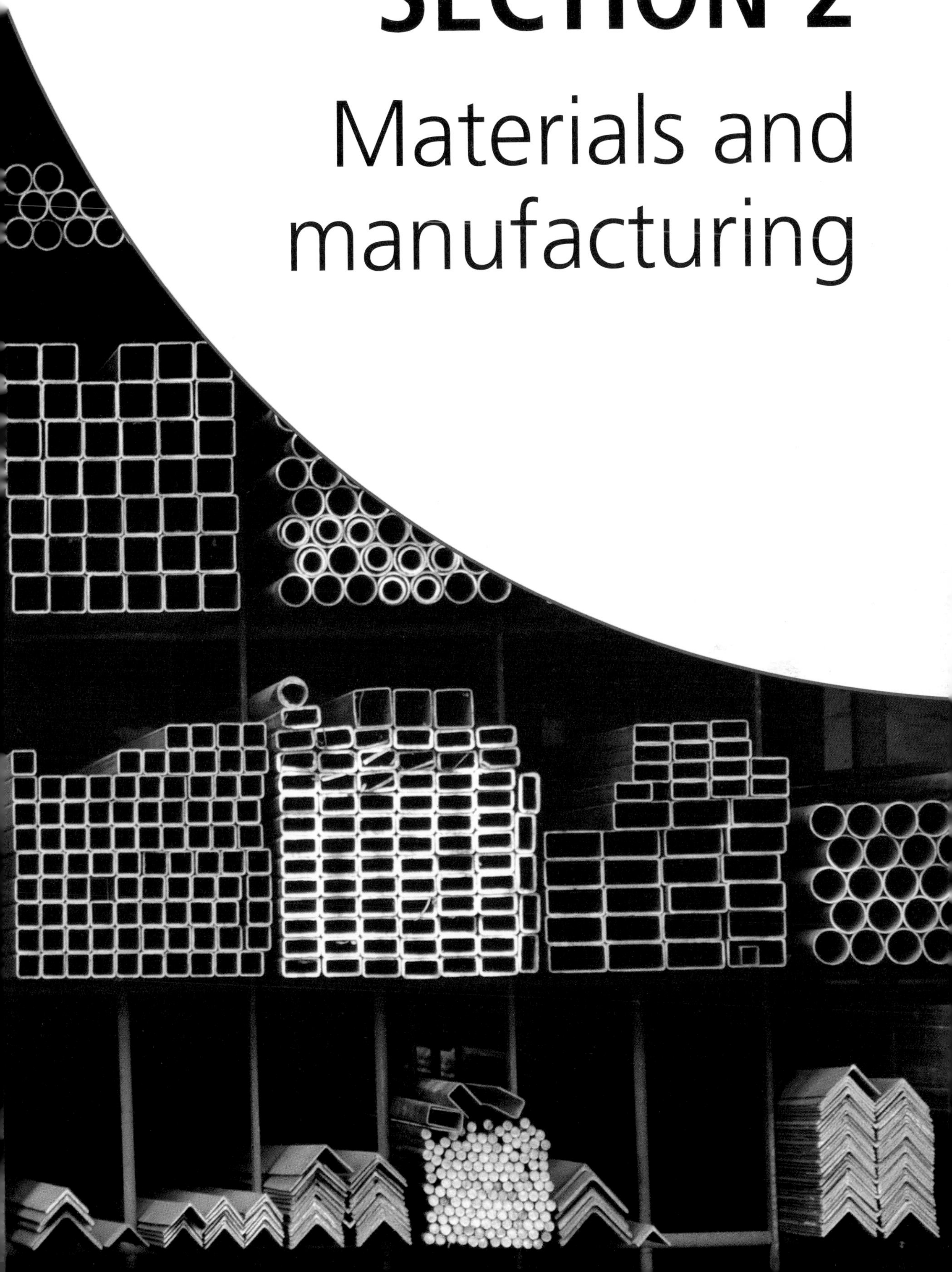

5 An introduction to materials

By the end of this chapter you should be able to:

- describe the sustainability issues related to materials
- describe the properties and identifying features of a range of woods and manufactured boards
- describe the properties and identifying features of a range of metals
- describe the properties and identifying features of a range of plastics
- explain why a material is appropriate for a manufacturing task
- explain the purpose of testing materials before selecting them for manufacture
- describe methods of testing materials in terms of workability, practicability, function and performance
- explain reasons why a material is suitable for the manufacture of a component or product.

Selecting a material

When selecting a material for a product there are lots of considerations, such as:

- availability
- properties
- environmental impact and sustainability issues
- conditions of use of the product
- suitable manufacturing processes
- cost of the materials
- source.

The properties of the material must match the needs of the product. For example, a wood with a high natural oil content should be used for outdoor furniture as it will last longer outside in bad weather.

The volume of products to be produced should also be considered. For example, using an entire board of MDF to make one small key rack will waste a lot of material. It would be less wasteful to use a material which is supplied in smaller sizes, such as a plank of pine.

Hint

Check which materials are available before making any decisions, to avoid disappointment.

Alternatively, a batch of 20 key racks could be manufactured from one board of MDF. Clever material use is an environmental consideration. When selecting a material, designers should try to find a sustainable source and aim to use local materials to cut down on pollution from distribution lorries.

Complex products require challenging manufacturing processes, which may limit the type of material being used. For example, chipboard can be difficult to work; it may not be possible to cut a good dovetail joint with this material. To avoid potential problems, take the demands of the manufacturing process into account before selecting a material.

Hint

When selecting a material, match the properties to the required features.

Properties

Materials have special characteristics and features, or **properties**. Properties can include, for example, being strong, soft, brittle, shiny, waterproof, lightweight, malleable, durable, and many others.

Once a material has been selected, it must be tested to check that the properties match the requirements of the product. If the material isn't suitable for some reason, then another material should be selected. You must be able to explain why you have recommended a particular material using the evidence you gathered when testing it.

Copper is used for central heating pipes because it has suitable properties: it is easy to bend, is corrosion resistant and keeps its shape even at high pressure and high temperature.

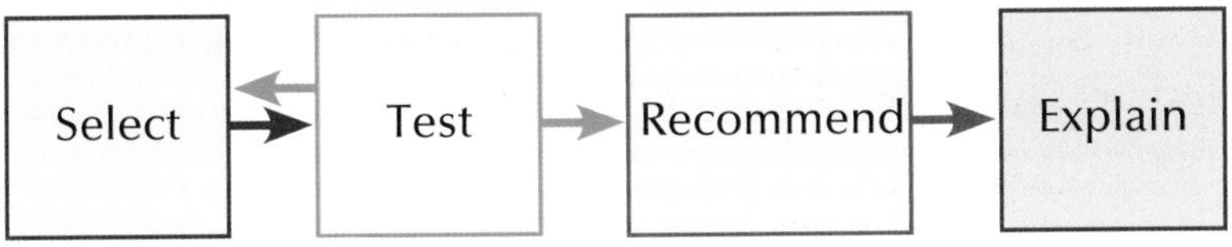

Forms

Materials are available in a variety of forms. The **form** is the shape of the material when it is supplied. Examples of forms include sheet, bar, plank, tube, rod, wire, etc.

Uses

The term 'uses' refers to the products or purpose for which the material is used. Aluminium is a suitable material choice for a drinks can as it is lightweight and does not rust. Aluminium can be recycled more cheaply than it can be made from mined raw materials. It is an unusual material in that it keeps it original properties when it is recycled; it does not get **down-cycled** (downgraded when recycled), also making it ideal for drinks cans.

Some synthetic materials were developed for a specific use and have since been put to other uses. For example, Nylon was invented in 1939 as a replacement for silk; there was a shortage of silk during World War 2. Originally, it was used as a fabric, mainly in the manufacture of tights. It is now a common plastic, used for brushing teeth, carpeting floors and parachuting.

The neutral and plain birch wood used for this button-shaped pot stand allows other design features, such as shape and style, to stand out.

Identifying features

The visual characteristics of a material are its **identifying features**. These are the elements of materials which make them recognisable and they have a big impact on the aesthetic of the product. For example, the identifying feature of copper is the distinctive reddish-brown colour, and a glossy shine is characteristic of acrylic. There are many features of a material that make it identifiable, including the colour, pattern, weight, texture and even the way it responds to testing, such as burning.

Standard sizes and standard components

Designers and manufacturers use universal components and material sizes, meaning that all suppliers provide the same materials in common sections, widths and lengths. This makes it easier to order parts or materials and compare costs as every supplier works with the same sizes and part names.

Materials are supplied in standard sizes. These are the common sizes of boards, planks, rods, sheets, etc. When designing, it is important to consider standard sizes and to design with them in mind. For example, dowel rod is available in 6, 12 or 15mm diameters; to design a product with 13mm diameter dowel rod would not make sense. While it is possible to order materials to be cut to size from some suppliers, this will cost more. Therefore, it is cheaper to purchase standard sizes and use the material wisely.

Make the Link

Chapter 7 explains the ways in which products can have identifying features as a result of processes during commercial manufacture, such as ejector pin marks left by injection moulding.

A metal store stocks metal in standard lengths and widths.

Standard components are the common parts used in products. To design every part from scratch would overcomplicate the design, waste time and money. Standard components make the manufacture of a product easier and mean that it is possible to get replacement parts. Standard components include wheels, brackets, fitting and fixing components, washers, handles, electronic parts, etc.

Make the Link

Standard components called 'knock-down fittings' are commonly used to join flat pack furniture. This keeps the cost of the product low as the furniture is not built by a skilled worker in a factory.

Test your knowledge

Link to suggested answers
www.leckieandleckie.co.uk/tykanswers

Standard sizes and standard components

A pupil has designed a clock to be laser cut and manufactured in small batches to sell at an enterprise craft fair.

The clock, size 200 × 105 × 3mm, has been manufactured from a sheet of acrylic, which is bought in by the manufacturing company in a standard size of 1200 × 800 × 3mm. The company will cut 32 clocks from one sheet.

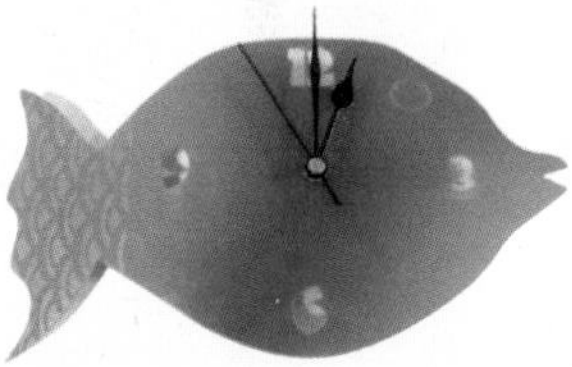

1. Explain the meaning of the term 'standard size'.
2. State **two** benefits of buying in standard sizes of material.

The clock mechanism is a standard component which was attached through a hole in the plastic.

3. Explain the meaning of the term 'standard component'.
4. Explain **two** benefits of standard components.
5. The clock mechanism measures 50 × 55 × 25mm. Describe **two** ways in which the dimensions of the standard component influence the design of the clock.
6. State the names of **five** other products that have been manufactured using standard components and state which part is the standard component in each product.

Sustainable materials

From sourcing a raw material from nature, to the end of a product's life, every material has an impact on the environment. A sustainable material can be regrown or replaced, can be recycled and will not harm the environment.

Finite resources

Sourcing materials to manufacture products can cause environmental damage. Mining materials from the Earth, such as ore for metal, must be done responsibly as these are **finite** or **non-renewable resources**. Over-mining can ruin landscapes, affect wildlife by causing loss of habitats and, in extreme cases, bring about landslides. Finite resources form over very long periods of time and cannot be replaced in a human lifetime. Therefore, they must be used responsibly and be recycled if possible.

Renewable resources

Renewable resources are the materials which we have the capability to produce, such as wood or biopolymers. For example, wood is said to be a renewable resource as a new tree can be planted to replace one that is cut down. This is a sustainable approach to managing materials, ensuring wood will be available for years to come. However, if the trees are not replaced, use of wood becomes unsustainable and such harvesting causes irreparable environmental damage.

Recycling materials

Assuming that all the materials used in the product are recyclable and that the user has taken the time to separate the materials correctly, then the product's materials can be used again. This is the best case scenario. The worst case scenario is when the materials used in the product are not recyclable (some manufactured boards for example). Or, when the user does not recycle and the product ends up in a landfill.

Landfill waste is buried and compacted to rot away over hundreds of years.

Cradle-to-grave

When products are designed without any consideration of how the materials can be reused, it is said that these are *cradle-to-grave* products. These products use raw materials which either cannot be recycled, are very difficult to recycle or the parts of the product are difficult to separate for recycling. They waste our natural resources and cause pollution in landfills. Such products are part of a **linear economy** because they reach an end point, and this type of manufacturing is sometimes referred to as 'take, make, dump'.

Make the Link

Plastic products should be marked with a recycling symbol to identify their type of plastic, making them easier to recycle.

Cradle-to-cradle approach

The term 'cradle to cradle' is used to describe design and manufacture in total harmony with the Earth; whatever we take from the land must eventually be returned to nature. This approach is about designing for disassembly, to allow the separation of the materials, so they can be reused, reprocessed or recycled. The materials can be cascaded through different uses until they can be returned to nature. Therefore, when selecting an appropriate material, the entire life cycle of the product must be considered.

Some materials, such as biopolymers made from corn starch, are designed for the **biological cycle**. These materials are biodegradable and are safely returned to the Earth through composting as they contain no harmful toxins.

When all the materials can be reused or returned to nature, this is called a 'closed loop' or 'circular-economy approach'. This means that products must:

- be 100% recyclable
- not damage the Earth with any chemicals or toxic waste
- not disturb or damage the Earth's ecosystem
- be manufactured using renewable energy sources.

These seedling pots will decompose after the seedlings have grown, making them a sustainable biological material.

The cradle-to-cradle approach can preserve our natural resources, minimise air pollution and have an overall neutral or positive impact on the environment.

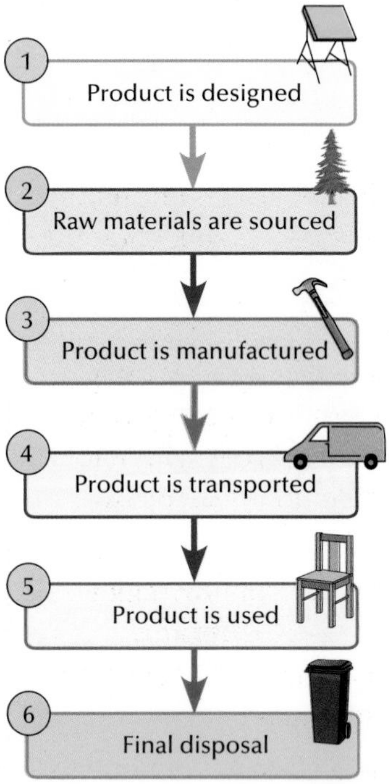

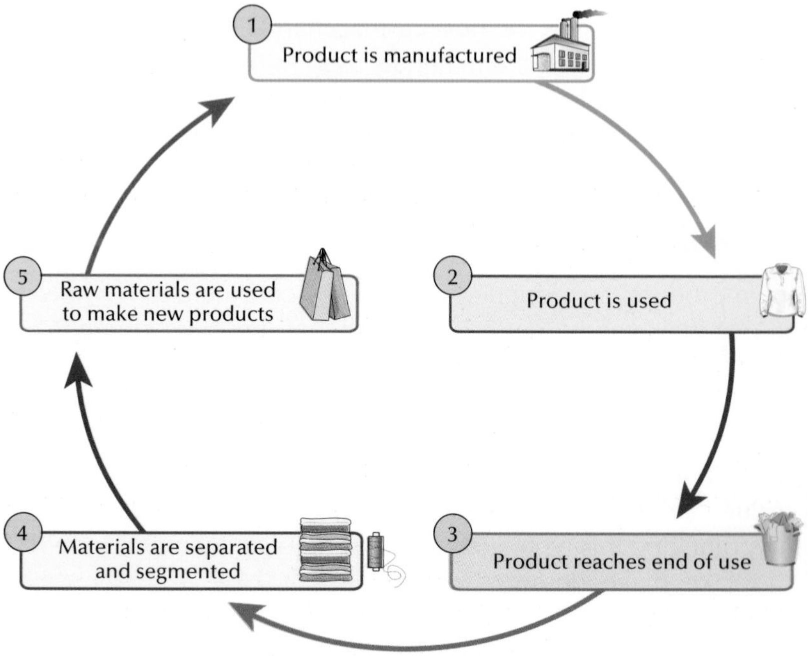

Products can follow a linear path whereby they are not broken down for reuse or recycling or they can follow a circular life cycle in which they are reused or recycled. The circular path is said to be sustainable as it reuses materials instead of wasting them.

Upcycling materials

It is popular for designers to use materials from discarded products instead of using raw materials. This is called **upcycling**, as it gives old products a new lease of life. It is an extremely good way of working sustainably as it incorporates the **six Rs** of recycling:

- **Rethink**
- **Reuse**
- **Recycle**
- **Repair**
- **Reduce**
- **Refuse!**

Upcycling is a positive approach compared to recycling. With recycling, materials can degrade in quality each time they are recycled. Recycling may also involve energy and water consumption, and often transportation.

Case study

Forestry Commission Scotland
Coimisean na Coilltearachd Alba

Scotland's forests are the most productive in the UK. They make a significant contribution to Scotland's economy through jobs in the wood-processing industry, forest management, wood transportation and other associated industries.

Forestry Commission Scotland (FCS) aims to maximise the economic potential of Scotland's timber resources. It encourages continued investment in timber processing by sustaining a predictable and stable supply of good quality timber. It plants 24 million trees every year, to create new woodland and to replace the trees harvested. Some of these trees will help to regenerate blighted industrial landscapes, such as former coalfield communities, and to bring new woodlands closer to urban areas.

A sustainable forest is a forest that is carefully managed, so that as trees are cut down they are replaced with seedlings which eventually grow into bigger, mature trees. The forest provides raw materials for furniture and construction, and wood pulp for paper. Great care is taken to ensure the safety of wildlife and to look after the natural environment.

Sustainable forests make business and environmental sense as raw materials can continue to grow, they provide habitats for wildlife, and they also attract walkers and hikers.

Sustainability is at the heart of FCS, setting the standards for the sustainable management of the UK's forests based on internationally recognised science and best practice. Britain was the first country in the world to have all its public forests independently certified as being sustainably managed.

FCS sustainably harvests almost five million tonnes of wood every year from Britain's public forests. That's around 44% of total domestic production or 300 truckloads every day. This reduces our dependency on imported wood and provides low-carbon materials for domestic wood-using industries, and for fuel and energy. The income from timber helps to offset the costs of managing the forests.

As Britain's largest land manager, FCS is custodian of one million hectares of land, including some of our best-loved and most spectacular landscapes. Two-thirds of FCS estates lie within national parks, areas of outstanding natural beauty or sites of special scientific interest (SSSIs).

Wood

Some wood, such as walnut, is used for its unique grain and vibrant colours.

Choosing a type of wood demands careful consideration as there are lots of varieties. Different types of wood have different strengths, visual features and colours. There are two main categories of wood: **hardwood** and **softwood**. Additionally, a third material, which is made from timber, is **manufactured boards**.

Wood is a natural material and, therefore, each piece is unique. The fine lines on the wood are called the **grain**. Sanding in the direction of the grain will smooth the surface of the wood. Sanding across the grain will scratch it.

Wood also has knots – dark circles on the wood where a branch once grew. Knots are tough and can be difficult to work with but look very interesting and give a unique aesthetic quality to the material.

Wood properties

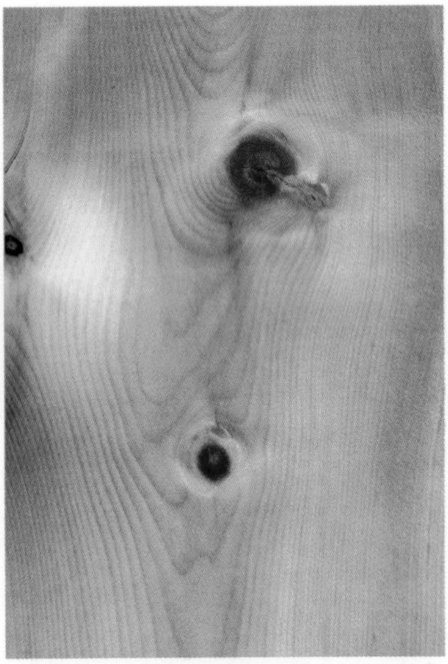

When selecting a wood for a product involving lots of cutting and shaping, avoid woods which are known for having lots of knots as they are difficult to work with.

The properties of wood and manufactured boards vary depending on the type of material; each wood and board has its own unique set of properties. The properties of wood can include:

- Buoyant – able to float.
- Durability – the resilience of the material (perhaps when outdoors or with wear).
- Density – the combined weight, strength and durability, ranging from soft to hard.
- Natural oil content – natural oil provides natural weatherproofing.
- Porous – the grain is open and has small 'pores', making it absorbent.
- Stable – flat and smooth, so doesn't warp or twist. Stable materials will paint or stain well.
- Strength – the ability to withstand force without breaking, ranging from weak to very strong.
- Toughness – the ability to withstand sudden blows or shicks without breaking.
- Weight – the heaviness, ranging from lightweight to heavy. When a material has a good strength to weight ratio then it strong for a lightweight material.
- Workability – the ease of cutting, shaping, etc.; ranging from easy to work to difficult to work. Usually, if wood is difficult to work it is due to the grain or knots. Manufactured boards can be difficult to work due to the way they are made.

Hardwoods

Hardwoods usually come from deciduous trees, which are trees with leaves, not needles. Hardwood trees can be identified by their leafy branches in summer. In winter, most shed their leaves.

Despite their name, hardwoods are not all hard. The lightest wood in the world, balsa wood, is a hardwood. The term 'hardwood' comes from their higher resistance to water, compared to softwoods, making them less likely to rot. As they are slower to grow than softwoods, hardwoods are generally more durable, but also more expensive.

Hint

Not all hardwoods are hard.

Name	Properties	Identifying features	Uses	Forms
Birch	Strong and durable but soft and easy to work with. Hard to stain.	White or pale yellowish colour with a close grain and smooth texture.	Used for furniture, tool handles and to make plywood.	Plank, square batten, strip.
Beech	Strong and durable but easy to work with and finish.	Pale brown colour, distinctive flecks in the grain.	Toys, tool handles, furniture (used for steam bending).	Plank, square batten, strip.
Balsa	Lightweight, porous, soft and buoyant.	Pale white and feels velvety to the touch.	Used for model making.	Small scale square battens, strips and sheets for model making.
Mahogany	Moderately strong, easy to work with, durable and finishes well with oil, wax and varnish particularly.	Light brown to reddish brown with a close and even grain, which gives a smooth and even surface.	Furniture, shop fittings, bar tops, solid wood flooring.	Plank, square batten, strip, veneers (wide planks are also available due to the large size of trees).
Oak	Strong, tough and durable but very difficult to work with.	Open grained with distinctive markings. Looks expensive.	Furniture, building beams, barrels, solid wood flooring.	Plank, square batten, strip, veneers.
Ash	Strong, tough and durable with good elasticity (suitable for bending).	Pale brown with a straight grain which can have a coarse texture.	Furniture, hammer handles, garden tool handles, hockey sticks, boat oars.	Plank, square batten, strip, veneer.
Teak	Strong, tough and durable with a high natural oil content.	A golden to dark brown colour with an oily feel.	Outdoor furniture, sheds, boats.	Plank, square batten, strip.
Walnut	Strong, tough and durable but can be hard to work.	Dark brown with an open, wavy grain which looks expensive.	Expensive furniture.	Plank, square batten, strip and veneers.

Softwoods

Softwoods come from coniferous trees, which are trees with needles and cones (e.g. pine cones). Softwood trees can be identified as being evergreen all year round.

Softwoods are quicker to grow than hardwoods and so they usually cost less than hardwoods. They are ideal for sustainable forestry (in which a new tree is planted when another is cut down), because they are fast growing. Approximately 80% of woods used are softwoods. They grow in Scandinavia, northern Europe, Russia and North America.

Name	Properties	Identifying features	Uses	Forms
Scots pine	Strong, straight-grained and easy to work.	Pink to reddish colour with a pale yellow grain.	Used for DIY, furniture, construction work and simple joinery.	Plank, square batten, strip, dowel.
Red pine	Strong, straight-grained but difficult to work due to knots.	White to pale yellow colour, straight grain and lots of brown coloured knots.	Used for DIY, furniture, construction work and simple joinery.	Plank, square batten, strip.
Cedar	Durable outdoors as it has high natural oil content, easy to work but not strong.	Reddish orange colour with distinctive growth rings.	Garden fencing, outdoor furniture, sheds, building exteriors.	Plank, square batten, strip.
Spruce	Strong, resistant to splitting and easy to work.	Pale white, small knots and sometimes contains resin pockets.	Used for general indoor work and furniture.	Plank, square batten, strip.
Douglas fir	Durable with good workability. Doesn't take stain well (use with paint instead).	Yellow to reddish brown with a pronounced grain.	Used for furniture, construction work and simple joinery.	Plank, square batten, strip.

Larger trees can provide wider planks. However, they take longer to grow and so are quite expensive.

Manufactured boards

These boards are made from wood pulp, blocks, chips or strips. They are mostly inexpensive compared to solid wood as they are made from wood which would normally go to waste. The main benefit of manufactured boards is that they are available in large sheets, whereas the size of solid wood planks is limited by the tree trunk diameter. Manufactured boards are said to be stable, meaning they have a flat and even surface, which is ideal for a smooth finish. Also they do not warp, twist or bow.

Name	Properties	Identifying features	Uses	Forms
Plywood	Stable and durable. Strong due to alternate grain direction in each layer.	Thin layers of wood, each layer placed at 90° to each other.	Furniture, cabinets, worktops, building construction and under flooring.	Boards.
Blockboard	Stable, durable and resistant to bending. Strong due to thickness but difficult to cut and shape.	Veneered top and base with blocks of wood sandwiched in between.	Large structures, building construction and heavy duty shelving.	Very thick boards.
Veneered chipboard (also available without a veneer)	Prone to splitting when used with screws. Difficult to cut and shape. Edges chip easily.	Compressed wood chips with a solid wood veneer on the top.	Worktops, cabinets, desk tops, low-cost furniture and shelving.	Boards. Laminated boards (with a plastic top layer) are also available.
MDF	Stable, stiff, easy to cut and shape. MDF dust is extremely harmful to breathe.	Wood fibres pressed together, satin smooth surface texture, rougher edges.	Furniture, worktops, cabinets, desk tops, low-cost furniture and shelving.	Boards. Laminated and veneered MDF boards are also available.
Hardboard	Very soft with little strength, bends easily and stable on one side only.	Wood fibres pressed together. Top is smooth and the back is soft and almost furry.	Templates for use in manufacturing, frame backs.	Thin boards (3 and 6mm thick only).

GO! Activity

Selecting wood

A coffee table made from wood is shown.

1. Discuss the features which would identify beech as the material for the table top, then decide and write down the top **two** identifying features.
2. Discuss other types of wood suitable for the table top, then write a list of **five** of the most suitable types of wood.
3. Complete the table below to find a suitable manufactured board for the table top.

Manufactured board	Suitable or unsuitable	Reason for suitability/unsuitability
Hardboard		
Blockboard		
Laminated MDF		
Chipboard		

Wood supply

The common sizes of timber materials are:

- **Manufactured boards** – available as a standard size of 2440 × 1220mm or 1220 × 607mm with a thickness of 6, 9, 12, 16, 19, 22mm.
- **Planks** – available in various sizes depending on the type of wood.
- **Strips of wood** – available in various sizes depending on the type of wood.
- **Square battens** – available in 35 × 35mm, 45 × 45mm, 75 × 75mm, 100 × 100mm.
- **Dowel rods** – available in diameters of 6, 8, 10, 12, 15 and 25mm.

Advantages of using wood

Designers use wood as it has a unique aesthetic and it is considered to be a comforting and warm material. Wood products have a handcrafted feel, adding a sense of skill, quality and care. Using a wood with an interesting or unique grain pattern brings a distinctive style which no other material can match. As trees can be replanted, wood is a sustainable material. Wood can also be recycled and reusing it is a fashionable way of sourcing material.

Disadvantages of using wood

As wood is a natural material, it typically requires a finish to protect and waterproof it. Applying a finish adds cost and time to manufacturing. Under pressure, wood can split along the grain and loose wood knots can fall out. Using wood can also mean working with unwanted natural characteristics, such as bowing, splitting, warping and twisting, which can add cost and time to manufacturing.

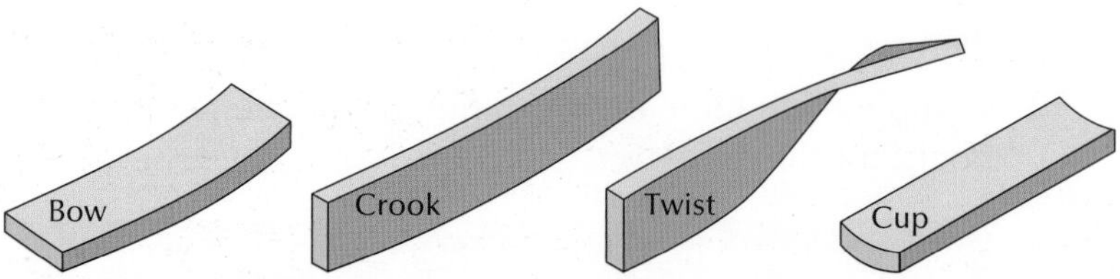

At the sawmill, wood is seasoned to dry it out. However, irregular grain and tension within the wood can cause it to bow, split, warp or twist. Storing wood at the wrong temperature or moisture level can also cause these defects.

Metal

Metal ores are rocks which are mined and then processed to refine them into metals. Some metals are mined as pure metals, such as copper, while some are mixed together to improve their properties, such as brass (copper with added zinc). A metal made from a mixture of two or more metals is called an **alloy**. All metals, including alloys, are classified into two main groups; **ferrous** and **non-ferrous**.

Make the Link

The tables on pages 132 and 133 show the properties of each metal.

Metal properties

The properties of metal vary depending on the type of material; each metal has its own unique set of properties. The properties of metal can include:

- Brittle – cracks or breaks easily.
- Corrosion resistant – does not rust.
- Ductility – can be stretched out without breaking to make long, thin lengths of metal.
- Durability – the resilience of the material and its resistance to wear and tear.
- Thermal insulator – able to maintain temperatures.
- Electrical conductor – able to pass an electric current through the metal.
- Malleable – soft enough to be shaped by pressing or pushing without the metal breaking or springing back into shape.
- Strength – ability to withstand force without breaking, ranging from weak to very strong.
- Toughness – the ability to withstand sudden blows or shocks without breaking.

Ferrous metals

A ferrous metal is a metal which contains iron. It is, therefore, magnetic. Iron reacts with oxygen in the air and in water by developing iron oxide on the surface of the metal. This is known more commonly as rust. To avoid rusting, ferrous metals require a finish, such as paint, to protect the metal.

Wrought Iron can be forged and bent, whereas cast iron is heated until it becomes molten metal and is then poured into a mould.

Name	Properties	Identifying features	Uses	Forms
Cast iron	Strong, tough, cannot be bent or forged. A hard outer skin.	Usually painted to avoid rust, very dark grey to black with a matt texture.	Baths, garden benches, pots, weights, drain covers, railings machines.	Ingots, bar and pipe.
Mild steel	Ductile and malleable yet tough. Easy to weld.	Silvery grey with poor corrosion resistance.	Car bodies, nuts, bolts, nails, screws, wire fencing.	Ingots, wire, bar, pipe, sheet.
Tool steel	Brittle, difficult to cut, resistant to wear.	Silvery grey with poor corrosion resistance.	Tools: saw blades, files, screwdrivers chisels, etc.	Ingots, wire, bar, sheet.
Stainless steel	Corrosion resistant, tough, difficult to cut and shape.	Silvery grey. Can appear dull or shiny.	Sinks, cutlery, saucepans, furniture, lighting, bikes, kitchen appliances.	Ingots, wire, bar, pipe, sheet.

Make the Link

Non-ferrous metals are not magnetic. However, depending on the amount of iron, a ferrous metal, in stainless steel it may or may not be magnetic. Stainless steel is well known for being corrosion resistant.

Non-ferrous metals

A non-ferrous metal is a metal which does not contain iron. It is, therefore, not magnetic. As they do not contain iron, most non-ferrous metals are corrosion resistant, which means they do not rust. Non-ferrous metals can tarnish (dark coloured spots or smears appear on the surface) but this can be polished off most metals and it only occurs after many years.

Copper tarnishes green with exposure to oxygen.

Name	Properties	Identifying features	Uses	Forms
Aluminium (pure metal)	Good strength-to-weight ratio, malleable, conducts heat and electricity well, ductile.	Shiny silvery grey colour which polishes well.	Kitchen foil, drinks cans, boat hulls, sports equipment.	Ingots, wire, bar, pipe, sheet.
Brass	Rigid, polishes well, conducts heat and electricity well, solders well.	Golden tones which polish well.	Taps, plaques, ornaments, instruments, household fittings.	Ingots, wire, bar, pipe, sheet.
Copper	Tough, ductile, malleable, conducts heat and electricity well, solders well.	Deep orange brown colour but tarnishes green with exposure to oxygen.	Electric wires, pipes, circuit boards, jewellery, roofing, cooking pans.	Ingots, wire, bar, pipe, sheet.
Duralumin	Stronger than pure aluminium, good strength-to-weight ratio.	Shiny silvery grey colour which polishes well.	Aircraft, greenhouses, window frames, high quality sports equipment.	Ingots, wire, bar, pipe, sheet.
Zinc	Weak, ductile, malleable, poor strength-to-weight ratio, casts well.	Silvery grey. Tends to have a matt surface finish.	Guttering, roofing, coins, watering cans, bins.	Ingots, wire, bar, pipe, sheet. Coating (galvanising).

Metal supply

When selecting a metal there is a wider range of forms and standard sizes compared to wood and plastic. The most common sizes of metals are:

- **Wire** – available in a range of thicknesses and lengths.
- **Bar** – metal bar is available in a range of cross sections (the shape at the end of the bar) such as round, square, flat (rectangular) and hexagonal. These are available in varying sizes from 5mm to 50mm. Lengths of bar are 1000 or 2000mm.
- **Pipe** – 5mm to 40mm diameter. Lengths of pipe are 1000 or 2000mm.
- **Sheet** – metal sheets can come in extremely thin sheets, just 0·1mm thick, up to 10mm thick. However, thicker metals are also available.
- **Ingots** – large blocks of metal which are melted down to use for moulding metals.
- **Powder** – fine metal powder is used for 3D printing.

Advantages of using metal

Metals come in a range of colours – from greys to golden yellows. Painting or plastic dip-coating metal gives even more scope for colour choice. Without a finish, metals can be polished to a high shine, which makes products appear glossy and new; therefore, metal products are said to have a hygienic and sterile appearance. Metals are excellent for conducting heat and electricity, and some metals, such as aluminium, have a good strength-to-weight ratio.

Disadvantages of using metal

Ferrous metals are prone to rusting and so a finish must be applied to them, adding time and cost to manufacturing. Once a finish has been applied, it will require maintenance to ensure it does not chip or flake off and further coats may be required, perhaps on an annual basis.

Although all metals can be recycled, metals are a finite resource, meaning that once all the metals have been mined from the Earth they cannot be replaced. Therefore, metal products should be designed so that they are easy to disassemble, reuse or recycle.

Test your knowledge

Link to suggested answers
www.leckieandleckie.co.uk/tykanswers

Metal and wood

A pupil designed and manufactured a key rack from metal and wood. The pegs were attached to a wooden plinth. Small metal ornaments were made in the shape of an office, car and house which were attached above each peg.

1. State **one** feature which would identify aluminium as the material for the pegs.
2. Explain **two** benefits of using aluminium for the pegs.
3. State the name of an alternative metal which could have been used for the pegs and explain why it would be suitable.
4. The pegs were attached with a mild steel nut at the back of the plinth. Explain **one** reason why mild steel is a suitable material for the nut.
5. State **one** feature which would identify birch as the material for the wooden plinth.
6. State the name of an alternative wood which could have been used for the wooden plinth and explain why it would be suitable.

Plastic

Plastic is a synthetic material. The basic raw materials used in the manufacture of plastics are made from oil, natural gas and coal. Modern developments in the plastics industry have seen the introduction of bioplastics or biopolymers. Biopolymers are plastics which are made from renewable resources, such as starch, sugar and cellulose sourced from animals or plants. These are ideal for disposable items, such as carrier bags and packaging, as they can decompose and the nutrients return to the soil. Such items are part of the cradle-to-cradle circular economy. Plastics are classified into two main groups; **thermoplastics** and **thermoset plastics**.

Make the Link

The tables below and on page 137 show the properties of each plastic.

Properties of plastic

The properties of plastic vary depending on the type of material; every plastic has its own unique set of properties.

The properties of plastic can include:

- Buoyant – able to float.
- Brittle – cracks or breaks easily. Non-brittle plastics are shatter resistant.
- Chemical resistant – does not wear away or break down when exposed to chemicals.
- Durability – the resilience of the material, resistance to wear and scratching.
- Flexible – how bendy the plastic is; from soft to rigid.
- Good heat insulator – able to maintain temperatures by keeping cold items cold and hot items hot.
- Heat resistant – able to withstand high temperatures without deforming, burning or melting.
- Moisture resistant – the ability to repel liquids.
- Strength – ability to withstand force without breaking.
- Toughness – the ability to withstand sudden blows or shocks without breaking.

Thermoset plastics

Thermoset plastics can withstand high temperatures.

When they are heated and shaped, thermoset plastics set. They cannot be returned to their original shape by reheating them. This means that they can withstand higher temperatures than thermoplastics and are used for products which are exposed to heat, such as oven dishes, electric plugs and sockets. Due to their ability to withstand heat, they are extremely difficult to recycle. Recycling a thermoset plastic involves grinding it down into a powder or small chips, which uses a lot of energy and the grainy end result has very few uses.

Name	Properties	Identifying features	Uses	Forms
Epoxy resin	Strong, chemical resistant, heat resistant.	Transparent, extremely strong chemical smell when used.	Adhesive for permanently joining different materials.	Two transparent liquid adhesives.
Melamine formaldehyde	Rigid, tough, scratch resistant, heat resistant.	Grainy texture.	Table tops, work tops, cooking utensils.	Veneers
Urea formaldehyde	Rigid, strong, heat resistant.	Matt or glossy finish.	Adhesive, electrical plugs and sockets.	

Thermoplastics

Thermoplastics soften when heated, allowing them to be shaped. They harden into shape as they cool. With this type of plastic, the softening and hardening can be repeated many times over. **Re**heating a thermoplastic will **re**turn it to its original shape, unless it has been permanently damaged by excessive heat or deformation. This unique characteristic of thermoplastics on reheating and reshaping is known as plastic memory (i.e. the material **re**members its original shape).

Hint

Reheat, **re**turn, **re**member.

Name	Properties	Identifying features	Uses	Forms
Polymethylmethacrylate (Acrylic)	Rigid, very durable, polishes to a high shine.	Glossy and smooth texture.	Shop signs, picture frames.	Sheet, rod, tube, granules, powder.
Polyvinylchloride (PVC)	Rigid, tough, chemical resistant.	Matt texture.	Pipes, guttering, window frames, cosmetics containers.	Sheet, rod, tube, granules, powder.
Polyamide (nylon)	Tough, resistant to wear, chemical resistant.	Waxy texture.	Gear wheels, machine parts, clothing, combs, tights.	Sheet, rod, tube, fibres, granules, powder.
High-Impact Polystyrene (HIP)	Lightweight, rigid, moisture resistant.	Glossy and smooth. Can be transparent.	Model kits, packaging, CD cases, plastic cutlery, toys.	Sheet, rod, tube, granules, powder.
Expanded polystyrene	Very lightweight, buoyant, good heat insulator.	Extremely light and spongy. Usually white.	Insulation, packaging, bean-bag filling, model making.	Blocks, strips, beads (small round pellets, normally used in packaging).
Polypropylene	Lightweight, flexible, resists cracking and tearing.	Waxy surface, often transparent or semi-transparent.	Ice cream tubs, straws, kettles, climbing ropes, crisp packets.	Sheet, rod, tube, fibres, granules, powder.
Polythene (HDPE)	Very tough, chemical resistant.	Waxy surface, coloured, transparent or semi-transparent.	Plastic bags, plastic films, containers, buckets, traffic cones, grit bins.	Sheet, rod, tube, rolls of film, granules, powder.
Acrylonitebutadienestyrene (ABS)	Very tough, scratch resistant, chemical resistant.	Shiny surface, colourfast.	Casings for electronics, car body parts, toys, luggage.	Sheet, rod, tube, granules, powder.

Plastic supply

When selecting a plastic, the supply types and sizes are complex.

- **Sheets** – available as a standard size of 1220 × 607mm, with a thickness of 4mm.
- **Rods** – available in diameters of 3 to 100mm. Lengths vary.
- **Tubes** – available in sizes of 5 to 100mm. Lengths vary.
- **Powder** – available for mass manufacturing processes in large volumes.
- **Granules** – available for mass manufacturing processes in large volumes.
- **Synthetic fabrics** – a standard width of 150mm and available in any length.

Plastic granules used for industrial manufacturing processes.

Advantages of plastic

Plastic is a very useful material as it is generally very lightweight but strong, and therefore it has a good strength-to-weight ratio. There is no need to apply a finish to plastic as it is waterproof and has built-in colour. It can also be transparent, making it the only alternative to glass. Plastics can resist chemicals in a way that wood and metal cannot. They have a smooth surface which can be wiped clean and so are said to be hygienic.

Disadvantages of plastic

Some plastics can be tricky to cut and shape as they can easily crack or shatter, and plastic dust is extremely dangerous to inhale. The surface of some plastics can also scratch easily (this is why most sheet plastics are supplied with a thin protective film on them).

Over time, plastics can become weaker with wear and sunlight can bleach the colour. Plastics cannot withstand extreme temperatures. They will deform, blister or burn if they are exposed to heat, while low temperatures can actually make plastics more brittle. Petroleum-derived and non-bio plastics can have an extremely negative environmental impact if they end up in landfill.

Case study

Sustainable packaging materials

In addition to considering the sustainability of the materials used for the product, designers must consider the environmental impact of packaging. Pallets, crates and packing trays are commonly reused when transporting products and traditional packaging materials, such as paper bags and cardboard boxes, can be recycled.

Some plastic carrier bags take at least 20 years decompose. However, the plastic bags now provided by most local councils for food waste are biodegradable. These are made from corn starch, biopolymer is called polylactide (PLA). The bags decompose along with the food waste.

Biopolymers make an extremely sustainable packaging material as they use renewable resources and are not harmful to the environment when they are disposed of correctly. Other biodegradable packaging materials include loose corn starch 'peanuts' which replace polystyrene balls, bubble wrap and air bags. Fungi or mushroom packaging is made from waste cornstalks and seed husks mixed with fungal mycelium, which grows and bonds the corn material. This material replaces styrofoam and polystyrene, and can be used to secure the contents, such as computers, in packaging boxes.

Test your knowledge

Link to suggested answers
www.leckieandleckie.co.uk/tykanswers

Plastics

A pupil evaluated a set of plastic and metal kitchen utensils.

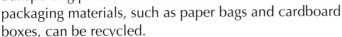

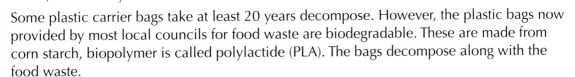

1. Describe **one** feature which would identify polystyrene as the material used.
2. Explain **two** benefits of using polystyrene for the utensils.
3. State the name of an alternative plastic which could have been used for the utensils and explain why it would be suitable.
4. State the name of a plastic which could have been used as an adhesive to join the metal whisk to its handle.

Make the Link

Measuring and recording is an ideal method to use for testing materials.

Testing materials

Materials should be tested to check their suitability for a design before they are used in manufacture. This is important as the material influences the success of the product.

Testing materials can take place as part of the research throughout the design development. By carrying out simple tests, appropriate materials can be identified. Experimenting with small material samples can provide enough information to make informed decisions. Aim to test just a few materials with one or two tests to gain results which are easy to analyse. Testing a wide range of materials with a wide range of techniques will provide a lot of results, which will be time consuming and difficult to collate.

To select an appropriate material there are four aspects to consider:

- **Workability** – selecting a material which can be cut, shaped or formed.
- **Practicability** – selecting a material which is affordable, sustainable, maintainable and available.
- **Function** – selecting a material with properties that suit the product's use.
- **Performance** – selecting a material which suits the circumstances of use.

Make the Link

The experience of working with materials gained during testing can be used when writing a plan for manufacture.

Workability

A material's workability is its capacity to be cut, shaped, drilled, etc.

Example: A letter rack with a curved edge is designed to be made from a manufactured board.

Test: Samples of MDF, chipboard and plywood are cut using a coping saw. This test aims to find out which material is the most suitable for manufacture, by testing the ease of sawing the curves. This test, therefore, aims to find out which material has the best workability and should result in a recommendation of the most suitable material.

Results:

- The MDF cut well with good quality, clean cuts.
- The plywood was harder to cut than the MDF but had better quality cuts.
- The chipboard was easy to cut but fell apart at the edges.

Recommendation: MDF was selected as it was the easiest manufactured board to cut and had good quality, clean cuts.

A student is using a coping saw to test the ease of sawing a piece of red pine.

Practicability

A material's practicability is its ability to be put into practice. It should be a sensible choice of material which is available for use.

Example: An egg cup is designed to be manufactured from metal.

Test: Samples of copper, aluminium and brass are cut. They are left in water to test their corrosion resistance, comparable to frequent dishwasher use.

Results:

- Copper was not affected by the water.
- Copper will oxidise and turn green over time with exposure to air.
- A few small, hardly noticeable, tarnish marks showed up on aluminium.
- Corrosion marks became evident on brass, which worsened throughout the test.

Recommendation: Of all three materials, aluminium has the most resistance to corrosion, therefore it would be easy to maintain and would not need to be replaced.

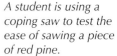

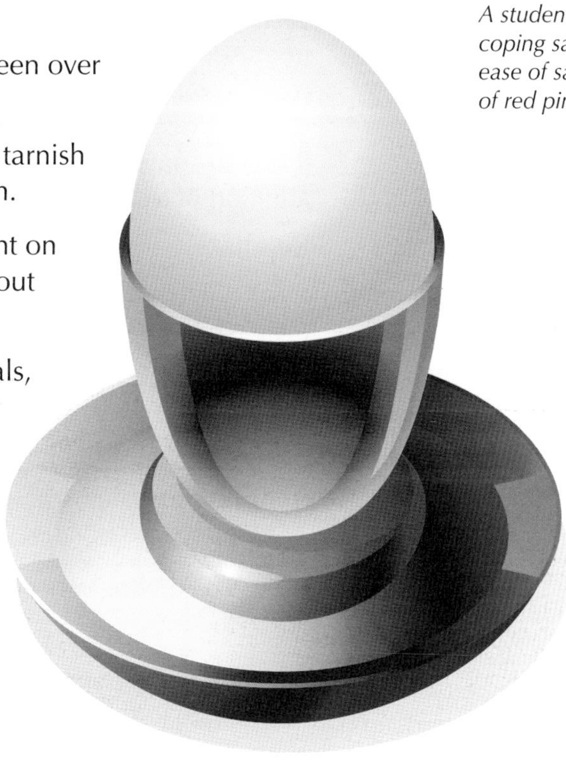

Function

Selecting a material which is suitable for a particular function depends on the location of the product, the conditions of use, the frequency of use and many more factors.

Example: A bird box is designed to be made from wood.

Test: Samples of cedar, red pine and mahogany are nailed to a tree. Additionally, samples of the same woods, coated with an exterior paint, were also nailed to the tree. The test imitates an outdoor location and aims to find out which material is able to function outdoors through its durability and whether the addition of a surface finish provides any benefit.

Results:

- The cedar retained its density and didn't appear to be affected by the weather.
- The cedar with paint felt the same.
- The red pine sample felt a little spongy to the touch.
- The red pine with paint retained its density and didn't appear to be affected by the weather.
- The mahogany sample also felt a little spongy to the touch.
- The mahogany with paint retained its density and didn't appear to be affected by the weather.

Make the Link

A situation analysis will identify the functional requirements of the material. When more than one material is recommended, the results from another material test may be considered to reach a conclusion; for example, using the results from a workability test to find out which material is most suitable.

Recommendation: The cedar, with its high natural oil content, proved to be the most suitable material without a finish. However, with the addition of a protective coat of exterior paint, all the woods tested would be suitable for outdoor use.

Performance

A material's performance is its ability to carry out a task and its reaction to an external element, such as force or heat.

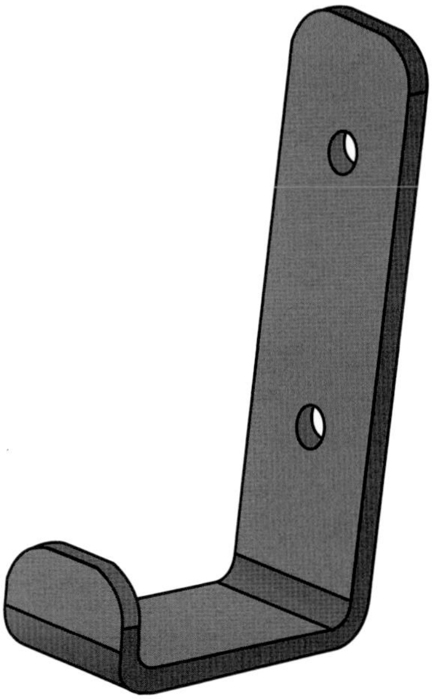

Example: A coat hook is designed to be made from metal or plastic.

Test: A strip heater was used to fold small sample strips of acrylic, recording the time it took to soften each material before shaping. A folding press was used to shape small sample strips of aluminium, annealed aluminum and brass. This test aims to find out which material is able to perform best under force.

Results:

- The acrylic required time to heat and soften before folding.
- Aluminium did not require heat to fold it.
- The acrylic bubbled if left on the heat for too long.
- The acrylic could be reshaped if mistakes were made.
- The aluminium cracked slightly along some of the folds.
- The brass also cracked slightly along some of the folds.
- The annealed aluminium did not crack along the folds, but additional time was required to carry out the annealing process.

Recommendation: Choosing the most appropriate material was a close decision between the brass and the acrylic. Aluminium was ruled out as it would require to be annealed to strengthen it to prevent cracking before bending, and this took additional time. Acrylic was selected for its ease of bending.

Recommending final selection of materials

Once testing has taken place and the results are gathered, it is then time to explain why a material is appropriate. A designer will describe the reasons clearly for the material selection by identifying the properties of the material, along with any test results to justify their choice.

The reasons for choosing a material can be based on:

- Aesthetic qualities
- Sustainability
- Workability
- Practicability
- Function
- Performance

Here are some examples:

The rich reddish brown colour of mahogany makes it suitable for a spice rack as it works well with the traditional style of the kitchen and complements the orange, red and brown tones of the spices.

The cookie cutter will be made from aluminium because it is malleable and easy to shape. It did not rust in the dishwasher test and was found to have a sharp enough edge to cut the dough.

After testing a few different woods on the wood lathe, it was decided that beech would be the best material to make the candle holder. Both the red pine and walnut proved difficult to turn due to the number of knots and grain pattern. The close grain of the beech made it easy to work and suits the design aesthetically.

Hint

Along with the properties of the material, the tests should identify an appropriate material.

GO! Activity

Testing materials

A pupil has designed a plaque for the front door of their home which has numbers on the front, holes in each corner for screws, rounded edges and two slots, which are aesthetic design details.

1. Select **three** suitable materials for the door plaque and justify your choice of materials.
2. Cut samples of these materials.
3. Test the material samples for one of the following criteria:
    - Workability
    - Practicability
    - Function
    - Performance
4. Record your results and state the most suitable material.
5. Explain why this material is appropriate.

Check your progress

I can:	HELP NEEDED	GETTING THERE	CONFIDENT
• describe sustainability issues in relation to materials			
• describe the properties and identifying features of a range of woods and manufactured boards			
• describe the properties and identifying features of a range of metals			
• describe the properties and identifying features of a range of plastics			
• explain why a material is appropriate for a manufacturing task			
• explain the purpose of testing materials before recommending them for manufacture			
• describe methods of testing materials in terms of workability, practicability, function and performance.			

6 Manufacturing in the workshop

By the end of this chapter you should be able to:

- describe methods of preparing for manufacture
- state the names of appropriate tools, equipment and manufacturing processes for working with wood
- state the names of appropriate tools, equipment and manufacturing processes for working with metal
- state the names of appropriate tools, equipment and manufacturing processes for working with plastic
- describe how to evaluate the success of a manufacturing process.

Prepare for manufacture

Once a design proposal has been finalised and a plan for manufacture has been completed (see page 108) it is time to begin manufacture. There are a few tasks to carry out before this plan is implemented:

- **P**urchase or order all the materials and components.
- **R**ead the working drawings.
- **E**stablish a practical sequence for manufacture.
- **P**repare materials – by cutting material to size, smoothing rough sawn edges, etc.
- **A**ssure quality of materials – by checking for flaws and overall quality.
- **R**ecognise tools, equipment and processes.
- **E**xamine tools and equipment to check they are in a safe working order.
- **M**anufacturing plans and drawings are checked for accuracy.
- **E**valuation preparation is in place.

Hint

What do I need to do to PREPARE ME for the workshop?

Make the Link

The cutting list (page 111) is an essential part of the plan for manufacture (page 108).

Purchasing materials and components

A designer will work with the engineer to create a cutting list to order materials for the manufacturer. Without a cutting list, no materials can be ordered.

Read the working drawings to select tools and equipment

The working drawings are a useful resource in the workshop. They can be used to find the sizes when marking out and they can be used to select tools and equipment for manufacturing tasks.

Establish a practical sequence for manufacture

The **plan for manufacture** is used to guide you through the construction of the product. However, it may need to be redrafted a couple of times before it is in an order which makes sense. This sequence can be difficult to predict as the project is new to you and you may be unfamiliar with some of the processes involved. Sometimes the sequence of manufacture is simple. For example, the hole must be drilled in a clock before the clock mechanism can be assembled. Sometimes the sequence of manufacture is more complex. For example, in this key cabinet (below) the plastic backing had to be cut on a laser cutter before the project was assembled. This required further thought as the key cabinet was to be painted and, therefore, the plastic had to be carefully covered with masking tape before painting.

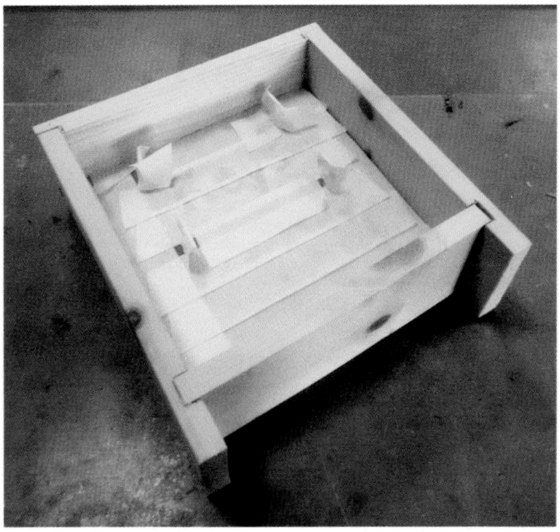

Key cabinet before assembly and then masked off before painting.

Once a sequence for manufacture has been decided, you should be able to justify the reasons for the order of tasks. The sequence must be the most practical method, in that it must be easy to put into practice, and it must be the most efficient method, in that it must make good use of time and resources.

Hint

In order to justify a sequence of manufacture, it must be practical and efficient.

Some reasons to justify your sequence may be:

- The process was researched and this sequence was found to be a common approach.
- A practice or test was carried out to investigate the best possible method.
- Common sense was applied.
- Time can be used more effectively by following this sequence.
- Grouping similar tasks together saves time.
- The time taken to complete this sequence is the quickest.
- The quality of work from this sequence will be the best.

Prepare materials

It is necessary to prepare some materials before manufacture. This may involve cutting longer lengths of material to size or, perhaps, smoothing rough edges or saw marks. When preparing for manufacturing a large wooden product, it may be necessary to build up wide panels of wood by gluing planks of wood together with PVA glue.

Planks of red pine are glued together to create a wider board. The sash clamp on top prevents the boards from bowing while the scrap wood at each end protects the red pine from being damaged when the clamps are tightened.

Make the Link

Quality assurance checks are completed by manufacturers in industry (see pages 196–198).

Assure quality of materials

When you receive your materials, you must check them over to assure their quality. This involves checking for any flaws in the material and assessing its general overall quality. This is the best time to identify any faults with the material as it is easier to fix or replace at this stage.

Recognise tools, equipment and processes

For successful manufacture, it is important to learn and use the correct names for tools, equipment and processes. This will help you to communicate effectively the manufacturing processes and techniques you will use during manufacture.

Hint

Asking for help is much easier when you know what tools, equipment or processes you need help with.

Examine tools and equipment

Before starting any practical work, it is extremely important to examine tools and equipment to check they are in safe working order. Using faulty or broken tools and equipment is very dangerous and can lead to accidents.

If a tool or piece of equipment breaks during use, the responsible thing to do is to report it. Some common faults and breakages with tools and equipment are:

- File handles can come loose or come apart completely.
- Plane blades are adjustable and so can become loose or angled.
- Mallet heads can come loose from the handle or come apart completely.
- Coping saw and jigsaw blades can snap.

Make the Link

Safety in the workshop is covered later in this chapter.

Manufacturing plans and drawings are checked for accuracy

Producing manufacturing plans which are accurate takes practice. A good manufacturing plan will incorporate requirements for tools, equipment, materials and fixings, as well as manufacturing techniques and processes.

A good quality **working drawing** is essential for marking out material for cutting or shaping, which usually takes place during the first stages of manufacture.

If an **orthographic drawing** is used as a working drawing, the following standards must be followed:

- Drawings are to scale.
- Third angle projection layout is used.
- Dimensions are placed to the side of the drawings, not on top of them.
- Dimensions are not repeated.
- Keep the number of views to a minimum.
- Dimensions are all in mm.
- Construction lines, heavy outlines, centre lines and hidden detail line types are used.

Hint

Ask your teacher to check your manufacturing plan before beginning any practical tasks.

Make the Link

A plan for manufacture includes a detailed drawing with dimensions and a cutting list (see pages 108–112).

In this orthographic drawing, third angle projection is applied. This means the plan is above and in line with the elevation. The end elevation is to the side of and in line with the elevation.

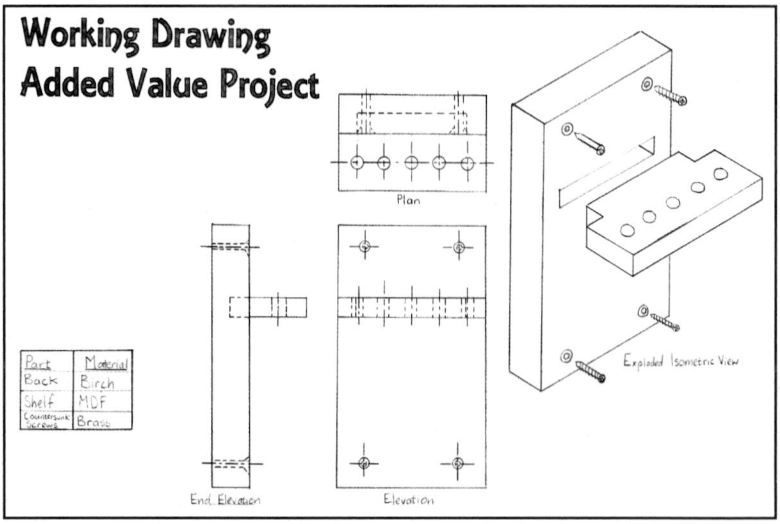

Make the Link

Writing an evaluation of the manufacturing plan is covered on page 184.

Evaluation preparation

When manufacturing is complete, the plan for manufacture can be evaluated. This evaluation can make suggestions to improve the plan in terms of the practicality and efficiency. To make the evaluation easier, it is a good idea to record your thoughts as you are manufacturing. This may include ideas of an alternative method or a record of any changes you made, if perhaps your original manufacturing plan did not quite as you expected. Your record may be a log sheet, a video diary or even just a list of notes. The key thing is that it is kept up to date and regularly added to. Keeping a record of the success of the manufacturing plan during manufacturing simplifies the evaluation task.

The signs you see around the workshop are colour coded: blue signs are for mandatory rules (must do), red signs identify a danger, yellow signs are to warn you of a hazard and green signs are for safety and first aid.

Safety in the workshop

The general safety rules for a workshop are:

- Keep jackets and bags out of the work area, to avoid tripping hazards.
- Remove all loose clothing, earphones and jewellery and tie back long hair.
- Don't run around in a workshop.
- Keep tools in the middle of the bench or put them away when they are not in use.
- Safely carry tools down by your side.
- Keep calm in a workshop and don't rush work. A productive pace is a safe pace.
- Report any breakage or accident, even if very small.
- Pay proper attention during demonstrations to ensure you understand how to safely use the tool, machine or equipment.

Personal protective equipment (PPE)

Special safety equipment must be worn in many different jobs – people from lumberjacks to doctors wear PPE. It is a responsible approach to avoid accidents at work and employers will insist PPE is worn for the health and safety of their workers. PPE is worn in the workshop too:

- Safety goggles protect eyes when using machinery.
- A face mask is used when sanding wood or when using toxic finishes such as spray paint.
- A face shield is required when working with hot metal.
- Heatproof suede apron and gloves are needed when working with hot metal.

In many jobs PPE is part of the uniform.

Manufacturing with wood

Woodwork is a popular hobby which millions of people enjoy, and a life-long skill. Good woodwork requires the right tools for the job. Most homes have a basic toolkit and you may already be familiar with some of the woodwork tools in this section.

When working with wood and manufactured boards, the main processes are:

- **Cutting, sizing and shaping**
- **Drilling**
- **Turning**
- **Assembly and joining methods**
- **Finishing**

Cutting, sizing and shaping wood

Cutting, sizing and shaping wood requires a range of different tools, depending on the shape and size of the project. First, the raw material may need to be cut to size using a saw, simply called sizing. Wood can then be measured and **marked out**. This involves accurately drawing the component parts or woodwork joints onto the wood or manufactured board. The table on the next page shows some of the most common tools for marking out.

Tool	Image	Use
Tape measure		Checking material sizes
Steel rule		Measuring
Try square		Drawing lines at 90° to the edge of the wood or checking for 90° angles
Sliding bevel		Similar to a try square, but adjustable to any angle
Marking gauge		Drawing lines parallel to the edge of the wood
Mortise gauge		Similar to a marking gauge, but with two pins for marking mortise joints
Bradawl		Marking hole positions

Hint

A coping saw can cope with curves.

Once it is marked out, the material can be cut using saws that are suitable for wood. A tenon saw or mitre saw is used for straight cuts, while a coping saw can cut curves. The table opposite (top) shows some of the most common tools used for cutting wood.

Tool	Image	Use
Tenon saw		Sawing straight cuts
Coping saw	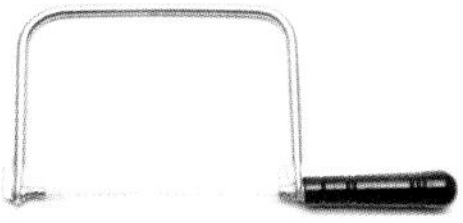	Sawing curved cuts
Mitre saw		Sawing at a specific angle, with a range of angles

To cut woodwork joints, a chisel can be used with a mallet. There are many variations of plane, which can remove waste material, smooth surfaces or cut grooves. A rasp or surform can be used to smooth edges or remove waste material. These are some of the most common tools used for shaping wood.

Tool	Image	Use
Jack plane	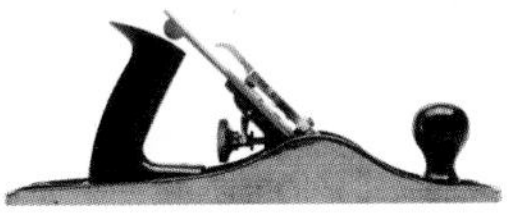	Adjusts the thickness of wood by removing a layer of material
Smoothing plane	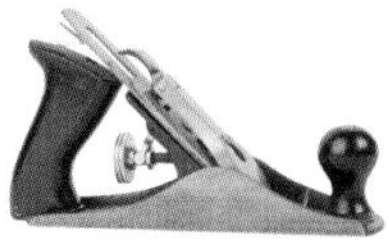	Smooths wood by removing a thin layer of material
Rebate plane		Removes a thin section of wood (rebate) along one edge
Mortise chisel		Cutting out wood, especially suited to mortise joints
Bevelled-edge chisel		Cutting out wood
Mallet	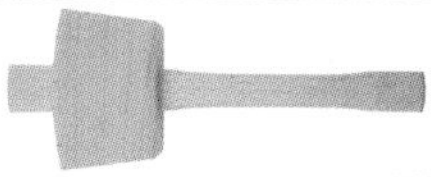	Used to hit a chisel
Rasp/surform		Roughly smoothing the edge of wood and for forming curved edges

Card templates are a quick way of marking out complex or curvy shapes and they can be reused, allowing for small batches of identical products to be produced.

A range of machines and power tools can be used to shape wood. These make manual tasks faster and easier. However, extra safety precautions must be followed when using them:

- Wear appropriate PPE (e.g. wear safety goggles when using the mortise machine).
- Test the emergency stop button before using a machine.
- Keep a safe distance from others.
- Be aware of the power cable when using power tools.
- Keep fingers away from sharp or moving parts.

Each workshop has different machinery. These are some of the most common workshop machines.

Tool	Image	Use
Woodwork lathe	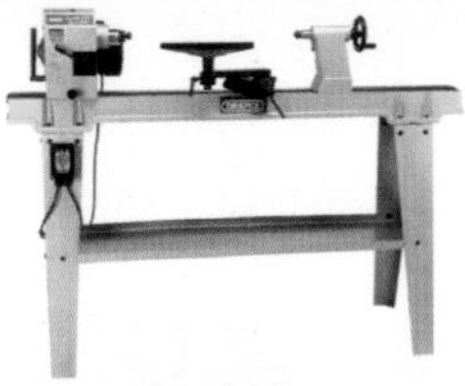	Creates cylindrical wooden shapes by turning wood
Sanding machine		Smooths the edges of wood
Band saw		Large machine saw for cutting materials
Fret/scroll saw	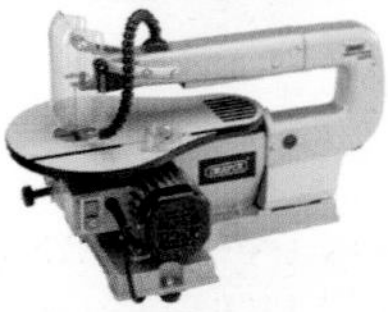	Smaller saw used for thin material, and intricate cuts and tight curves
Mortise machine		Cuts square or rectangular holes or slots in wood

Power tools can be used to cut and shape material when greater flexibility is required, where a machine is unsuitable or to speed up a manual task. The table below shows some of the most common power tools.

This picture frame has a curved edge, which was cut using a router.

Tool	Image	Use
Orbital sander	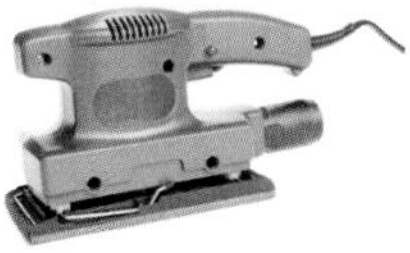	Sands wood to an extremely smooth finish
Power drill		General drilling, can act as a screwdriver with a screwdriver attachment
Jigsaw	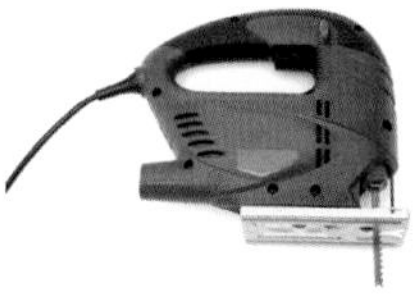	Cutting curved cuts or quick rough cuts
Biscuit jointer		Cuts a groove for a biscuit joint
Router		Cuts a curved profile along an edge; can also cut a rebate

Drilling wood

To make a round hole in wood, a drill is used. A hand drill, brace, power drill or pillar drill can be used to drill wood. There is also a range of different drill bits suitable for drilling wood, depending on the shape and size of the project. For example, a forstner bit will drill a flat-bottomed hole, while a flat bit can be used for larger holes. A steel rule and try square or marking gauge should be used to mark out the location of the hole accurately. The table on the next page shows some of the most common tools used for drilling wood.

Tool	Image	Use
Twist drill bit		Drilling general holes
Forstner drill bit		Drilling flat-bottomed holes
Flat drill bit		Drilling larger holes
Countersunk bit		Drilling countersunk holes
Hole saw		Drilling and creating round discs
Brace		Drilling by hand
Hand drill		Drilling by hand, comes in handy for tight corners

When marking out a hole, a cross is marked on the material, allowing for the tip of the drill bit to line up with this exact point.

Make the Link

The pillar drill is also used for drilling metal and plastic.

Hint

Use a small piece of scrap wood under the G-clamp to avoid denting wood. Remember to remove the chuck key as this can cause a serious accident if left in the machine.

The pillar drill (below) is ideal for most woodwork drilling tasks and can also be used to drill metal and plastic. While using this machine, the material must be clamped to the table using a G-clamp. A machine vice can be used to hold small pieces of wood. However, the vice can dent the wood if it is overtightened. The drill should be adjusted to suit your work by setting the depth stop and table height. A small hole is drilled first. This is called a **pilot hole** as it guides the way for a larger hole to be drilled and prevents the material from cracking. A pilot hole is usually 1–2mm in diameter.

The same process is followed for drilling plastic.

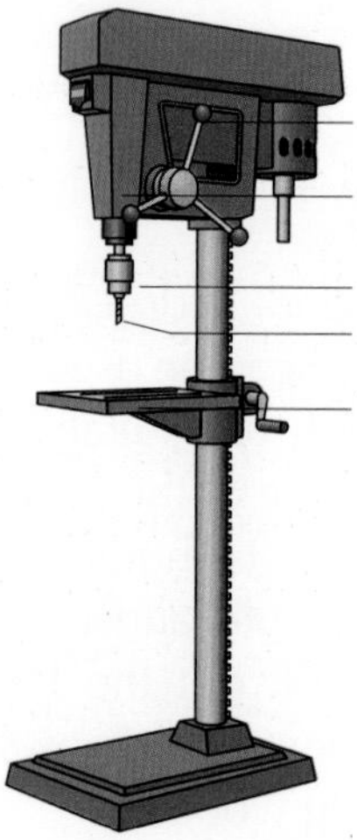

A pillar drill

Turning wood

The wood lathe is used for turning between centres (to make long cylindrical shapes such as table legs), or for face plate turning (using round blocks of wood to make e.g. bowls). To prepare for using a lathe, a length of wood, known as a blank, is marked out and planed to a cylindrical shape.

Make the Link

When selecting wood for turning, look for a piece of wood which is free from knots.

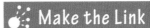

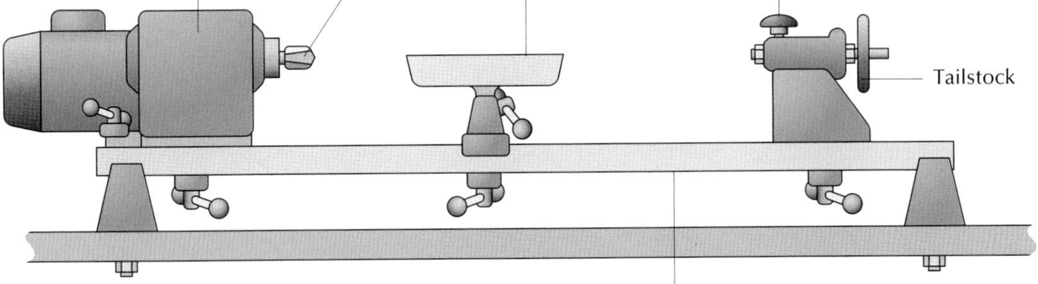

The wood lathe.

When wood is manufactured on a wood lathe, the process is called turning as the machine spins the wood around. The wood is held tightly between the fork centre and the revolving or dead centre. Before using a wood lathe the following checks must be made:

- The material is held tightly on the machine.
- No loose clothing or jewellery is in the way.
- The speed is set correctly for the task.
- The material can turn freely without hitting any machine parts.
- Safety goggles are worn.
- The material is held exactly in the centre.
- The tailstock is secured or locked in position.

Make the Link

Follow these same safety checks when using a metal lathe.

Make the Link

Chapter 7 explains wood turning in mass manufacture.

Once prepared, the blank is then held between the fork centre on the headstock and the dead centre or revolving centre at the tailstock end. The operator holds a tool on the tool rest and can shape the wood by moving it in different directions. A range of curves, indents, angles and shapes can be created with a range of different wood-lathe tools. A gouge and/or a scraper is used to roughly round the product off, then other shaping tools can be used to create more detailed shapes. The table on the next page shows some of the most common tools used for turning.

Tool	Image	Use
Skew chisel	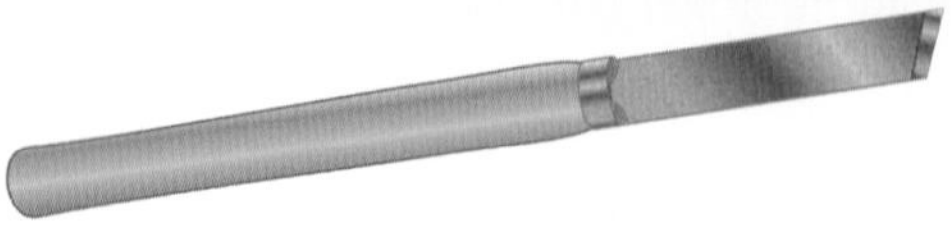	Sharp-edged tool for accurate rounding and shaping
Parting tool	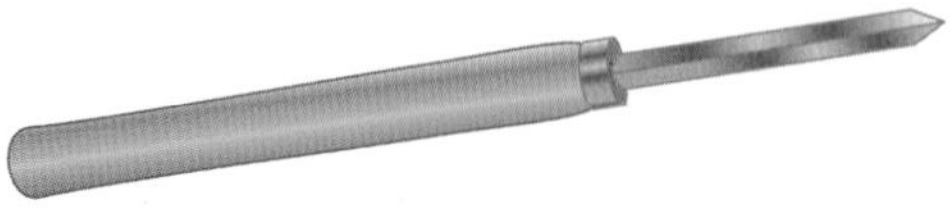	Pointed tool for cutting notches or cutting/removing wood from the lathe
Rounded scraper	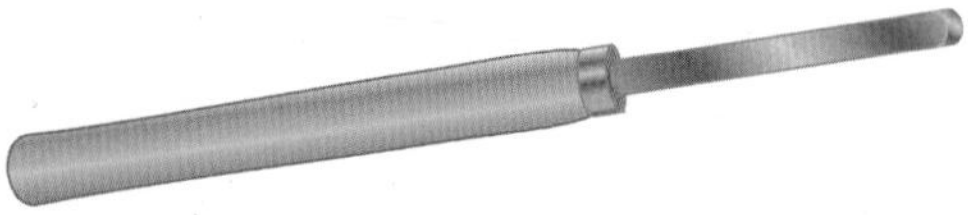	Rounded-edge tool for removing wood quickly and creating convex curves
Gouge	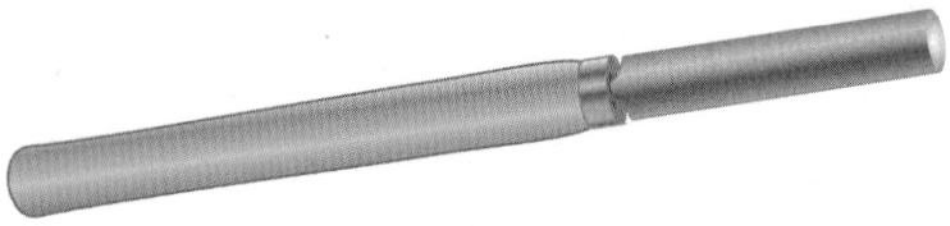	U-shaped tool for removing waste wood quickly and creating convex curves
Inside callipers		Measuring inside diameters on the woodwork lathe
Outside callipers	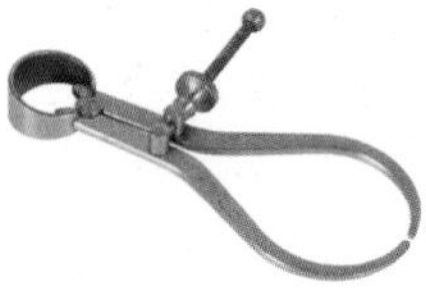	Measuring outside diameters on the woodwork lathe

Test your knowledge

Link to suggested answers
www.leckieandleckie.co.uk/tykanswers

Turning

1. State the checks that are made on the machine before using a woodwork lathe.
2. State the checks that are made on the operator before using a woodwork lathe.
3. Describe the **four** stages required to prepare the wood for the lathe.
4. State a suitable wood for the turned wooden bowl on the right.
5. Explain why this is a suitable wood for turning.

Assembly and joining methods for wood

There is a range of woodwork joints. Designers select woodwork joints based on their:

- strength
- aesthetic qualities
- functional suitability
- ease of manufacturing.

Most woodwork joints are held together by an adhesive to strengthen the joint. However, panel pins or screws can also be used to reinforce a joint. Aesthetic qualities of a joint can be that they are simple or that the joining method is hidden.

- A **mitre joint** has a small surface area with just two surfaces to coat with adhesive. Therefore, the joint will be weak.
- A **finger joint** has many surfaces which interlock. This gives a large surface area to coat in adhesive, so the join will be stronger.
- A **stopped housing joint** hides the joint, simplifying the overall look and improving the aesthetic of the product.

Some woodwork joints are more complex to manufacture. However, they can be more attractive as their complexity and detail indicates craftsmanship and skill. A **dovetail joint** is extremely challenging to manufacture. It brings a sense of skill and quality to the product.

The most common wood adhesive is PVA, which is a white glue that dries clear. It is a non-toxic, non-flammable, water-based adhesive. As it is waterproof, any excess glue must be wiped away with a damp cloth or paper towel before it dries. It is, however, unsuitable for outdoor use. It is best to leave PVA for around 24 hours to dry properly.

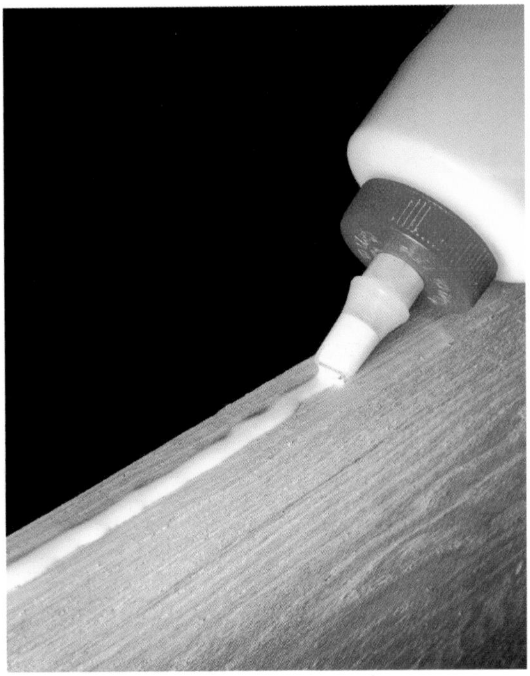

Adhesives which are suitable for outdoor use are harder and more durable. However, they are generally toxic and must be used with care.

Joints range in terms of their strength and difficulty of manufacture. The correct joint to choose will depend on the function of the frame that is being constructed; the wooden framework for a building obviously has different requirements to that of a picture frame. The table on the next page shows some of the most common framework joints.

Joint	Image	Strength	Manufacture
Butt	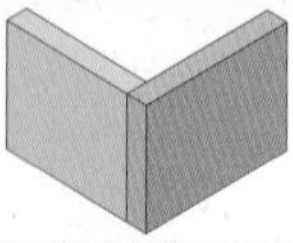	Very weak	Easy and quick
Mitre	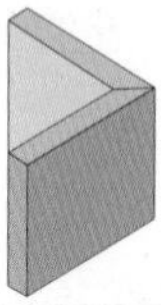	Weak	Easy and quick
Lap	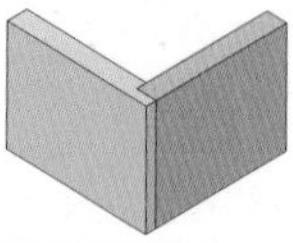	Moderate	Fairly easy and quick
Dowel	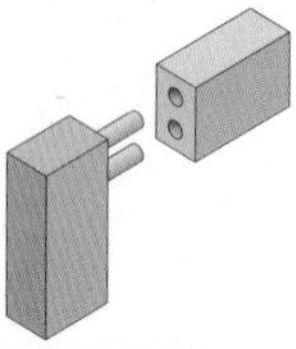	Moderate	Moderate difficulty and time requirement
Halving	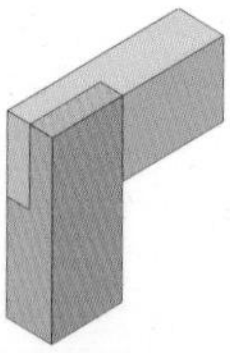	Moderate	Moderate difficulty and time requirement
Bridle	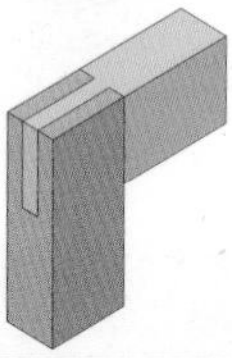	Strong	Challenging and time consuming
Mortise and tenon	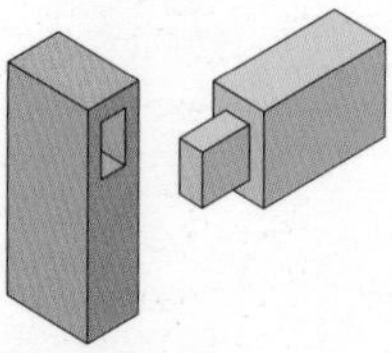	Strong	Challenging and time consuming

Cabinet joints also have a range of strength and difficulty. Cabinet joints can sometimes be called **carcass joints**. The table opposite shows some of the most common cabinet joints.

Joint	Image	Strength	Manufacture
Butt	See table opposite	Very weak	Easy and quick
Dowel	See table opposite	Moderate	Moderate difficulty and time
Through housing	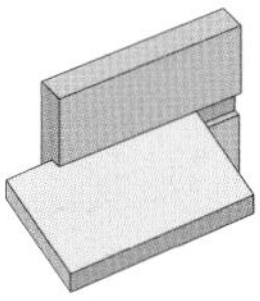	Moderate	Moderate difficulty and time requirement
Stopped housing	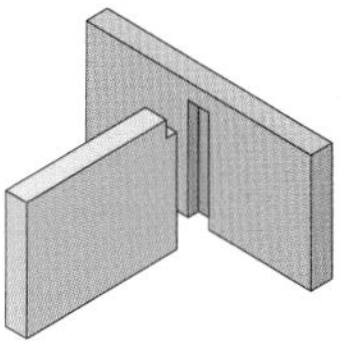	Strong	Somewhat challenging and time consuming
Finger	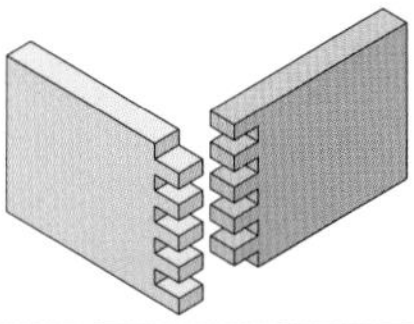	Extremely strong	Challenging and time consuming
Dovetail	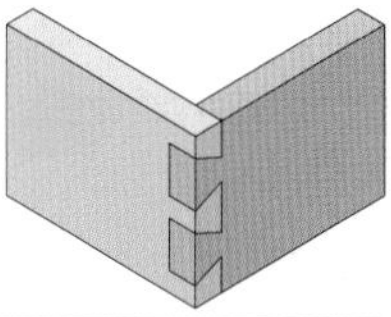	Extremely strong	Very challenging and time consuming
Biscuit	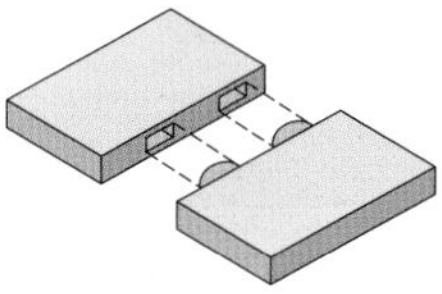	Moderate	Easy and quick but requires machinery

When joining materials, they should be **dry clamped** first. This involves putting the whole project together without glue to check the assembly.

When assembling, the four things to check are that the project is:

- **Square** – check the corners with a try square or measure the diagonals and check they are equal.
- **Level** – check the project is sitting flat on the surface and is not wobbling. You can also check horizontal parts are level using a spirit level.
- **True** – check all the parts are correctly and accurately aligned.
- **Secure** – check that all parts are properly fitted together, especially wood joints and boards which fit into slots. Use extra clamps when necessary for extra accuracy.

Hint

Before gluing any wood clamp it together without glue to check it is square and fits properly. This is called dry clamping.

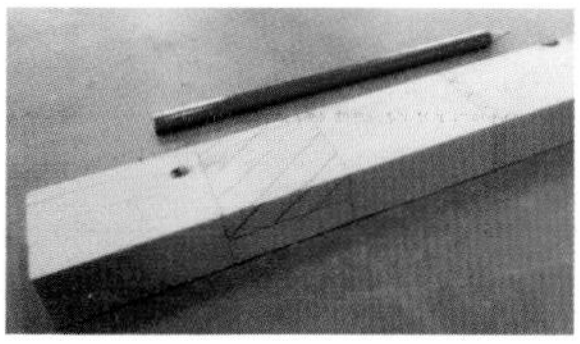

When marking out a joint, use cross hatching to show the waste wood.

Hint

Put your project on a large flat board to avoid assembling on uneven workbenches.

Here are some common tools that are used in the assembly of products.

Type of hammer	Image	Usage
Claw hammer		Nailing or removing nails or panel pins; also good for levering items apart
Warrington hammer		Nailing small nails or panel pins
Screwdriver		Attaching screws
Nail punch		Drives nails below the surface of the wood
G-clamp	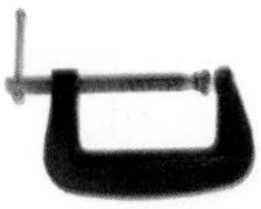	Holds wood in place while cutting or for assembly
Sash cramp	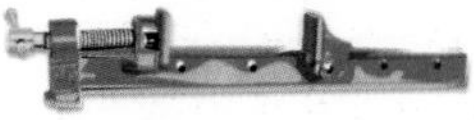	Holds wood in place during assembly

A range of fittings and fixings is available for woodworking projects. Here are some of the more common items.

Type of fitting/fixing	Image	Usage
Roundhead screws	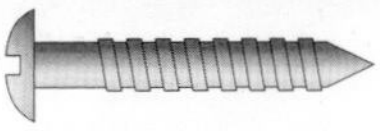	Rounded tops have aesthetic qualities
Countersunk screws		Sit flush (level) with the surface, hiding the screw
Panel pin	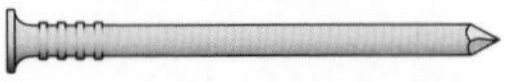	A general purpose nail
Lost head nail		Nails which can be hit below the surface of the wood
Butt hinge	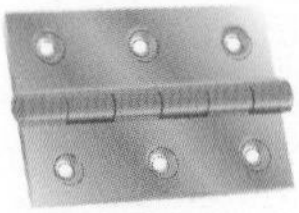	Classic hinge which must be let-in (set in a chiselled-out recess)
Piano hinge		A long-length hinge
Knock-down fittings		A range of joining fittings used as easy alternatives to joints

Finishing wood

When deciding on the type of finish for a product or component part, it is important to consider the following factors:

- **aesthetic**
- **function**
- **lifespan** required
- **location** (interior or exterior)

Certain wood finishes will make the wood more durable or waterproof, while others will simply offer a different colour or shine.

Well-prepared surfaces create a good quality finish. Sandpaper, also known as glasspaper, is a type of abrasive paper used to remove small amounts of material from surfaces, to make them smoother, remove pencil marks or remove dried glue. Sandpaper is available in different grades from coarse, which feels rough to the touch, to fine, which is smoother.

> **Hint**
>
> Check the edges of the wood for diagonal saw marks (left by the circular saw) and remove them.

Always sand *with the grain* of the wood (in the direction of the lines).

Sanding across the grain will scratch your wood and damage it. When sanding the end grain (where the annual rings are), sanding in a circular motion will achieve the best finish.

Belt and disc sanders are machines which can smooth the surfaces and edges of wood to a very high standard. The sandpaper moves extremely quickly and it provides a much faster finish than hand sanding. However, a final sand by hand gives a higher quality finish.

Sand the wood until it has the same level of smoothness all over using a sanding block, or cork block.

Here are some of the most common pieces of equipment for applying a finish.

Equipment type	Image	Usage
Brushes		Applying paint, varnish, stain or sanding sealer
Steel wool		Smoothing between varnish coats or for applying wax
Sanding block		Sandpaper is wrapped around it, providing even pressure
Sand/glass paper		Abrasive paper for smoothing wood
Cloth		Applying wax, oil or polish

A natural finish can be achieved by simply sanding the wood smooth.

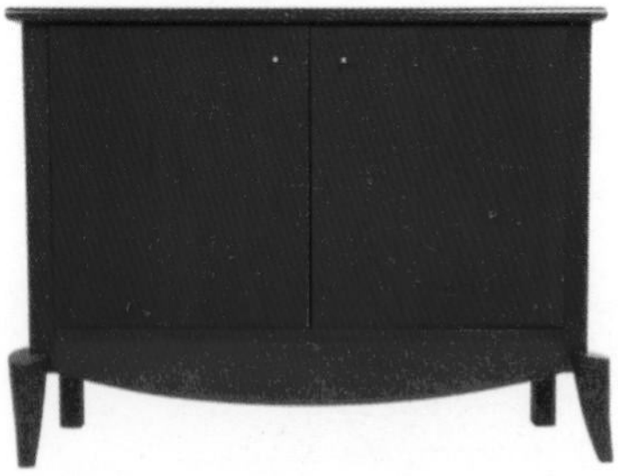

Using wood stain is a clever way to make a low-cost wood appear more expensive or to add colour.

Hint

Avoid applying half a coat as it can appear patchy when it dries.

Many mass manufactured wooden products have a lacquered finish as it is the fastest drying finish.

Oil will enhance a natural finish or protect the wood. There is a range of different types. Vegetable oil is safe to use on products which will be in contact with food. Danish oil and teak oil add a depth of colour and contain minerals which help to preserve wood. To prepare for oiling, the wood must be clean and clear of dust. Oil is applied with a clean, dry cloth or with steel wool, using quick strokes up and down the grain. Oiled wood must be left for about 24 hours to properly dry but will only need one coat, if done properly.

Wood stain requires extra preparation as it is water-based. This extra preparation is called *raising the grain*. Before applying the stain, the wood is dampened with a wet cloth. This makes the wood swell up. Once dry, the wood will be slightly plumper and so it is sanded back down to create a level and smooth surface. The stain can then be applied with a clean, dry cloth using quick circular motions or with a brush. Most stained wood can be lacquered or waxed to give a glossy finish and protect the wood; however, be aware that some stains react badly with lacquer or wax.

Paint and varnish are applied with a brush. Dip the brush into the finish and wipe off the excess on the side of the tin. Brush a thin layer in the direction of the grain and allow plenty of time to complete one full coat. Leave lots of time between coats for the finish to dry properly. Before applying a second coat, give the wood a very light sand with fine sandpaper to remove any bumps or flaws. Steel wool or fine grade sandpaper is excellent for smoothing varnish between coats.

Wax is a common finish used to bring a high quality finish and extra shine to wooden products. There is a range of colours and types of wax available. These can be used to enhance the shine or to protect untreated wood. Many woodworkers are fond of wax because the aroma of the wax gives an impression of traditional woodworking and craftsmanship. To apply wax, a base layer of sanding sealer (a watery sealant) or a light varnish is advised to provide a base for the wax. Once the wood is dry, ensure it is clean, then apply the wax with a clean, dry cloth or steel wool, using quick circular motions to give an even finish.

Lacquer is a glossy, clear finish. Traditionally, lacquer was applied with a brush. However, this can leave brush marks on the surface and spraying lacquer onto wood achieves a smooth and glossy finish.

Before using a spray lacquer, open all the windows in the room for ventilation as the fumes are toxic and dangerous to inhale. To apply lacquer from an aerosol can, first read the directions on the can. Usually, the can must be about 300 to 400mm away from the wood. Spray in even strokes, coating thinly.

As the finish dries quickly this can be repeated almost immediately, coating the surface with many more thin layers. To apply lacquer with a brush, follow the procedure for painting or varnishing.

Test your knowledge

Link to suggested answers
www.leckieandleckie.co.uk/tykanswers

Manufacturing with wood

A pencil box is made from plywood.

1. State a suitable joining method for the corners of the box.
2. Describe the method of marking out the holes on the sides of the box.
3. State the name of a suitable drill bit for the holes.
4. Explain the process of drilling the holes.
5. A slot was cut in the sides to allow the base to fit in. State the name of a suitable hand tool which could cut this slot.
6. Describe why the box was dry clamped before it was assembled.
7. State the name of a suitable adhesive to use when assembling the pencil box.
8. After assembly, some dried glue was found on the sides. Describe a method of removing this dried glue.
9. Describe a benefit of using wax as a finish for the box.
10. Explain the meaning of the term 'raising the grain' when applying wood stain to the box.
11. State a method of applying oil as a finish for the box.
12. Describe a method of applying lacquer to the box which will leave a smooth and glossy finish.
13. Explain the stages of applying paint to the box.

Manufacturing with plastic

Plastic has a bright, colourful and shiny appearance which makes it appealing to use. However, it can be a tricky material to work with. It cracks and snaps under pressure during manufacture and it can scratch easily. Most plastic sheets come with a plastic covering to protect them and this should be kept on for as long as possible.

When working with plastic the main processes are:

- **Cutting and shaping**
- **Drilling**
- **Forming, bending and twisting**
- **Moulding**
- **Finishing**

Cutting and shaping plastic

When cutting and shaping plastic, care must be taken as it can easily crack or snap. However, there are many techniques which can be used to avoid damaging the plastic during manufacture.

To mark out on plastic, a non-permanent marker or chinagraph pencil is required; a pencil will not work. Tools which scrape into the plastic, such as a scriber or a marking gauge, can be used to mark out, but only for waste plastic. A compass can be used for drawing circles or curves. However, the point will also scratch the plastic, so it is common to use a template for this job. The most common tools for measuring and marking out on plastic are shown here.

Hint

Keep the protective film on sheets of plastic for as long as possible, to protect the plastic from scratches.

Tool	Image	Usage
Tape measure		Checking material sizes
Steel rule		Measuring
Scriber		Drawing lines on waste material

Plastic curves are cut using a coping saw, while straight cuts are cut with a junior hacksaw. These saws leave a raw edge on plastic, and so files are used to smooth away the rough edges. Then the edges can be finished using wet-and-dry paper and a cloth with polish on it. The most common tools and workshop equipment used in plastics work are shown in the table opposite.

A pupil has covered their plastic with masking tape to mark out a line parallel to the edge of the plastic using a marking gauge.

Tool	Image	Usage
Coping saw		Sawing curved cuts
Junior hacksaw/ abrafile		Sawing at a specific angle, with a range of angles
File		Smoothing the edge of plastic
Wet-and-dry paper		Abrasive paper for smoothing plastic
Cloth		Applying polish

The edges of plastic are smoothed using the four stages (CDEF):

- **C**ross file to remove any large bumps, by moving the file across the material.
- **D**raw file for a smooth finish after cross filing, by drawing the file along the material.
- **E**ven out with a wet piece of wet-and-dry paper to make it super smooth and shiny.
- **F**inish with a polish.

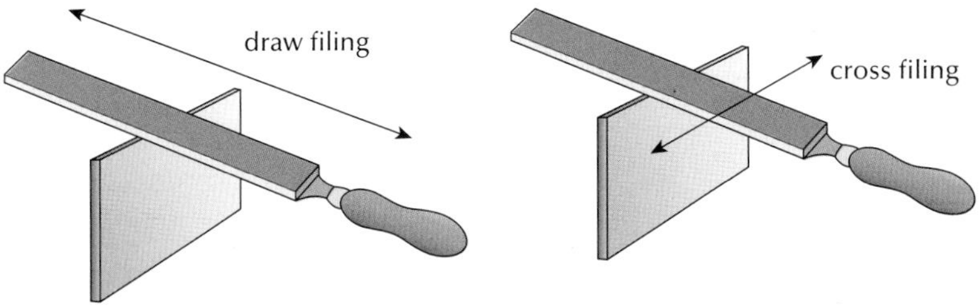

Files are available in a range of shapes and sizes and can be used to shape the edges of the material. For example, a half-round file can be used to file a curve.

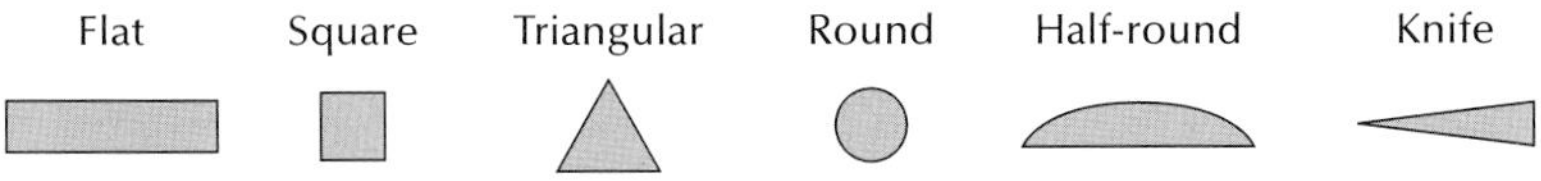

A fret/scroll saw or a bandsaw can also be used to cut plastic. However, they leave rough edges. A laser-cutter machine can cut plastic to a very high quality, is very quick and can produce identical products, but these machines are expensive and not always available. The table on the next page shows some of the most common machines used for cutting plastic.

Hint

Cross filing and draw filing are *techniques*, not types of files.

Make the Link

Metal is also filed using these four stages. However, wood should not be filed, as sandpaper and planes achieve a better quality finish.

When filing plastic sheets, keep the sheet as low to the woodwork vice as possible or sandwich the plastic between two pieces of scrap wood in the vice to support the sheet and avoid cracking it.

Machine	Image	Usage
Bandsaw		Large machine saw for general cutting of materials
Fret saw		Smaller saw used for thin material, intricate cuts and tight curves
Laser cutter		Cuts and engraves plastic, wood, paper, glass, metal and fabric sheets

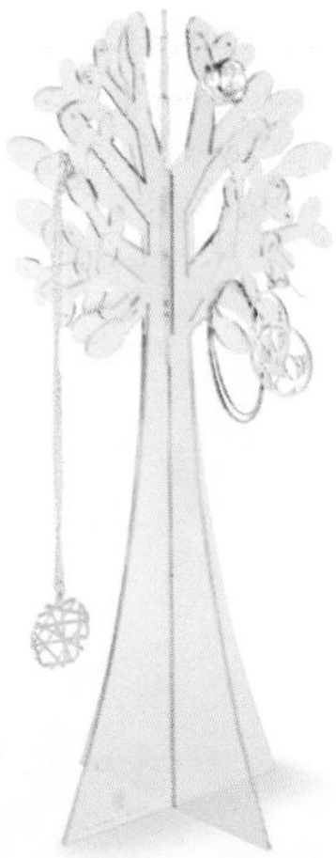

Joining plastic

Although joints are not used on plastic, it is possible to cut slots in plastic to slot pieces together, like this jewellery tree. To permanently join plastic to plastic, use an adhesive such as liquid solvent cement, epoxy resin or impact adhesive (superglue). These adhesives are suitable as they can create a strong bond on the relatively non-porous surface found on plastic.

To join plastic to wood, a groove can be cut into wood using a multi plane or rebate plane. The blade size can be changed to suit the thickness of the plastic. This technique is used for attaching plastic to picture frames and door panels.

Drilling plastic

To mark out a hole on plastic, place a small tab of masking tape on the plastic and mark it with a pen. During drilling, the drill bit can become hot and the masking tape will prevent any small bits of waste plastic (produced when drilling out the hole) from welding onto the surface of the plastic, giving a cleaner edge.

Make the Link

Epoxy resin is a type of thermoset plastic which is also an adhesive (see page 136).

When drilling plastic, a pillar drill or power drill can be used. However, plastic can easily crack during drilling and so the following precautions must be taken:

- Drill a pilot hole before drilling a large diameter hole.
- Support the plastic with scrap wood underneath it.
- Drill slowly.

Make the Link

Drilling plastic is similar to drilling wood or metal. However, a centre punch should not be used on plastic as this can crack it.

Forming, bending and twisting plastic

Thermoplastic becomes soft when heated and then it can be easily bent, formed or twisted into shape. When the plastic cools to room temperature, it sets into the formed shape. With a thermoplastic, if the shape produced is not quite as required, heat can be reapplied and the process repeated. Two ways to heat plastic are to use a strip heater or an oven.

The strip heater can only apply heat along a narrow strip. This allows one bend or fold to be made at a time. These are the four main stages of using the strip heater.

Hint

Remove the protective film from the plastic before using the strip heater.

Hint

Running the plastic under a cold tap will speed up the cooling process.

1 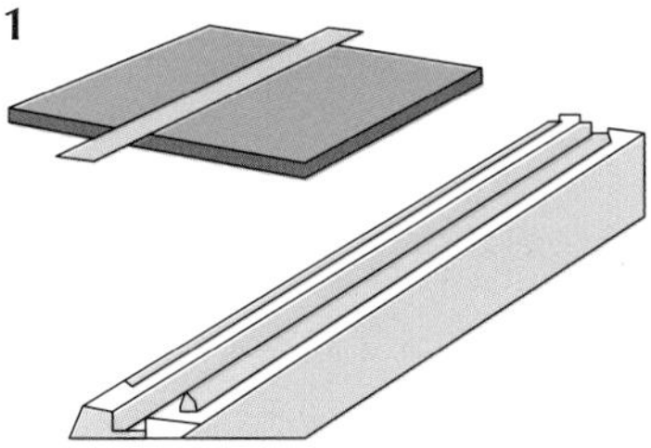 Mark a line where the bend is required.	2 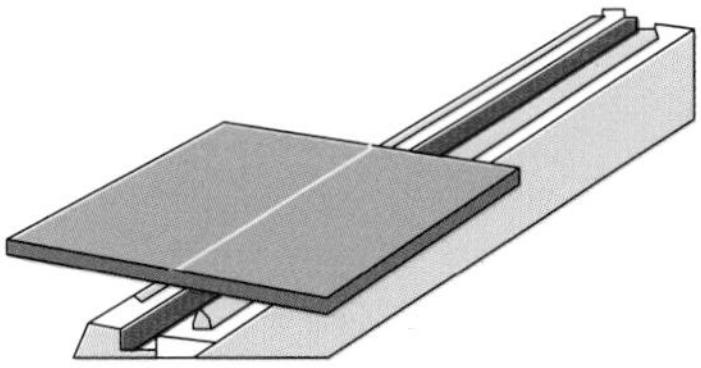 Place the acrylic over the heated element, turning regularly (about every 30 seconds) to avoid the plastic bubbling or burning.
3 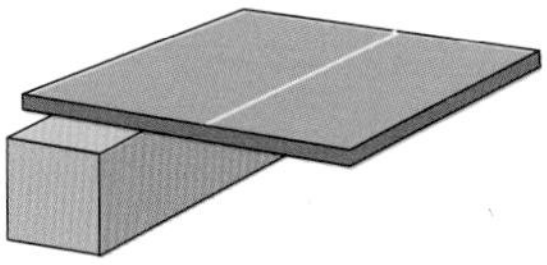 Remove the plastic and quickly place it on a wooden jig or former.	4 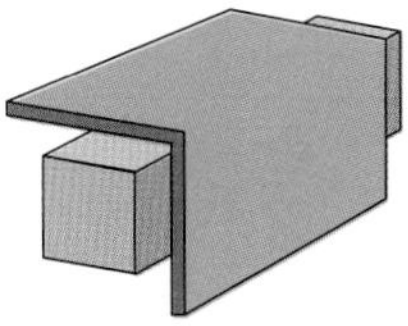 Press the plastic around the jig and hold for a few minutes until it is set.

Identifying features:

- Plastic bent along a line
- Thin sheets of plastic (around 4mm thick)

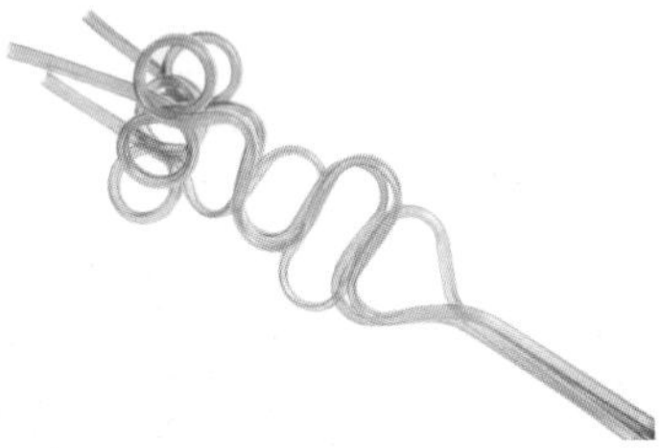

Plastic twists can be achieved by using the oven to soften the plastic.

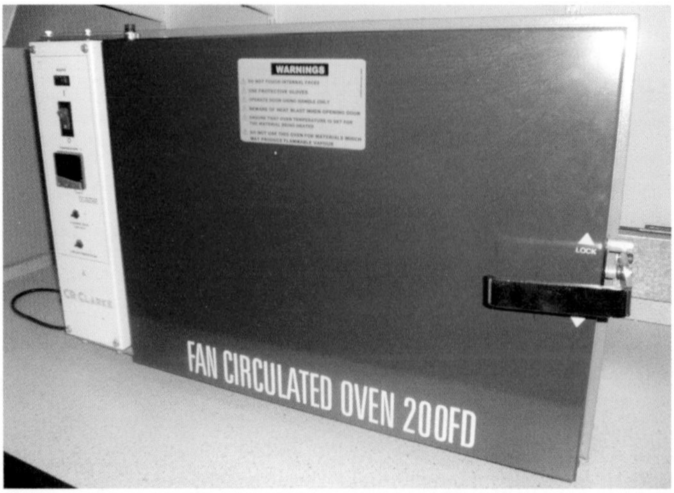

An oven can be used for more complex shapes. The thickness and type of plastic will determine the time it takes for the plastic to become soft enough to shape. For example: to shape a 3mm thick sheet of acrylic, set the oven at a maximum temperature of 170°C and place the plastic in the oven for about 3 minutes, before forming it to the required shape. A jig or former can be used to shape plastic into complex shapes, or to make a batch of identical items.

Make the Link

Chapter 7 covers the plastic processes which are suitable for mass manufacture.

Identifying features:

- Complex 3D shapes
- Sheet, rod, bar or tube of plastic

Finishing plastic

Plastics require very little finish as they are waterproof, colourful and are very durable. Polish is the only finish that may be required. This can be applied using a clean, soft cloth or a mop-head linisher.

Make the Link

Mass manufactured plastics can have intricate details (such as symbols, patterns and text) imprinted on products during the moulding process.

The patterns on these injection-moulded plastic buttons were imprinted on the surface during the moulding process.

Test your knowledge

Link to suggested answers
www.leckieandleckie.co.uk/tykanswers

Manufacturing with plastic

A pupil has manufactured a set of four fridge magnets using workshop tools.

1. A card template was used to mark out the fridge magnets. State **one** benefit of using a card template.
2. State the name of a suitable saw to cut out the fridge magnets.
3. Describe the **four** stages to smooth the edges of the plastic.
4. A small magnet was attached to the back of each piece of plastic. State the name of a suitable adhesive for this.
5. Some small scratches were found on the surface of the plastic. Explain **one** method which could have prevented this.

Manufacturing with metal

Metalwork requires a lot of care and attention as it has many unique hazards. Working with hot or molten metal is extremely dangerous and there are a few additional safety rules which must be followed. It is, therefore, important to pay close attention to instructions or demonstrations to learn how to use tools safely.

When working with metal the main processes are:

- **Cutting and shaping**
- **Drilling**
- **Turning**
- **Heat treatments**
- **Casting**
- **Assembly and joining methods**
- **Finishing**

Cutting and shaping metal

There are several ways to shape metal. First, the metal must be measured and marked out. As lines marked out on metal can be difficult to see, a quick-drying ink called 'engineer's blue' can be used to coat the surface of the metal. The metalwork tools will scratch the ink away, making marking out much easier to see. The table on the next page shows some of the most common tools used for measuring and marking out on metal.

Tool	Image	Usage
Steel rule		Measuring
Scriber		Marking lines on metal
Engineer's square	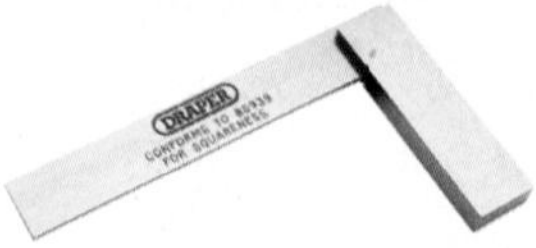	Drawing lines at 90° to the edge of the metal or checking for 90° angles
Combination square		Similar to an engineer's square, but adjustable to any angle
Odd leg callipers	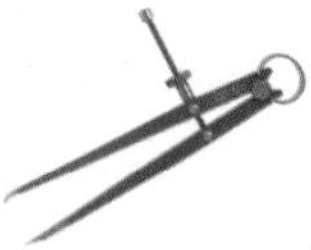	Drawing lines parallel to the edge of the metal
Dividers	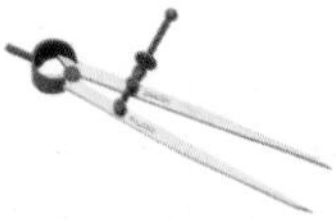	Marking circles and arcs on metal

Metal can be cut to size with a hacksaw, junior hacksaw or tin snips, depending on the thickness of the metal. Here are some of the most common metalwork tools used to shape metal.

Tool	Image	Usage
Hacksaw	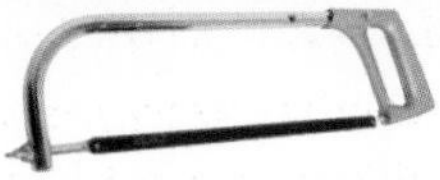	Sawing straight cuts
Junior hacksaw		Sawing straight cuts through medium to thin pieces of metal
Tin snips	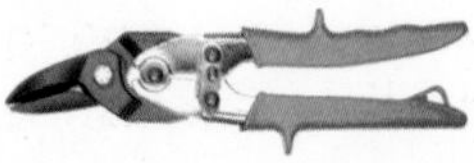	Cutting thin sheets of metal
Raw hide mallet		Shaping sheets, rods or bars of metal without denting the surface
Ball pein hammer		Shaping metal (flat end for flat work and rounded end for curved work)
File		Shaping metal and smoothing the edges

Large sheets of metal or strips of metal can be cut using a **guillotine**.

A factory worker feeds a sheet of metal into a guillotine to be cut to size.

A smaller version of the guillotine is the **notcher**, which removes little notches of metal to create an outline shape on a sheet or strip of metal. Tin snips can also cut thin sheet metal. The notcher is also known as the 'nibbler' because of the way that it removes metal with a sharp cutting tooth.

After all these processes, the edges of metal can be very sharp. Filing metal transforms rough and ragged edges into smooth edges in the four simple steps, CDEF (See page 167).

> **Make the Link**
>
> Metal is filed in the same way as plastic, using the four stages of smoothing the edges of material.

To shape metal it can also be bent or folded. Malleable metals, such as aluminium, can be bent or folded without the need to heat the metal. In mass manufacturing, metal is bent or folded in a **metal press** (or folding press). However, smaller workshop versions of these machines are common. To achieve a fold or bend in metal without a metal press, a wooden block or **former** can be used. Metal is forced around the former using a raw hide mallet. When bending or folding metal, the thickness of metal and the angle of the bend must be taken into consideration to avoid metal fractures (cracks along the bend line). Annealing the metal can aid bending as it softens the metal, reducing or eliminating fractures entirely.

Drilling metal

To drill metal, the same processes can be followed as with drilling wood and plastic (page 156).

A '**metal thread**' is the term used when a screw and thread are created with a **tap and die**. To cut an internal thread on metal a hole must be drilled. The diameter of the hole must be slightly smaller than the diameter of the bar that will fit into it.

> **Make the Link**
>
> Testing samples of different materials to select the most appropriate method for manufacture in terms of workability is explained in Chapter 5.

For example, to fit an 8mm diameter bar, a 7mm hole will be drilled. This is known as the **tapping size** as the tool used to cut an internal thread is called a **tap**. Once the hole is cut, three different taps will be used to cut the internal thread:

- **Taper tap** – used first, this tap has sloping sides to make an easy first cut of the thread.
- **Intermediate tap** – has less sloping sides, which cut deeper into the metal.
- **Plug tap** – used last, this straight-sided tap will cleanly cut the metal to the final shape.

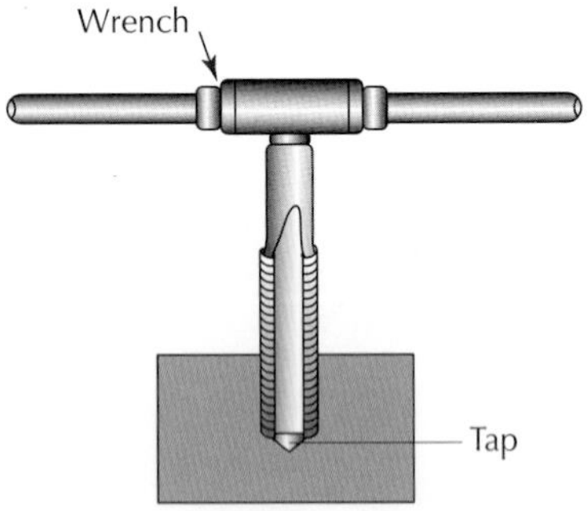

A tap wrench holds the tap

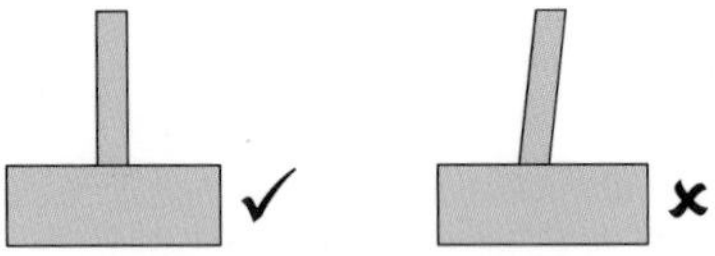

Cutting a thread at a wonky angle is difficult to fix and is known as a drunken thread.

The technique for using a tap is to first apply grease to the tap to prevent it becoming stuck inside the hole. Place the tap at the top of the hole, being careful to set it up vertically. Turn the tap wrench clockwise, pressing down to start the cut. For every full turn clockwise, turn the tap back a quarter turn. This clears the waste metal out of the hole. Forgetting to turn back and clear the waste metal can lock the tap in place and forcing it out can snap the tap, leaving half of it in the hole.

To cut an external thread on a bar of metal, a **split circular die** is used. It is held in a **die stock**, which has three **grub screws** on the outside.

- For the first cut, tighten the centre grub screw into the split. This widens the die by increasing the diameter of the hole which cuts the metal, providing a shallow first cut.
- For the second cut, the centre grub screw is loosened and two outer grub screws are slightly tightened, reducing the diameter of the die to cut deeper into the metal.
- Finally, the two outer grub screws are fully tightened to achieve a deep cut, good quality thread.

> **Hint**
>
> Turn the die in the same way a tap is turned, turning back to clear the waste metal, with grease used to lubricate the cut.

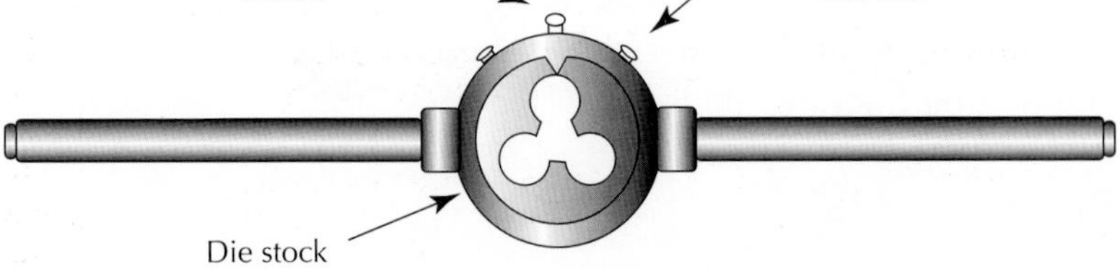

Turning metal

The metalwork lathe is used for shaping metal bars.

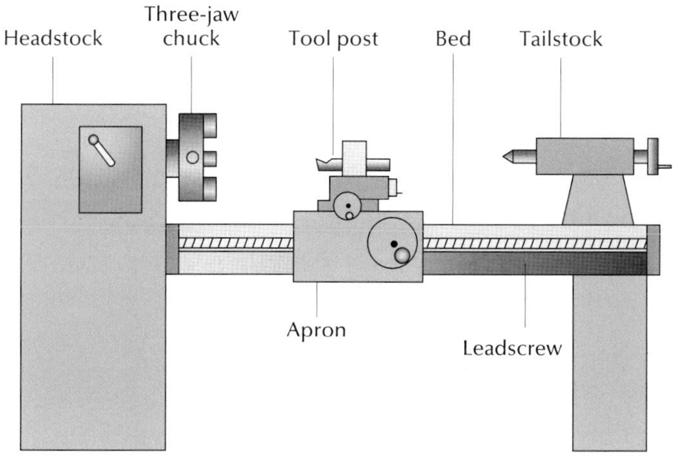

The metal blank is secured in the centre in the three-jaw chuck on the headstock using a chuck key. Unlike the wood lathe, the tools are not held by hand. A tool post holds the tools and this can be moved in different directions, using the wheels at the front of the machine. A range of indents, angles and patterns can be created with different tools attached on the tool post. The diameter of the metal can be accurately checked using a micrometer.

Here are some of the most common metal lathe tools.

Tool	Image	Usage
Cutting tools		A range of sharp-edged tools for accurate rounding and shaping
Parting tool		Pointed tool for cutting notches or cutting/removing metal from the lathe
Knurling tool		Creates an indented pattern on the metal
Centre bit		Drills a pilot hole in the face of a metal bar
Chuck key		Opens, closes and adjusts the three-jaw chuck which holds metal in the lathe
Micrometer		Accurate measuring diameters

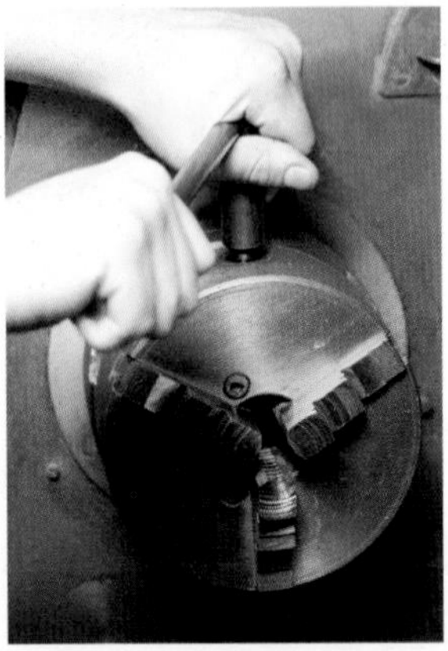

A chuck key is used to open the three-jaw chuck. Care must be taken to tighten the metal in the exact centre of all three jaws. Clamping the metal between two jaws will mean that metal will not spin centrally and the machine will be unsafe to use. Tighten the three-jaw chuck and slowly open it, trying to slot in the metal. If it doesn't fit, open it a little more. Keep repeating this until it slides in neatly, then tighten it in place.

Remember to remove the chuck key. Like the pillar drill, this can cause a serious accident if left in.

There are many different metal-turning processes, as shown in the table below. Each one creates different shapes and profiles.

Tool	Image	Usage
Step turning	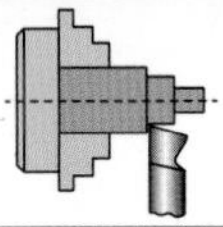	Reduces the diameter of the bar but also used to create stepped shapes
Facing off	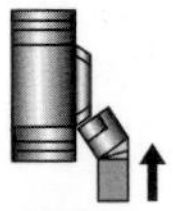	Smooths the end of the bar
Taper	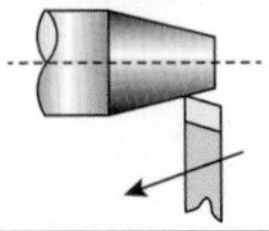	Cuts metal away at an angle
Knurling	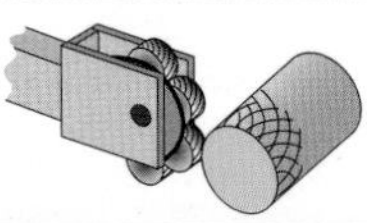	Imprints a texture onto the metal, generally used for extra grip
Drilling	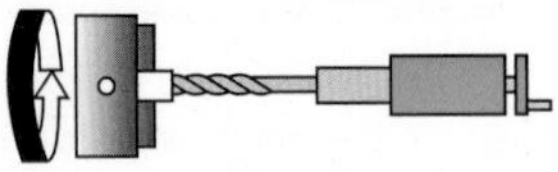	Drills a hole in the face end of the metal
Parting off	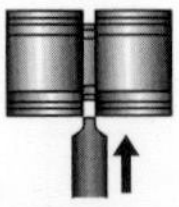	Removes the component part from the waste metal
Parallel turning	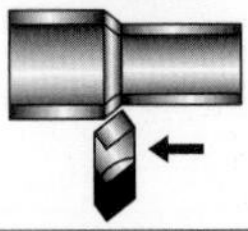	Reduces the diameter of the bar

Make the Link

Although the lathe can drill holes in metal bar, for drilling sheet or strips of metal, a pillar drill can be used. Follow the process for drilling wood on page 156.

Metal heat treatments

The properties of metal can be adjusted by applying heat to the metal by **annealing**, **hardening** or **tempering**. To heat the metal a **forge** is used.

Annealing will soften metal, making it more malleable and easier to shape. To anneal metal, it is heated to a specific temperature or colour, and then left to cool. Depending on the size and thickness of the metal, the cool-down time will vary.

Hardening will strengthen metal, making it more durable but more difficult to shape. To harden metal, it is heated to the point that it is glowing red hot and then quickly **quenched** into water. The metal will appear black. However, this is just on the surface and can be removed with emery paper. Although the metal is now tougher and stronger, it has also become extremely brittle. To be able to work this metal more, the hardening process is followed by tempering.

Hint

When heat-treating metal, wear heatproof gloves and an apron as the metal is extremely hot. Use tongs to hold the metal at all times and remember that the tongs heat up too!

Tempering will toughen metal, making it stronger but will also reduce the brittleness. To temper metal it is briefly heated to the point that it shows a blueish tint on the surface of the metal. The metal is left to cool. However, once cooled the blueish tint will remain and so again this can be removed with emery paper.

Casting metal

Pouring molten metal into a mould to create a solid metal product is called **casting**. Traditionally, sand casting was used. However, modern manufacturing methods are quicker, more accurate and have a better surface finish.

Sand casting

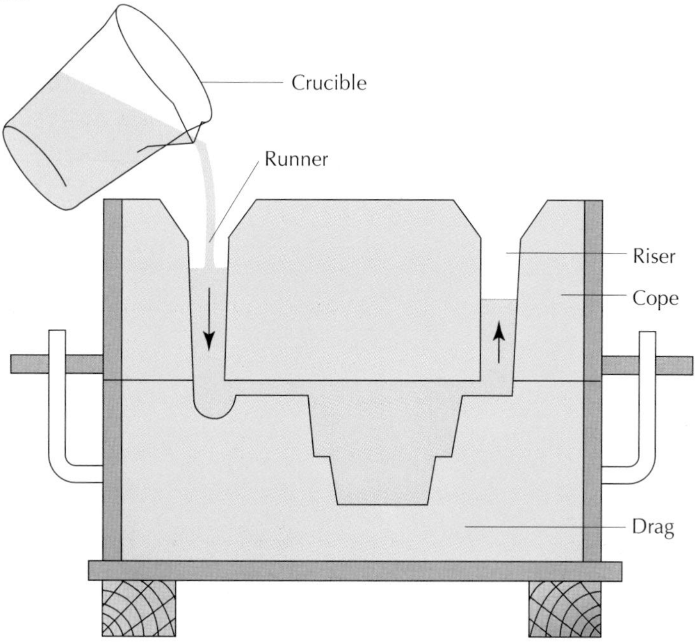

The sand-casting process involves first making a **pattern**. This is a full-scale block, cut to the exact shape which is to be cast. For the pattern to release easily from the sand, it must have sloped sides. This means that all sand-cast products have sloping sides, known as a **draft angle**.

A special type of casting sand is sieved to give a smooth finish to the final product. The bottom box, called the **drag**, is filled with this sand, which contains oil or water to bond it together. Sand is carefully packed around the wooden pattern to make the bottom half of the mould shape. Separately, the top half of the box, the **cope**, is filled with sand in the same way as the drag. The pattern is used to make the top half of the mould shape. The pattern is removed and the cope is then placed on top of the drag. Wooden pins, called **sprue pins**, are used to create cone-shaped indents in the sand, called the **runner** and the **riser**. Molten metal is poured down the runner and gathers in the mould. Once it is full, the molten metal will flow upwards out of the riser. This indicates that the mould cavity is full.

The cast metal requires time to cool and set, before it can be removed from the mould. The product or component then needs further finishing as the runner and riser also set as part of the casting. These two parts can be removed with a hacksaw and can be reused in future casting. The marks left on the metal by the hacksaw are called fettle marks.

Sand-cast products are generally big, solid, heavy metal items such as parasol bases, anchors, pipe fittings and machine parts. A batch of sand-cast products will take days to manufacture as the pattern has to be placed and prepared in the cope and drag every time.

Identifying features:

- Solid metal product
- Fettle marks
- A rough surface (caused by the texture of the sand)
- Draft angle (sloping sides)

Assembly and joining methods for metal

There are many different ways to join metal. Designers select a joining method most suitable for the product they are designing. While there are many non-permanent ways to join metal, such as nuts and bolts, permanent joining methods are a lot stronger. These methods can take more time but they create strong bonds and are extremely durable.

Rivets hold metal together permanently and are often used in large-scale construction, such as buildings and bridges. Smaller versions are used in metalwork.

The Forth Rail bridge was built between 1883 and 1890 using 54 000 tonnes of steel girders joined together by 6 500 000 rivets.

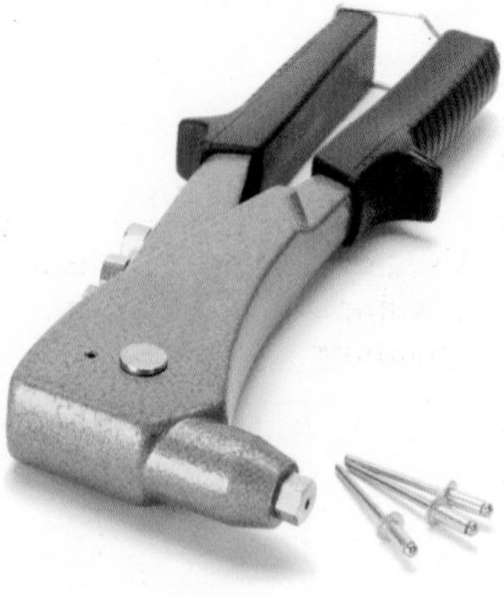

Pop rivets are a quick and easy way to join metal. Special pop rivets (which look like pins) are loaded into a pop-rivet gun (left). Both pieces of metal must be pre-drilled and then the rivet is simply 'popped' through using the gun.

Countersunk, flat-head and round-head rivets are different. They are pushed into a hole, then the back of the rivet is hit with a ball pein hammer and compacted over the hole at the back. This can take a long time, depending on the type of metal the rivet is made from. The join is formed by the rivet as it seals up the hole.

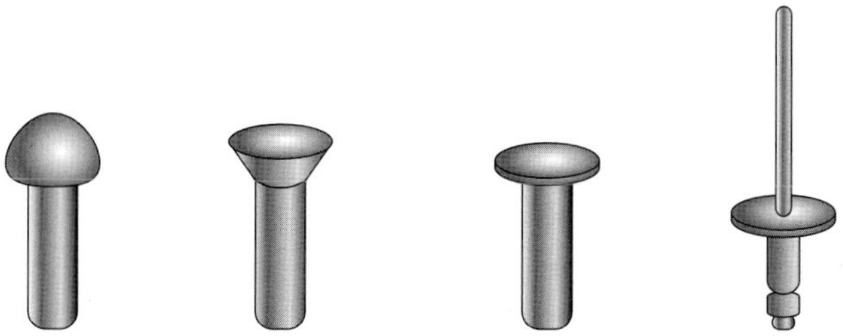

Machine screws, nuts and bolts can be used to non-permanently join metal. These are some of the most common metal fixings and fittings.

Fixture/fitting	Image	Usage
Machine screws	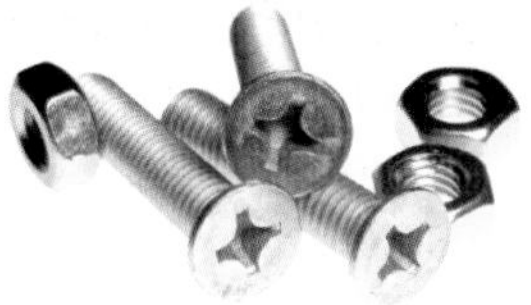	Screws which can fit into threaded holes
Nut and bolt		Bolts together metal – a spanner is required
Rivet		Permanently joins metal (see above for the full range of rivets)
Pop rivet		Permanently joins metal – used with a pop-rivet gun
Washer		Used with nuts and bolts to distribute the pressure of the fitting

Welding is also a permanent method of joining metal and is known as a **thermal joining method** as it uses heat to create the join. There are three types of welding: gas welding, arc welding and spot welding.

- **Gas welding** uses a gas torch to heat a welding rod, which is melted between the two metal parts. When it solidifies it joins the metal together.
- **Arc welding** works very similarly; however, it uses an electric spark to melt the welding rod.

Arc welding produces a very bright spark which can seriously damage your eyes and so a welding mask, with a special black lens, must be worn.

- **A spot welder** bonds metal together on one specific spot by passing an electric current through the spot. The combination of pressure and electricity creates the join.

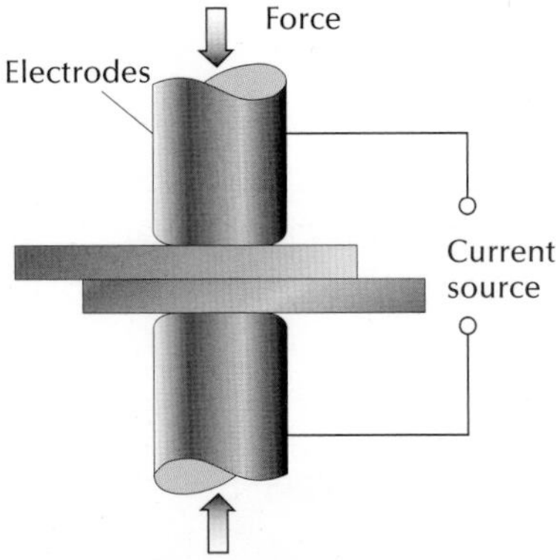

A spot welder uses two electronically charged points to soften and bond metal on one small point, almost like a large staple gun.

Soldering is another thermal method commonly used to permanently join metal.

The three types of soldering are soft soldering, silver soldering and hard soldering (brazing). Each method uses a unique alloy of metal solder wire or rod which is heated and melts into the join. As the metal cools it sets and bonds the metal together.

- **Soft soldering** uses solder that is a mixture of tin and lead, which melts at about 230°C (a low thermal melting point). This is ideal for small metalwork joins in most metal products and electronic circuit boards. The equipment used in soft soldering is small and so it is unsuitable for large pieces of metal.

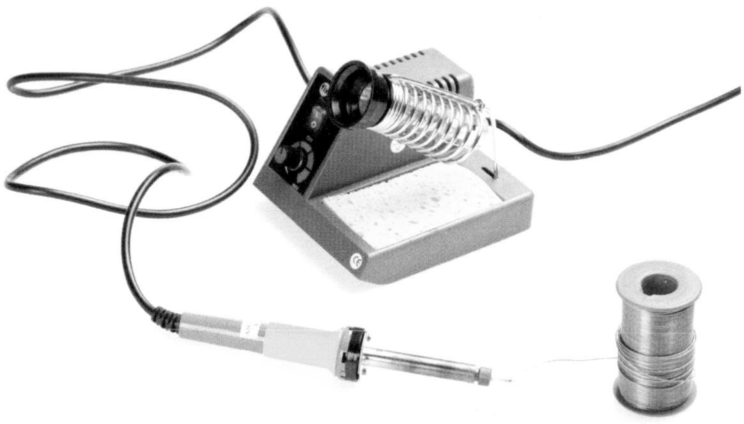

A soldering iron is used to melt the solder.

- **Silver soldering** uses a combination of copper, zinc and silver. This melts at around 600°C to 800°C, depending on the quantity of silver in the solder. This method of soldering requires a torch due to the high melting point of the silver solder.

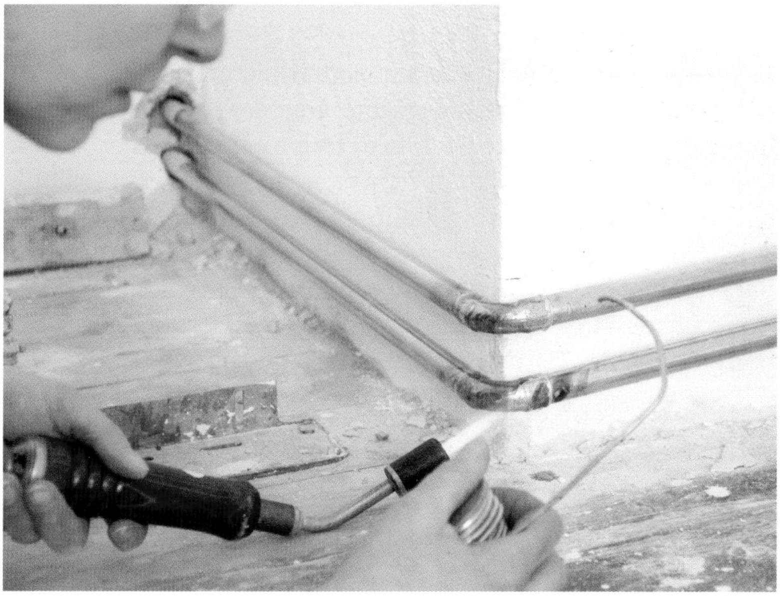

Silver soldering is widely used to manufacture jewellery. However, as it is also used to join copper and brass. It is common for copper central heating pipes to be silver soldered together.

- **Hard soldering** uses a similar solder of copper and zinc, and so requires a temperature higher than 800°C to melt. It cannot be used with non-ferrous metals as this temperature would melt them (ferrous metals have a higher melting point). This method of soldering also requires a torch due to the extremely high melting point of the solder.

When joining metal together, a clamp is used to hold components in the correct position. The table on the next page shows some of the most common tools and equipment used for clamping, holding and securing metal.

Tool	Image	Usage
Hand vice		Holds small or thin sheets of metal in place while drilling
Machine vice		Holds wood in place during assembly
Engineer's vice		Workshop vice for general metalwork
Spanner		Tightens and secures nuts and bolts

Metal finishes

To prepare metal for a good quality finish, it must first be clean. Some metalwork processes require grease, which is used as a lubricant. However, grease has to be properly cleaned off the metal before a finish is applied. Extremely rough edges should be filed smooth, following the four stages for smoothing edges (CDEF, page 167). Rough edges are smoothed using an abrasive paper called emery paper. Like sandpaper, emery paper varies from coarse to fine. Here is some of the equipment for finishing metal.

Tool	Image	Usage
Brushes		Applying paint, varnish, stain or sanding sealer
Steel wool		Smoothing between paint coats
Emery paper		Abrasive paper for smoothing metal
Wire brush		Brushes rust off the surface of metal
Fluidiser		Applying a plastic dip-coated finish

Painting metal requires a clean and dry surface. Before applying paint to metal, a primer should be used. Primer is a special undercoat which allows the paint to bond to the metal and enhances the durability of the finish. Applying paint with a brush can make it difficult to achieve even coverage and so aim to build up lots of thin layers. Covering the metal with one thick layer of paint may seem like a quick fix, but paint puddles will form. These puddles take much longer to dry and do not look good. Allow plenty of time to complete one full coat and ensure the paint is properly dry before applying a second coat.

A metal without a finish can be prone to rusting. The function and location of the product must be taken into account when selecting a finish.

Spray paint achieves a much smoother finish. However, the fumes are highly toxic to inhale. Manufacturers spray paint metal in specially designed painting booths, which have extractor fans fitted to remove the toxic fumes. It is common for manufacturers to galvanise (zinc coat) metal parts before painting as this improves their corrosion resistance.

Hint

Wipe off the excess paint from the brush on the side of the tin or pot to ensure there is not too much paint on the brush.

Plastic dip-coating is a process used to coat metal with a protective layer of plastic. This is ideal for adding extra grip to a metal surface or purely for aesthetic reasons. First, the metal must be thoroughly cleaned so that it is free from dirt and grease. Then the metal is heated to around 300 to 400°C. An oven is best for this as the hot air can circulate around the metal to obtain an even heat. The metal is then transferred from the oven to a metal box called a fluidiser. The fluidiser contains a fine plastic powder which is blown around inside. When the hot metal comes into contact with the plastic powder, they bond, creating a plastic coating. This process takes less than five seconds. The plastic will become smooth as it is left to cool.

These dumbbells have been dip coated in plastic.

Plastic dip-coating is a very quick process. However, there are a few common errors which can lead to a poor quality finish. Holding the metal in the fluidiser for too long will build up a thick and unattractive layer of plastic. Also, the plastic powder will not bond to metal that is greasy and so, if the metal is not cleaned properly, the plastic will be patchy. Lastly, the plastic coating will feel gritty if the metal has not been hot enough for it to soften and smooth out.

The shiny finish of this metal napkin holder contrasts with the soft, matt texture of the napkin, making the product stand out.

Unfinished metal is quite a common 'finish'. Applying metal polish with a clean dry cloth and lots of effort will help to make the metal shine.

Test your knowledge

Link to suggested answers
www.leckieandleckie.co.uk/tykanswers

Manufacturing with metal

A table set made from metal is shown.

1. The salt and pepper shakers were made from a metal bar. State the name of a suitable hand tool for cutting the bar to the correct length.
2. The bar was then turned on a lathe. Describe **two** processes that would be carried out on the lathe to shape the salt and pepper shakers.
3. The salt and pepper shakers are in two parts, to allow them to be opened and the condiments to be refilled. State a method of ensuring the two parts fit tightly together.
4. The toothpick holder was cut with a bandsaw, which left a raw edge. Describe the stages of smoothing the edges of the metal.
5. State the name of a suitable folding method to shape the toothpick holder.
6. Other than a polished finish, state the name of a suitable finish for the metal table set.
7. Describe the process of applying this finish.

Reviewing and evaluating manufacturing

Once the manufacture of the prototype is completed, the success of the project must be evaluated. This will involve reflecting on the:

- success of the manufacturing plan
- quality and success of the prototype.

Evaluating the success of the manufacturing plan

Once you have manufactured your prototype, you should be able to make suggestions to improve the plan for manufacture. If your original manufacturing plan did not work out as you expected, describe the issues with it. Otherwise, you may wish to suggest:

- improvements to preparations
- alternative manufacturing methods
- an alternative order of tasks
- alternative assembly methods
- different approaches towards manufacturing methods
- improvements for time management
- suitable commercial manufacturing methods.

Evaluating the quality of the prototype

Reviewing the quality of your own manufacturing skills requires honesty. Making suggestions for improvement in terms of craftsmanship can include anything from taking a little more time to smooth the edges of the plastic to totally changing the method of cutting a woodwork joint and replacing it with knock-down fittings. Consider the quality of your practical work and how the following have impacted on it:

- Tools and equipment – Were you using the right tool for the job?
- Pace and patience – Did you rush a job and ruin the quality of the work?
- Knowledge and understanding – Did improper use of tools and equipment have a negative impact on your work?

Evaluating the success of the prototype

The **prototype** is a stepping stone to mass manufacture. If it is successful, then it can be delivered to the manufacturer.

If the prototype was not successful, then some recommendations for changes that would improve it would be necessary. To turn a prototype into a mass-manufactured product, consider these alterations:

- Adjust the manufacturing process to allow the prototype to be mass manufactured.
- Reduce the price by reviewing the manufacturing equipment, tools and processes, using cheaper alternatives or cutting back on unnecessary elements.
- Reduce the price by reviewing the materials, using cheaper alternatives, using thinner materials, using fewer materials or removing unnecessary parts.
- Make the product work more efficiently by using alternative power sources, using different materials, improving the performance, removing unnecessary parts or reducing waste.
- Ensure the product is sustainable by using alternative sustainable materials, using thinner materials, using fewer materials, removing unnecessary parts or designing for disassembly.

Make the Link

Preparing for writing an evaluation of the manufacturing plan is covered on page 150.

Hint

There is a first time for everything. You will most likely be better at something the second time you attempt it, therefore making a practice piece is always recommended.

Make the Link

Personal evaluation can be difficult. Why not ask others to evaluate your work for you? Put together a questionnaire to guide others to evaluate the craftsmanship and finish of your prototype.

Check your progress

I can:	HELP NEEDED	GETTING THERE	CONFIDENT
• describe methods of preparing for manufacture			
• state the names of appropriate tools, equipment and manufacturing processes for working with wood			
• state the names of appropriate tools, equipment and manufacturing processes for working with metal			
• state the names of appropriate tools, equipment and manufacturing processes for working with plastic			
• describe how to evaluate the success of a manufacturing process.			

7 Commercial manufacturing

By the end of this chapter you should be able to:

- describe the benefits of Computer Aided Manufacture (CAM) and rapid prototyping
- describe the benefits and drawbacks of computer aided manufacture
- describe a range of commercial manufacturing processes for wood
- describe a range of commercial manufacturing processes for plastic
- describe a range of commercial manufacturing processes for metal
- describe the process of rapid prototyping
- explain the term 'quality assurance'
- describe the impact of global manufacture
- explain the impact of commercial manufacturing on the environment
- explain the impact of commercial manufacturing on society.

An introduction to commercial manufacture

The term 'commercial manufacture' means the manufacturing, assembly and finishing processes that are used to make commercial products or their components. There are four types of commercial manufacture:

- **One-off manufacture** – this is when one product is manufactured at a time and each product is unique. Highly skilled workers are required for this type of manufacturing. In a commercial setting, specialist machinery is used to create **bespoke** high-demand products. Consider a business which sells metal gates that are made to order in a specified size; the products on offer are in high demand, yet each product is unique.
- **Batch manufacture** – a small number of identical products are made at one time. One batch is manufactured before the next batch is made. Highly skilled workers are usually required for this type of production method, but it can also take place in a commercial setting using machines. An example of a product made by batch manufacture is a set of four matching handmade wooden chairs that are manufactured to order.

Make the Link

Consumer demand, as explained in chapter 2, can dictate the type of production method, as the volume of production should match the demand for the product.

Make the Link

At National 5 it is good to have an awareness of the different types of commercial manufacture, due to their social, economic and environmental impact. Higher Design and Manufacture looks in more depth at the production and planning systems related to these types of manufacture.

- **Mass manufacture** – large volumes of identical products or components are manufactured. The system is highly automated with a small number of workers and, usually, very little manufacturing skill required. An example of this is the manufacturing of kitchen utensils in high volumes using injection moulding machines.
- **Continuous flow manufacture** – extremely high volumes of products or components are produced 24 hours a day, 7 days a week. This system is also highly automated with a small number of workers and very little manufacturing skill. An example of this is the production of plastic water bottles in a factory. The consumer demand for this product is extremely high, therefore the production rate must also be high; one worker may be responsible for a machine which produces tens of thousands of products in one shift.

Computer aided manufacture

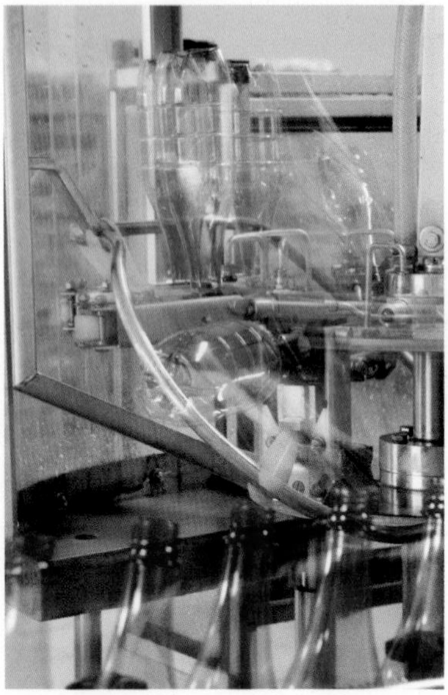

High speed CAM systems like this water-bottle production line will mould the bottle, fill it with water, cap it and label it by the time it gets to the end of the line.

In industry, automated mass-manufacturing processes produce a high volume of identical products at a fast pace. As the machinery is controlled by computers, this type of manufacture is named 'computer aided manufacture' (CAM).

The benefits of CAM are:

- high volumes of identical products can be produced
- costs are low when high volumes are produced
- products or components are produced at a fast pace
- a high level of detail is possible
- continual production is possible
- waste is minimised as precise amounts of materials are used.

CAM is extremely quick, compared to traditional methods, and gives high quality products. It can also eliminate human error in manufacture, reducing waste and assuring quality. Products or component parts can be made to an extremely precise level of detail, creating features such as threads or snap-fit joining fittings to the exact size. The set-up costs of CAM are expensive. However, the cost per product is low when thousands or millions of products are produced. This is called **economy of scale** as high volumes of identical products are produced at a fast pace.

The drawbacks of CAM are:

- machine breakdowns can cause production to stop completely
- a reduction in employment opportunities in manufacturing industry
- machinery, maintenance and tooling costs are high.

Occasional machine breakdowns interrupt manufacture and production is halted until repairs are made. Manufacturers employ or subcontract maintenance workers to keep machines in continuous production. They also train staff to repair machines and even to spot potential breakdowns before they occur. This incurs a cost to be set against profit.

With a CAM system, small numbers of people are required to manufacture extremely high volumes of products; fewer workers are required to operate the machines compared to traditional methods of manufacture. This means that staff costs are low. However, the machinery, the tooling (mould) and maintenance costs are high.

A series of milling machines are controlled simultaneously by a computer to mass manufacture table legs using CAM technology.

Of course, there are other costs to consider, such as retail, packaging and transportation. When all these costs are considered, CAM only becomes cost effective per product when large volumes are produced.

Commercial wood and manufactured-board processes

The wood processes and manufacturing methods explained in Chapter 6 can all be used in commercial manufacture. Many can be combined with automated systems to allow them to take place without a skilled worker. For example, a computer numerically controlled (CNC) drilling machine can be programmed to drill holes in a product as it passes through the production line. With a conveyor system or a robotic arm to remove the drilled item and replace it with a new piece of material to be drilled, wooden products can be manufactured automatically. In fact, a range of cutting, drilling, shaping and turning processes can be automated on a production line, allowing identical wooden products to be manufactured accurately with consistent quality. It is even possible to apply some types of finish with an automated system.

Make the Link

Applying lacquer on a mass-manufacturing production line is a way of finishing wood, as explained in Chapter 6.

Make the Link

There are many more plastics processes, such as: extrusion, laminating, compression moulding, calendaring and casting. These processes are part of the Higher Design and Manufacture course.

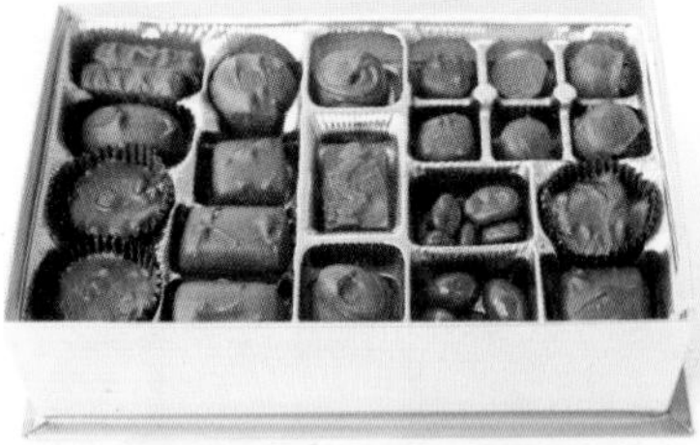

Hint

Remember vacuum forming as the process with a sweet tooth.

Commercial plastic processes

A range of cutting, drilling, forming, shaping and finishing processes for plastics can be automated to produce plastic products. In mass manufacture, large scale plastic moulding methods can produce thousands of identical products at a fast pace. The machines are all highly automated. The four main industrial plastic processes are:

- **vacuum forming**
- **rotational moulding**
- **injection moulding**
- **laser cutting**

Vacuum forming

This method is commonly used to manufacture packaging as it is suitable for creating complex shapes on thin sheets of plastic. The plastic trays and packaging found in selection boxes, chocolate boxes, biscuit packaging and chocolate advent-calendar trays are vacuum formed. In mass manufacturing, huge vacuum formers create many items at once and then they are cut apart using a guillotine. In one-off or batch production the waste plastic can be trimmed using a fret saw, coping saw, tin snips or even scissors if the plastic is thin.

Before vacuum forming, a pattern must be made. This is the block the plastic will be formed around and it is usually made from metal or wood. It is also possible to mould around plasticine or foam, if only a single vacuum form is required. The pattern must have rounded edges to prevent it from tearing the plastic and the sides of the block must be tapered to allow it to be removed easily at the end of the process.

The four stages of vacuum forming are shown below.

1

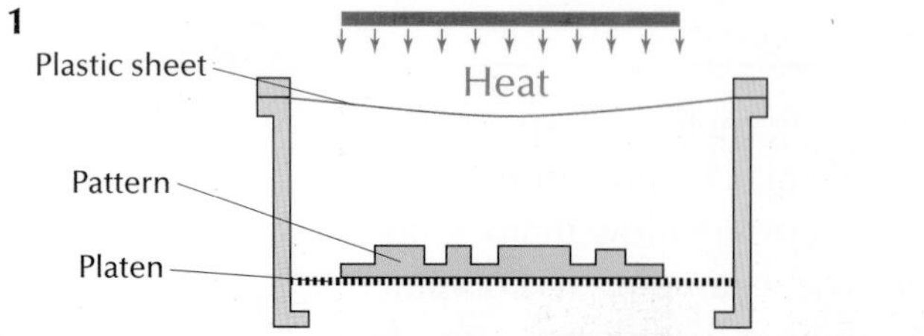

Place the pattern onto the platen (platform inside). Clamp the plastic down, creating an airtight seal. Apply heat to the plastic until it is soft and starts to sag under its own weight.

2

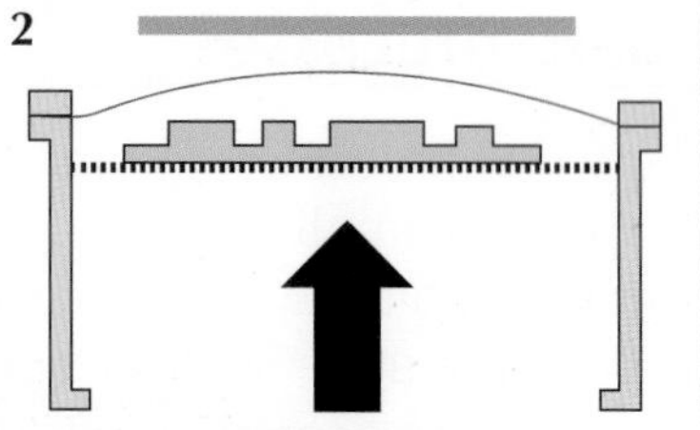

Raise the platen (with the pattern sitting on it) up to the level of the plastic.

3

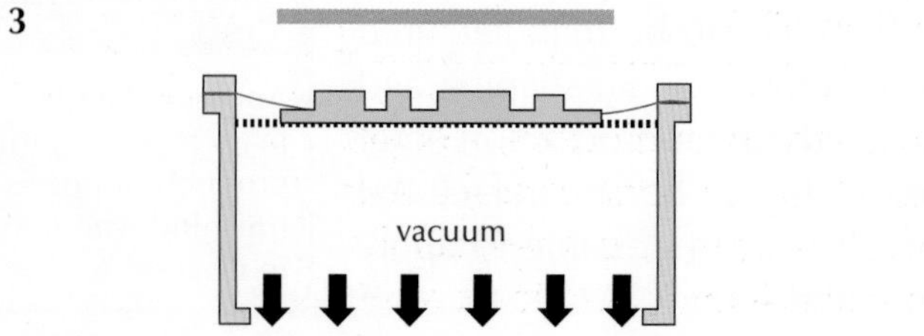

Vacuum the air from beneath the plastic, pulling the plastic around the pattern.

4

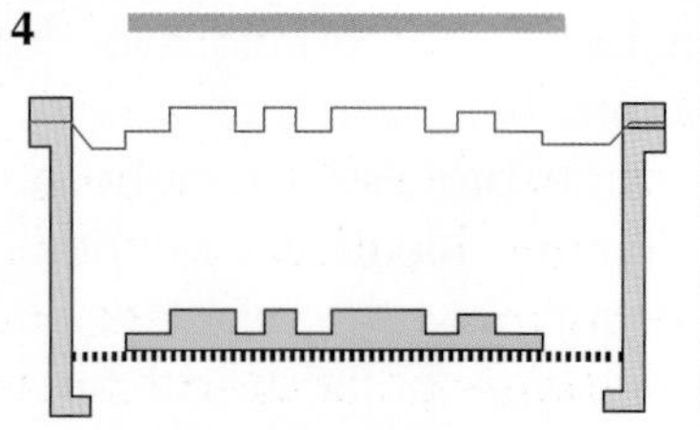

Lower the platen, removing the pattern from the plastic.

Identifying features:

- Rounded corners
- Tapered edges
- Thin sheet plastic
- No undercuts

Injection moulding

This method is used to produce plastic products with complex shapes. Plastic granules are heated until molten then they are forced into a mould where the plastic component or product quickly sets. The mould then opens up and small metal ejector pins force the plastic component or product out of the mould.

1

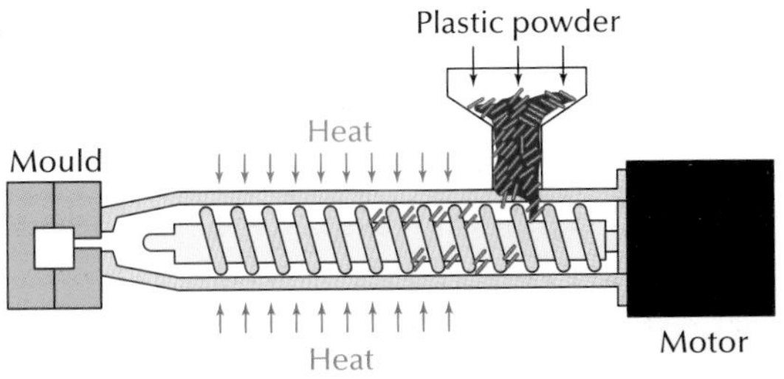

The powdered plastic is put into the machine and heated.

2

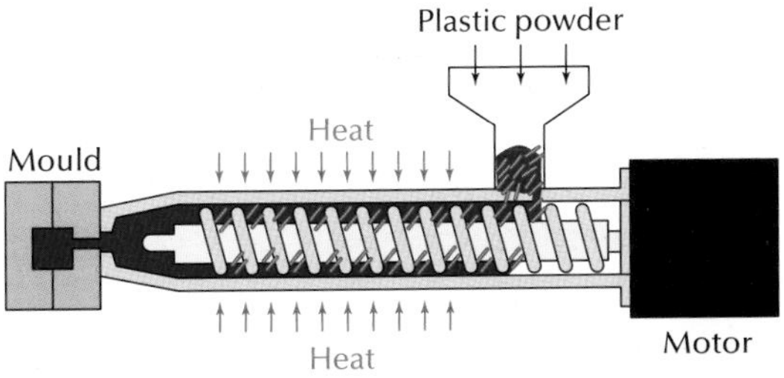

The molten plastic is injected into the mould.

3

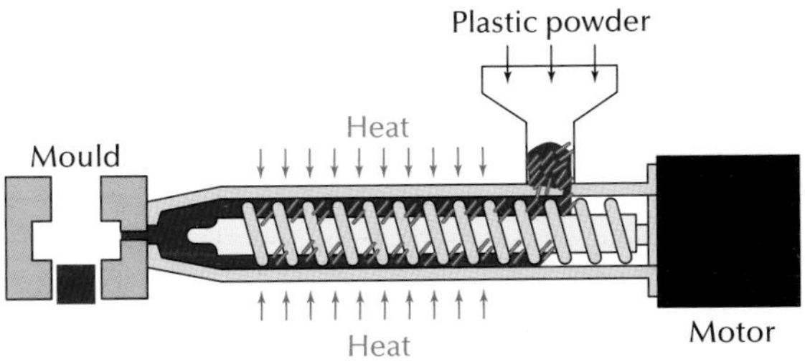

The moulded item is ejected from the mould.

Injection moulded plastic products include toys, remote controls, boxes, buckets, toothpaste caps, chairs, utensils, door stops, make-up packaging, water pistols, phone casings, combs, hairbrushes, car interiors, coffee-cup lids and a whole lot more!

Identifying features:

- An injection point or sprue mark (a protruding rough mark)
- Ejector marks (round indents)
- Tapered edges
- Complex detail
- Mould split lines (where the mould has joined)
- Webs which strengthen the shape

Rotational moulding

This method is used to produce larger hollow plastic products. A powdered form of these plastics is weighed and placed into the mould. The two halves of the mould are then joined together and sealed tightly. As the mould is rotated on a large frame, the plastic powder is pushed towards the internal surface of the mould. The mould is heated from the outside, which makes the powder melt, forming a thin plastic coat inside the mould. Gradually, the plastic layer becomes thicker as more of the powder melts, until all the powder has been used. The heat is then switched off and the plastic sets as the mould rotates around jets of cool air or cold water. When the two halves of the mould are separated, the hollow product or component can be released from the mould.

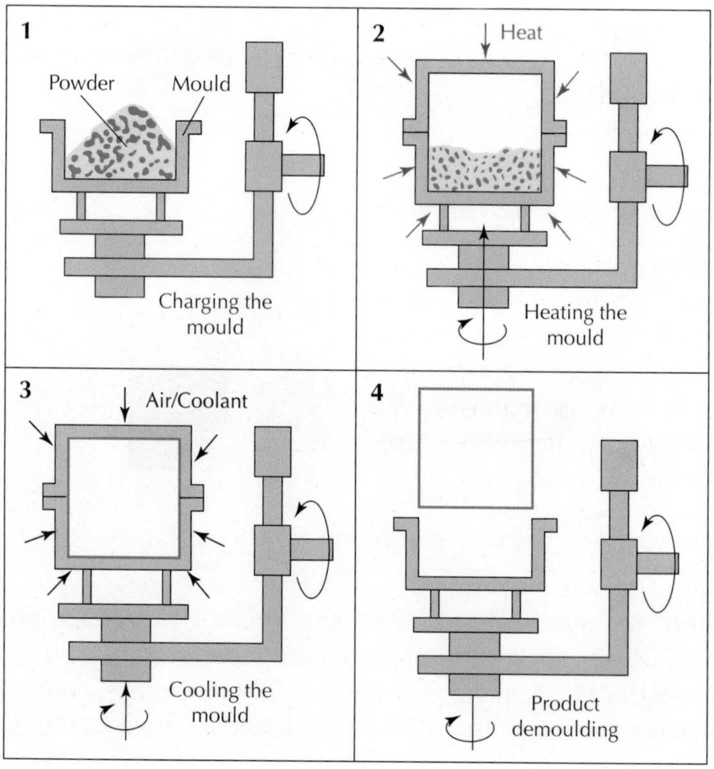

Rotational moulded products include children's play equipment (plastic slides and play houses), gritting bins, traffic cones, water tanks, canoes, floats and buoys.

Identifying features:

- Hollow plastic product
- Mould split lines (when the two halves of the mould have joined)

Case study

One Foot Taller

one foot taller

One Foot Taller is a product design company specialising in the design and supply of lighting and furniture. It began in Glasgow in 1995 and since 2007 it also has a studio in Saint Plancard, France.

The company tries to use local manufacturers (cutting down on transportation) and recycled materials in its super sleek modern designs. They believe in longevity, simplicity and sustainability.

One Foot Taller has dabbled very successfully in interior design, have worked with many other design companies and have an impressive list of products designed for local businesses. It has also designed products for large retailers, such as Marks & Spencer.

In 1999 it designed the Chasm chair (right), which was a rotational moulded hollow form that was then cut down the middle. The two halves were turned around and bolted together, creating two hollow sides. The chair won the Peugeot Design Award, the Blueprint Editor's award at 100% Design (a London design exhibition) and was also awarded Millennium Product Status.

Laser cutting

Designs drawn on specialist CAD software can be sent to a laser cutter, which can cut or engrave on plastic, paper, card, thin sheets of wood or manufactured boards. More powerful laser cutters can also engrave on or cut through metal. When cutting plastic, the laser cuts cleanly through the plastic, leaving a smooth and even finish. This means that, in some cases, there is no need to file or even polish the plastic.

A laser cutter cuts component parts from sheet metal.

Make the Link

A laser cutter can cut though a range of different materials.

Case study

Bonnie Bling laser cut plastic jewellery

Based on the Isle of Bute, Bonnie Bling is a range of quirky tongue-in-cheek acrylic jewellery and fashion accessories created by graphic designer Mhairi Mackenzie.

Since the company began, Bonnie Bling has featured in various magazines and website articles and attracted a celebrity audience including Lana Del Rey, Laura Whitmore, Olly Murs, Amelia Lily and even Sir Elton John!

In February 2011, Bonnie Bling scooped the prize for best new product in the jewellery category at Scotland's Trade Show. Since then, the brand has grown from strength to strength. Collaborations with Obscure Couture, RAKSA, Emily Moir and the Riverside Transport Museum have all created unique design-led pieces.

Bonnie Bling

Test your knowledge

Link to suggested answers
www.leckieandleckie.co.uk/tykanswers

Commercial manufacture of plastic products

A toy truck is manufactured from four different plastic components.

1. State the name of **one** method suitable for manufacturing all the plastic components of the toy truck.
2. Describe **two** identifying features of this manufacturing method.
3. Explain why this process is suitable for mass manufacture.

Make the Link

Aluminium can be extruded due to its low melting point.

A car production line with CNC robotic arms that are programmed to weld the car body.

Commercial metal processes

Just as with wood and plastic, a range of metalwork processes which are carried out in the workshop – such as cutting, shearing, notching, turning, drilling, folding and bending – can also be adapted for mass manufacturing. For example, in a factory production line a series of computer numerically controlled (CNC) robotic arms can place and then weld metal components to build a metal car body. Each weld, from one car to the next, will be identical in its quality and location, and the speed of welding will be extremely fast.

Most metal manufacturing processes can be carried out by machines. However, sand casting is not suitable for mass production. Instead, the process of die casting is used for casting of metal products to be mass manufactured.

Die casting

In die casting, a piston injects molten metal into a mould, called the die. When the metal solidifies, the two sides of the die separate and ejector pins push the metal product out of the die. Die casting moulds can be used over and over, giving a quick cycle time and large volumes of products.

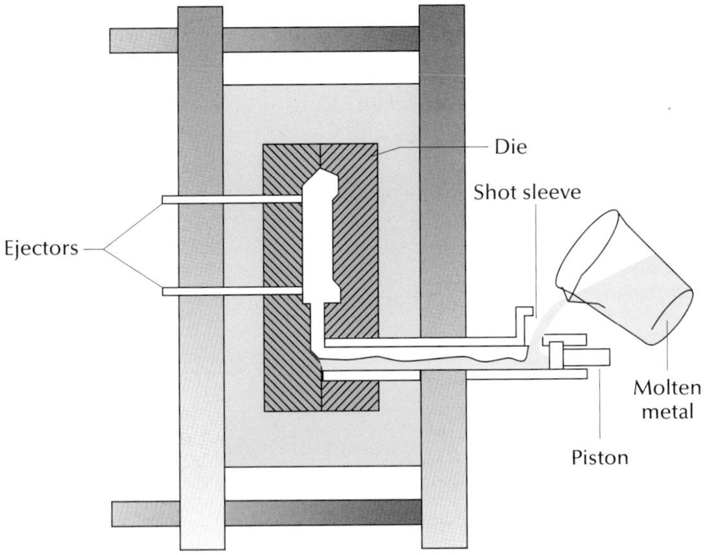

The diagram above shows how one product or component can be made by die casting. However, in commercial manufacture, one die could make numerous casts.

This process can be set up to run automatically and, therefore, high volumes of identical products can be produced at a fast pace. The volume of production, combined with the automation of the system, keeps staff costs down. However, the machinery, the die itself and maintenance costs can be high. Overall, die casting is usually cheap when production volumes are high.

Identifying features:

- Solid metal product
- Intricate details or surface pattern
- Sprue marks (small marks left when the sprue was snapped off)
- Ejector pin marks

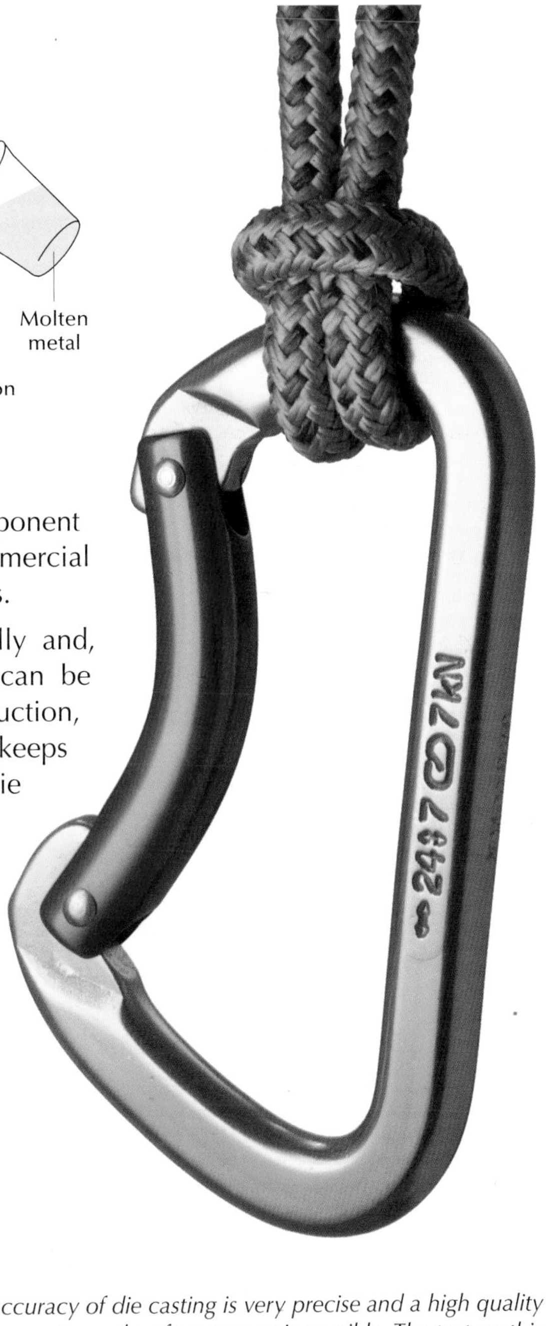

The accuracy of die casting is very precise and a high quality finish or patterned surface texture is possible. The text on this rock climbing carabiner has been formed into the metal during die casting.

Make the Link

For the benefits of modelling see pages 103–106.

Rapid prototyping

Rapid prototyping is a CAD/CAM process which generates a 3D model instantly from a computer aided drawing. The main benefits of rapid prototyping are:

- reasonably fast to produce a prototype
- the prototype can be made from the actual material that the product will be made from
- the end product can be used to make injection-moulding dies
- the level of accuracy is extremely high
- moving parts can be created
- models can be adapted and reproduced quickly
- the client can see the product as a high quality prototype.

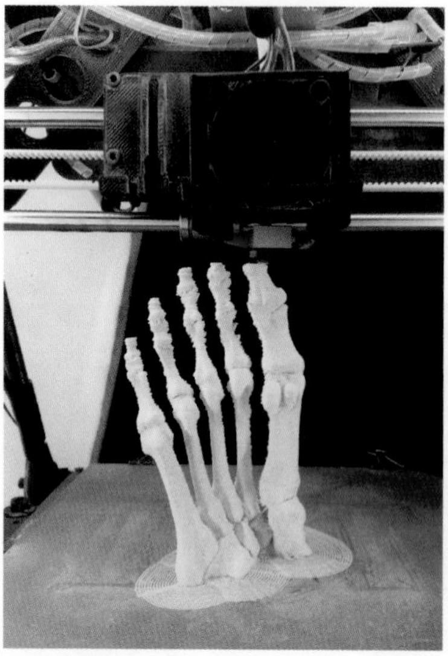

This model of finger bones was made by 3D printing. The parts are fully articulated, meaning they move like a real skeleton.

There are several different types of rapid prototyping and this list of processes continues to evolve as modern manufacturing techniques and capabilities develop. Each rapid prototyping method is different. However, they all tend to produce one thin slice at a time and these join together to form a 3D model.

The main methods of rapid prototyping are:

- Stereo-lithography apparatus – resin
- Fused-deposition modelling – ABS, PLA
- Thermojet – wax
- 3D printing – plaster, cornstarch or ABS plastic powder
- Selective laser sintering – metal

Quality assurance in commercial manufacture

Quality assurance monitors the quality of products. It involves a set of actions and paperwork which aims to deliver the best quality products to the consumer. The two main groups involved in the quality assurance process are the manufacturers and the consumers.

Quality assurance and the manufacturer

A set of actions must be carried out to ensure that the product which leaves the factory is the best quality.

Action 1 – Check materials

The quality of the materials must be checked when they arrive from the supplier to look for overall condition and any damage caused during delivery or by storage.

Action 2 – Check parts

Any parts ordered should also be checked over for damage and to ensure that the correct colour, size, quantity, etc. have arrived.

Action 3 – Train staff

To minimise human error, all staff should be trained to operate the machines or complete the manufacturing processes. This will lead to fewer materials being wasted during manufacture with fewer rejected or defective products. Training is a long-term investment, as it will cost the manufacturer time and money, but it will mean better quality products.

Action 4 – Maintenance

The manufacturer must maintain or replace their tools, machines and equipment regularly to ensure they work to their optimum standard.

A maintenance worker checks a machine is working efficiently.

Make the Link

A drawback of CAM is the need to shut down machinery for training. This costs the manufacturer in terms of time and money. However, in the long term, it will mean better quality products are produced.

Quality assurance and the consumer

Various documents are in place to ensure that the product the consumer purchases is the best quality.

Document 1 – Consumer rights

Consumer rights allow the consumer to return faulty products. The guarantee and receipt will ensure that the consumer can receive a refund if there is a fault with the product.

Document 2 – Instruction manuals

Instructions help the consumer to build or use their new product. They also reduce the chance of the product being broken through incorrect assembly or use.

Your consumer right to a refund is usually printed on the receipt.

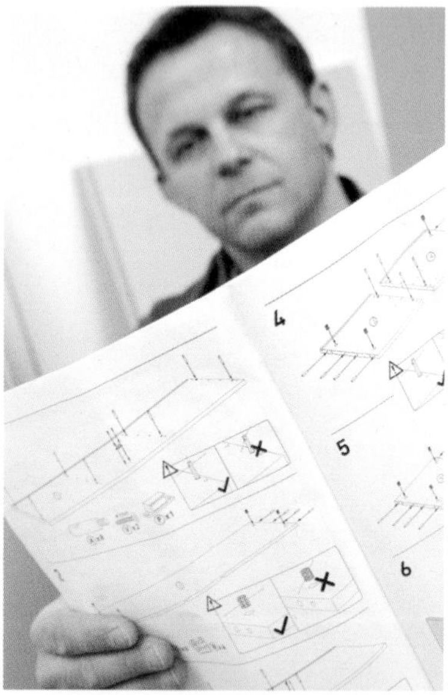

Flat-pack furniture instructions include a list of parts, assembly diagrams and the tools required.

Document 3 – Safety legislation

Safety legislation aims to protect consumers from injuries, thereby avoiding legal action against manufacturers. In a **product liability case** the manufacturer can be held responsible for the failure of a product which resulted in an accident, injury or death under the Consumer Protection Act (CPA) or simply under the common law of negligence.

Globalisation

Over the past century, there has been a rise in consumerism due to increased global population, and the introduction and availability of affordable products. As a result, design and manufacture has evolved into a global business.

This **globalisation** has brought consumers cheaper products and a wider choice. However, globalisation may also threaten the global economy – such as when an economic crash in one country has a global impact. There are also social issues, such as employment, associated with the movement of manufacturing from one country to another. The environmental issues surrounding globalisation are of huge significance to both designers and manufacturers.

Hint

Because in Europe labour costs are high and workers have a very different work/life balance, the Far East remains the prime location for low-cost manufacturing.

Global impact of commercial manufacture

When sourcing a mass manufacturer, large companies know which countries have the best factories at the most competitive prices. Countries in the Far East, such as China, Japan and Taiwan, have a different approach to work. The workers are highly efficient. Twelve-hour shifts are common (compared to an average eight-hour shift in Europe) and, in some factories, people work up to 80 hours a week with no days off. Many big factories employ whole towns of people and produce low-cost products 24/7.

Importing products also has its drawbacks logistically, such as damage during transportation and the time it takes for products to be imported from the other side of the world.

A modern Chinese electronics factory.

Social impact of commercial manufacture

With the introduction of manufacturing by highly automated machinery comes a reduction in staff numbers and, consequentially, loss of a skilled workforce. As machines become more complex and are increasingly capable of completing manufacturing tasks to extremely precise detail, the workforce becomes less skilled in manufacturing methods and more skilled in operating computer-controlled machinery. Therefore, the skillset of factory workers has shifted over the past century, while the number of employment contracts has fallen.

This can lead to:

- the loss of specialist craft skills
- unstable jobs
- increased unemployment
- the closure of factories
- the decline of industrial towns and villages
- economic decline of a whole geographical areas.

Environmental impact of commercial manufacture

Designers have a responsibility towards the environment, especially when creating a product which will be mass manufactured. During the development of a product, designers must consider the environmental impact of all their design decisions, working with the manufacturer to ensure that the commercial manufacture of the product can be sustainable.

In 2006, the Dundee Michelin factory was the first Michelin factory in the world to embrace wind energy with two wind turbine generators helping to reduce environmental impact and energy consumption.

Make the Link

The philosophy of cradle-to-cradle design, as explained in Chapter 5, considers the impact of the entire product and its potential recycling by-products on the environment.

Designers should make recommendations such as:

- using alternative materials which are recyclable
- reducing the volume of material (for example, thinner walls on plastic products)
- reducing the number of parts/components
- designing the product for disassembly
- using recycled components/parts.

The processes and materials used to manufacture, assemble, finish and package the product can pollute the air, water and land. Manufacturers have an environmental responsibility to eliminate pollution and strive towards **clean manufacturing**. This approach involves:

- non-toxic materials
- optimised raw material use
- water reductions, to create less waste water
- air emission reductions
- solid and hazardous waste reductions
- transport and packaging reduction
- energy efficiency, and use of solar, tidal, wind or other renewable energy sources.

Make the Link

In chapter 2, the product life cycle diagram shows the environmental impact of each stage, from sourcing raw materials to the disposal of the product at the end of its life.

Activity

Global manufacturing

1. Describe the advantages of manufacturing this MP3 player outside the UK.
2. Describe the disadvantages of manufacturing the MP3 player outside the UK.

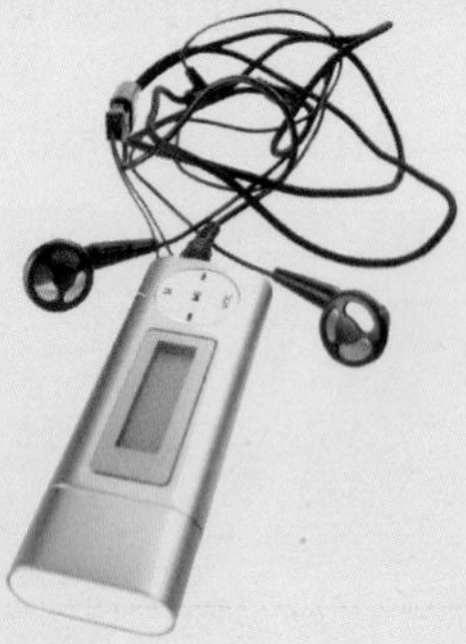

Check your progress

I can:	HELP NEEDED	GETTING THERE	CONFIDENT
• explain the term 'commercial manufacture'	◯	◯	◯
• describe the benefits and drawbacks of computer aided manufacture	◯	◯	◯
• describe a range of commercial manufacturing processes for wood	◯	◯	◯
• describe a range of commercial manufacturing processes for plastic	◯	◯	◯
• describe a range of commercial manufacturing processes for metal	◯	◯	◯
• describe the process of rapid prototyping	◯	◯	◯
• explain the term 'quality assurance'	◯	◯	◯
• describe the impact of global manufacture	◯	◯	◯
• explain the impact of commercial manufacturing on the environment	◯	◯	◯
• explain the impact of commercial manufacturing society.	◯	◯	◯

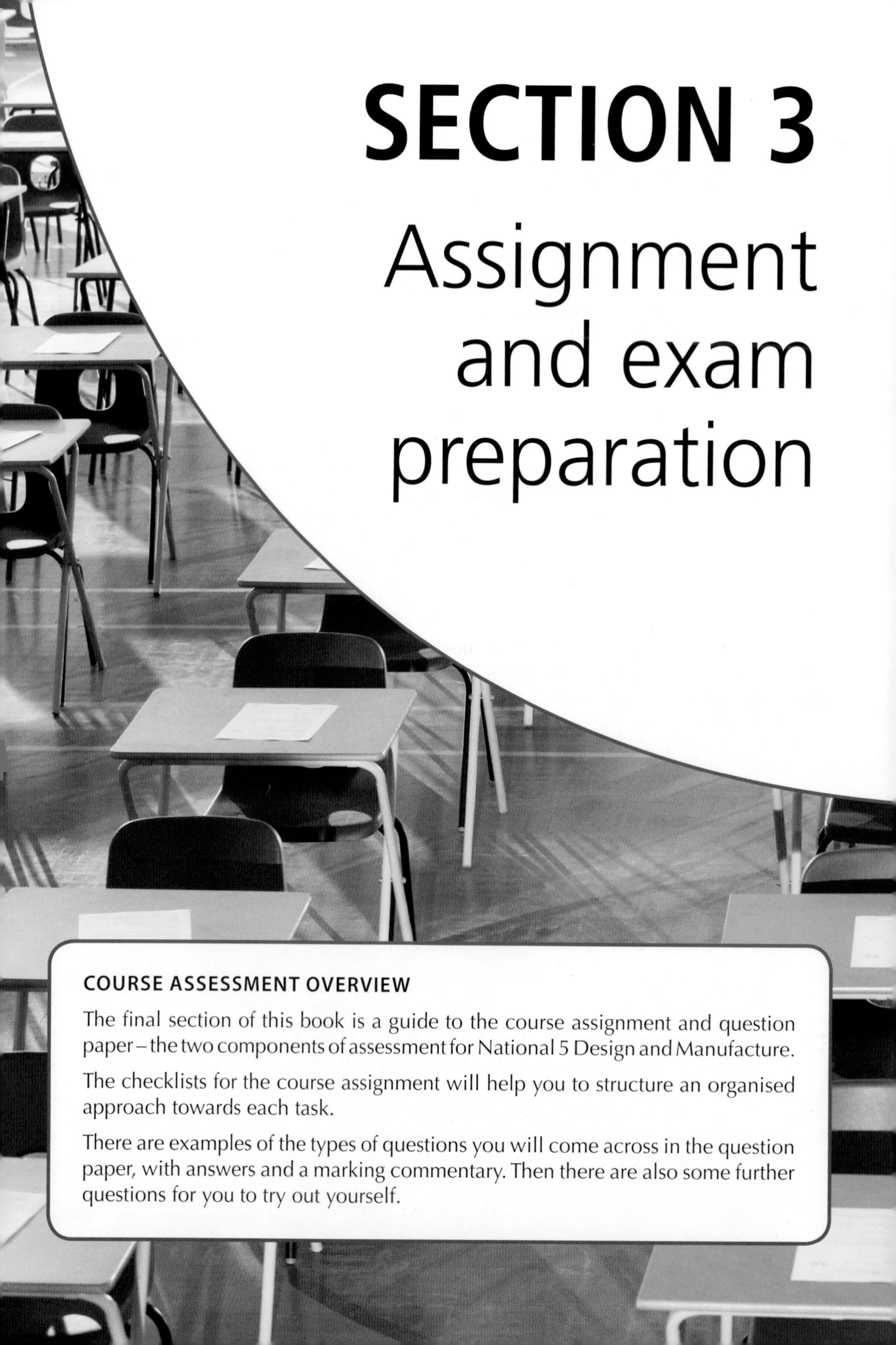

SECTION 3

Assignment and exam preparation

COURSE ASSESSMENT OVERVIEW

The final section of this book is a guide to the course assignment and question paper – the two components of assessment for National 5 Design and Manufacture.

The checklists for the course assignment will help you to structure an organised approach towards each task.

There are examples of the types of questions you will come across in the question paper, with answers and a marking commentary. Then there are also some further questions for you to try out yourself.

8 Assessment

By the end of this chapter you should be able to:

- understand the assignment and how to use the course assignment checklists
- understand the question paper and how to answer the questions.

Introduction to assessment

There are two units in Design and Manufacture; the **Design** unit and the **Materials and Manufacturing** unit. You are required to produce a range of evidence to demonstrate the skills, abilities and knowledge you have gained during your time studying these units. The units are assessed through the course assignment and the written exam, called the question paper.

Grades

The assignment is worth 90 marks and the question paper is worth 60 marks. Therefore, altogether you can achieve up to 150 marks. The question paper is set by the SQA and you are allocated 1 hour and 30 minutes to complete it on the day of the exam. The final grade you receive relates to the combined mark for the course assignment and question paper.

A marking structure which is *similar* to the one below will be used:

- A – 70% or above, within the range of 105–150 marks
- B – 60–69%, within the range of 90–104 marks
- C – 50–59%, within the range of 70–89 marks
- D – 40%–49%, within the range of 60–69 marks.

Course assignment

The course assignment is worth 90 of 150 marks, or 60%. A situation, a design brief, relevant research and a design specification are all provided by the SQA (not by your teacher). Your task is to design and manufacture a **prototype** in response to this information. There are 45 marks available for **designing skills** and 45 marks available for **practical skills**.

Hint

You have to provide evidence for every stage, so keep everything safe and organised.

Make the Link

Organise your work in a portfolio (see Chapter 1).

The course assignment should showcase your:

- design knowledge
- design skills
- knowledge of materials
- knowledge of manufacturing
- practical skills.

Course assignment checklists

During your course assignment, you could use these checklists to help you track your progress through each task. Of course, you may think of other work you can include which also demonstrates your designing or practical skills.

1. First steps

- ☐ I have made notes on or have underlined the key words in the situation, design brief, research and design specification.
- ☐ I have made an analysis of this information.

You may also wish to consider including additional evidence:

- ☐ I have used idea-generation techniques to produce some initial design ideas.
- ☐ I have a sketchbook *or* some sketches of my initial design ideas.

2. Develop a design proposal

- ☐ I have produced a wide range of design ideas which are all relevant to the design specification.
- ☐ I have communicated the designs using appropriate 2D and 3D sketching and drawing and modelling skills which communicate effectively.
- ☐ My written notes clearly communicate and justify design decisions, while also providing useful information, making use of the research materials provided.
- ☐ Throughout the design development, I have reviewed and evaluated the ideas.
- ☐ I have developed ideas that have evolved towards a design proposal which meets the needs of the specification.
- ☐ I have considered the practicalities of manufacturing the prototype. I have made a plan for manufacturing and have produced detailed working drawings with dimensions, which I can use in the workshop.

You may also wish to consider including additional evidence:

- ☐ Where appropriate, I have included additional research.
- ☐ I have used idea-generation techniques to develop my ideas.

3. Practical skills

- ◯ I have demonstrated care, accuracy and skill when measuring and marking out the materials, using my working drawing to find dimensions.
- ◯ My cutting, shaping and forming is precise.
- ◯ The resources I have selected and prepared for assembly are suitable for the task.
- ◯ The assembly techniques are accurate and I have checked that my work is square, level, true and secure.
- ◯ I have prepared surfaces for finishing and my finishing shows care, skill and attention to detail.

You may also wish to consider including additional evidence:

- ◯ To aid my evaluation, I have recorded any changes that I made to my prototype, or suggestions for design improvements to my prototype.

4. Evaluation

- ◯ I have used suitable methods to evaluate the success of my prototype.
- ◯ I have used the specification as a basis for my evaluation.

You may also wish to consider including additional evidence:

- ◯ Vocabulary that shows my ability to summarise and conclude.

Car mechanics use checklists to assess cars for their MOT tests every year.

Hint

Consider the layout of your evidence and use each page wisely. There is a limit of six A3 pages. Ideas should be on one or two A3 pages; Development on two to three A3 pages; Evaluating on just one A3 page.

Make the Link

People with practical jobs often use checklists in the workplace: for example, car mechanics, joiners, builders, plumbers and engineers.

Marking the course assignment

Marks are awarded for the course assignment as follows:

• Initial ideas	12 marks
• Development	18 marks
• Communication	9 marks
• Evaluation	6 marks
• Measuring and marking out	9 marks
• Cutting, shaping and forming	18 marks
• Assembly of components	9 marks
• Finishing	9 marks
	Total: 90 marks

The question paper

The question paper is a 60-mark written exam paper and is worth 40% of the overall grade. There are two parts to the exam, Section 1 and Section 2. You must complete both parts.

- **Section 1** is worth 24 marks and is mostly based on the Materials and Manufacturing unit. There will be a single extended question based on one product. Section 1 focuses on **materials, tools and manufacturing methods** and does not include any questions about commercial manufacturing.
- **Section 2** is worth 36 marks. There will be four or five questions in this part of the paper. Each question shows a different commercial product and has a range of sub-questions (such as 4a, 4b, 4c) based on that product. The questions cover a range of topics relating to **commercial products**.

Exam-style questions

Pages 207–213 show a typical question paper, with suggested answers written in blue and the marker's commentary in red. The key words and phrases in each answer are in **bold**.

Example of a Section 1 question with marking commentary

1. A pupil's project for a kitchen trolley is shown below.

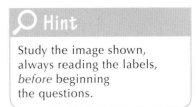

> **Hint**
>
> Study the image shown, always reading the labels, *before* beginning the questions.

(a) The kitchen trolley was made from a hardwood.

(i) State the name of a suitable hardwood for the trolley. **1**

Beech *is a suitable hardwood.*

Marking commentary: a mark is awarded for the identifying a suitable hardwood.

(ii) Give **two** reasons why this hardwood is suitable. **2**

Beech is a ***strong*** *wood. Therefore, it will be* ***durable enough to withstand*** *kitchen use, such as chopping on the worktop. It is also very* ***smooth and relatively knot free****, so it is an* ***easy hardwood to work****.*

Marking commentary: marks are awarded for the correct material properties matched to the needs of the product, or to the potential to manufacture with the identified material.

The pupil found out that hardwood is available in planks, but not in boards.

(iii) Explain four stages found in the plan for manufacture which the pupil followed to make the wide boards for the worktop and shelf. **4**

Stage 1 – First each plank of wood and two sash cramps were laid out. The planks were placed on top of them, ensuring that the ***end grain curved in the opposite direction, to keep the board flat and stop bowing*** *at a later stage.*

Stage 2 – Long lengths of ***scrap wood were placed between the planks and the cramps, to protect the wood from being damaged.***

[Turn over]

Stage 3 – Then ***PVA glue was put along each edge, the planks were put side by side, and the two bottom cramps were tightened*** *with a* ***third cramp on top to keep the boards flat.***

Stage 4 – Once the glue was dry, the cramps would be removed and ***a smoothing plane could be used to level off the board.***

Marking commentary: marks are awarded for a detailed explanation of each stage of making up a board from planks of wood.

(b) The pillar drill shown below was used to manufacture the bottle rack.

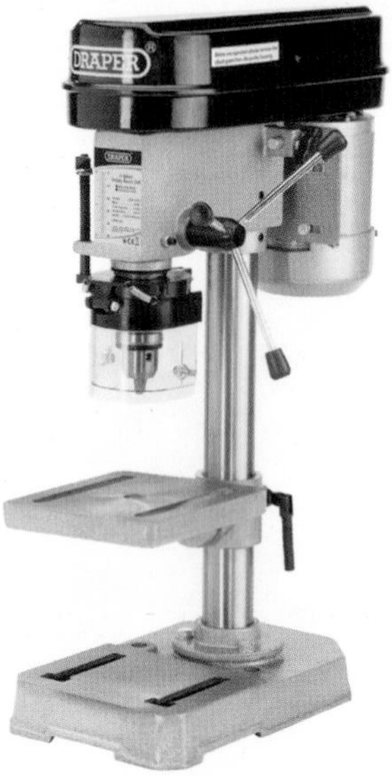

The holes drilled for the dowel rods were blind holes.

(i) Explain **two** benefits of a blind hole. **2**

The dowel rod will ***not be seen from the front or back*** *of the bottle rack. The bottom of the blind hole can be filled with* ***PVA glue to ensure a tight and secure permanent join*** *to the dowel rod.*

Marking commentary: marks are awarded for the explanation of two different benefits; similar responses will only be awarded one mark. The answer here is given in two separate sentences to clearly distinguish both points.

(ii) Describe **one** adjustment to the pillar drill that is necessary to drill a blind hole. **1**

The maximum depth of the drill can be adjusted by ***setting the depth gauge****, so that the drill doesn't go the whole way through the wood.*

Marking commentary: a mark is awarded for the description of using the depth gauge. This answer does not mention using a steel rule to measure the depth accurately, but describes drilling to a maximum depth and is, therefore, worth one mark.

[Turn over]

The forstner drill bit shown below was used to drill the holes on the bottle rack.

(i) Describe why this drill bit is suitable for drilling blind holes. **1**

A forstner bit can drill ***a flat-bottomed hole****, suitable for the end of the dowel rod to fit onto.*

Marking commentary: a mark is awarded for identifying that a forstner bit can drill a flat-bottomed hole.

(c) Vegetable oil was used as a surface finish for the hardwood.

(i) Describe **two** reasons for using vegetable oil as a surface finish for the hardwood. **2**

As vegetable oil is non-toxic, it is ***safe to use as a finish for any wooden kitchen product****. The vegetable oil will also* ***protect the wood from damage****, while enhancing the colour of the wood.*

Marking commentary: marks are awarded for identifying that vegetable oil is safe to use on wooden kitchen products. A second mark can be awarded for identifying that it will protect the wood. In this answer, a third reason has been given. Although it is correct that the vegetable oil does enhance the colour of the wood, only the first two answers given can be awarded marks.

(ii) Describe **one** method of applying the vegetable oil to the hardwood. **1**

It can be ***rubbed on with a soft cloth*** *in the direction of the grain.*

Marking commentary: a mark is awarded for indicating that the appropriate method of applying vegetable oil is to use cloth.

[Turn over]

(d) The drawer handles were made from a standard length of stainless steel strip.

(i) Explain the meaning of the term *standard length*. **1**

Standard lengths are the ***set sizes in which materials are available to buy*** *from suppliers, which you can then cut down to your own required sizes.*

Marking commentary: a mark is awarded for a clear explanation of the term 'standard length'. There may be reference to the ease of standard sizes to suppliers, buying a standard size then cutting it down to size, or that it is easy to work out material limitations due to standard size.

(ii) State **one** reason why stainless steel is a suitable metal for the handles. **1**

Stainless steel is ***corrosion resistant****.*

Marking commentary: a mark is awarded for the correct material property matched to the needs of the product, or to the possibility of manufacture with the identified material.

The pupil used a forge to carry out heat treatments to shape the stainless steel.

(iii) Describe the annealing process which is carried out on the forge to make the stainless steel more malleable. **1**

The stainless steel is first ***heated*** *to soften it by holding the metal with tongs in* ***the tip of the flame, until it glows red in colour, and then leaving it to cool down slowly.***

Marking commentary: a mark is awarded for the correct description of this heat-treatment process.

(iv) State the name of another heat treatment required during the manufacture of the handle. **1**

Hardening *would also be necessary.*

Marking commentary: a mark is awarded for the correct heat-treatment process. Another correct answer could be tempering.

[Turn over]

(v) Describe **two** steps the pupil followed to form the handle to the required shape using workshop hand tools. **2**

The metal could be marked out with an engineer's square and ***put into folding bars in an engineer's vice****. By* ***hitting the metal with a raw hide mallet*** *the handle shape could be made without denting the metal.*

Marking commentary: marks are awarded for the correct description of the manufacturing process. Two different steps must be identified.

(e) The wheels of the kitchen trolley are made from nylon.

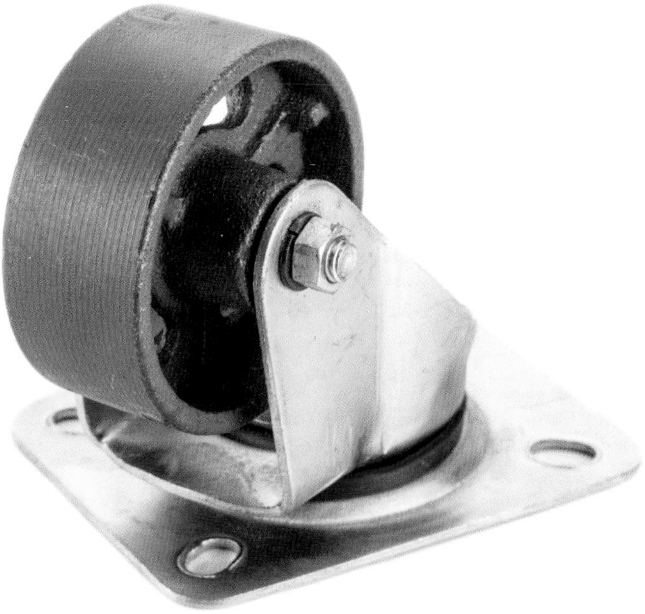

(i) State a benefit of using nylon wheels. **1**

Nylon is ***resistant to wear, so the wheels will last longer than other materials****.*

Marking Commentary: a mark is awarded for the correct material property matched to the needs of the component.

(ii) Explain how the pupil joined the wheels to the legs. **3**

First, the holes would be ***marked out on the legs using a tri square and steel rule****. The pupil could measure the bracket to get the location of the hole. Then a* ***pilot hole would be drilled using a power drill with a small twist drill bit****. The plates on the wheels have holes, so* ***countersunk screws could be used to screw them onto the legs using a screwdriver****.*

Marking commentary: marks are awarded for the correct description of the manufacturing process. Three different steps must be identified and the joining method described must be suitable.

Total marks 24

Example of a Section 2 question with marking commentary

2. A foldable grater is shown below.

(a) Before producing a design specification for the foldable grater, the designer would have researched various design factors. Explain why the following design factors would be researched when designing a foldable grater. **3**

(i) Durability

Durability would be researched because the user would need the grater to ***withstand the grating of different foods without becoming blunt****.*

(ii) Ergonomics

The designer would research ergonomics because the ***folding feature would need to be easy to understand and easy carry out without the user trapping their fingers or cutting themselves.***

(iii) Function

Function would be researched as a variety of ***different grating options*** *are available and the designer would need to* ***find out which ones to include****.*

Marking commentary: marks are awarded for the explanation of why each design factor is to be researched. Simply writing a definition of durability, ergonomics or function is not sufficient to gain any marks.

(b) The grater was mass produced. Describe two benefits to the manufacturer of mass-manufacturing techniques. **2**

Mass manufacture is ***cheaper as high volumes*** *of products are made. Also all the products are* ***extremely accurate and are all the same****.*

Marking commentary: marks are awarded for the identification of two benefits *to the manufacturer* of mass manufacture. Other answers would include the fast pace of production, the consistently high quality of the products and the potential reduction in the workforce, lowering labour costs.

[Turn over]

(c) The grater was made using CNC and CAD/CAM. Describe the impact these technologies have on the manufacturer. **3**

*The **set-up costs of the equipment are high** and so large volumes of product have to be made to recoup this money. Also, the **cost to fix broken machines** can be high and, if manufacturing stops, this also impacts on profits. **Staff need to be trained** so that they know how to work the machinery, which again costs the manufacturer money.*

Marking commentary: marks are awarded for the correct identification of three ways in which modern technology has an impact on the manufacturer. These may be positive or negative impacts. The response correctly identifies set-up costs and repair costs. For a third mark, it identifies the additional cost of staff training. Another valid answer is the time away from manufacturing for this training to take place. Other answers could include sustainability issues relating to increased production and disposal of old equipment. Also related to sustainability is a potential reduction in materials used and waste produced as a result of technology. Further answers relating to the social impact of these technologies could include reduced labour costs, quicker production methods and the ability to stay ahead of other manufacturers by lowering costs or by offering cutting-edge technologies. Other answers which explain the benefits of these technologies could include faster manufacturing, increased complexity and accuracy of production, and a reduction in joining techniques when a product is designed and manufactured with fewer parts.

Total marks 8

Practice exam-style questions

Now that you have read over the examples, it is time to attempt some exam-style questions on your own. Here are two tips to remember when practising exam questions (and when sitting the exam for real):

- Time yourself: there are 60 marks allocated to the written paper and 90 minutes to complete it. Therefore, you should spend about one and a half minutes on each mark, or three minutes for two marks.
- Always read the question carefully; also study the diagrams, photos and any labels.

The following questions (pages 214–220) are exam-style questions which you may work through yourself.

1. A pupil's project for a mirror with a drawer is shown below.

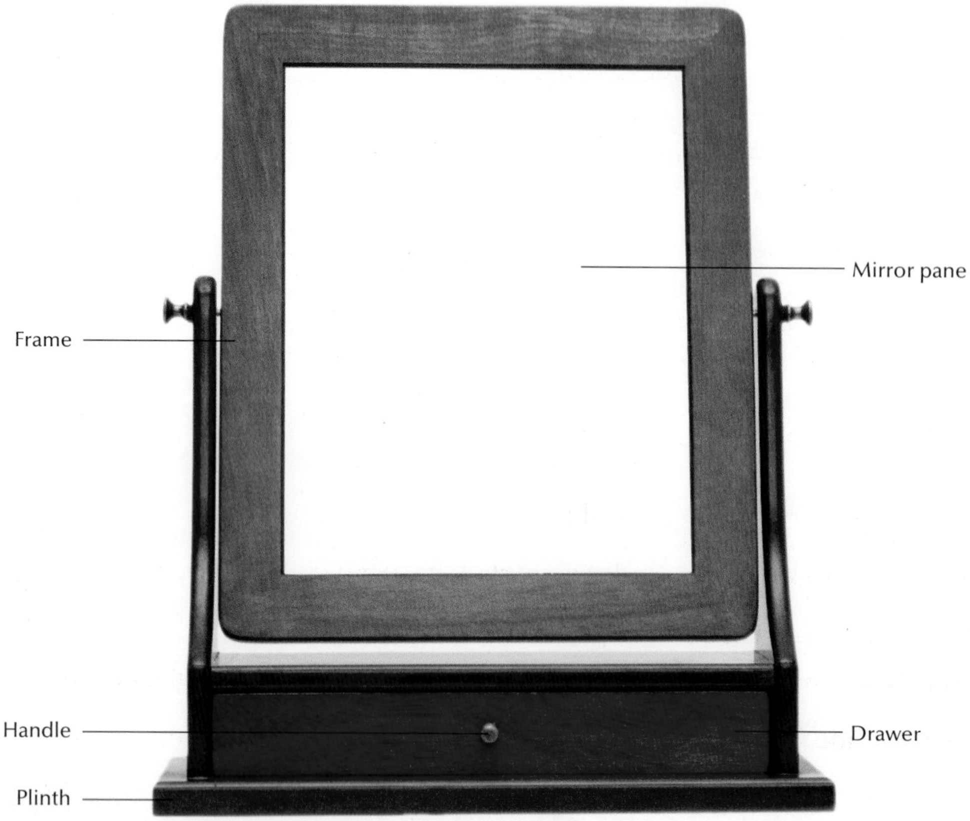

(a) A sheet of mirrored acrylic was used for the mirror pane.

(i) State two reasons why mirrored acrylic is a suitable material for the mirror pane. **2**

(ii) Describe a suitable method of cutting the acrylic to the correct size. **1**

(iii) Explain the four stages required to create a smooth surface finish on the edges of the piece of acrylic. **4**

(iv) State a suitable method of attaching the mirror to the frame. **1**

(b) The sides, drawer and plinth were all made from a light coloured softwood and were finished with a dark wood stain.

(i) State the name of a suitable softwood. **1**

(ii) Explain two benefits of using a softwood instead of a hardwood. **2**

(iii) Describe three stages of applying the wood stain to achieve a good quality surface finish. **3**

[Turn over]

(c) The photo below shows the dovetail joint which was used to join the front of the drawer to the sides of the drawer.

(i) Give a reason why this joint is suitable. **1**

(ii) Explain **one** reason why the pupil did not stain the drawer sides. **1**

The base of the drawer was fitted with a manufactured board.

(iii) Describe **two** benefits of using a manufactured board for the base of the drawer. **2**

(d) The handle was made from a brass bar which was shaped on a centre lathe.

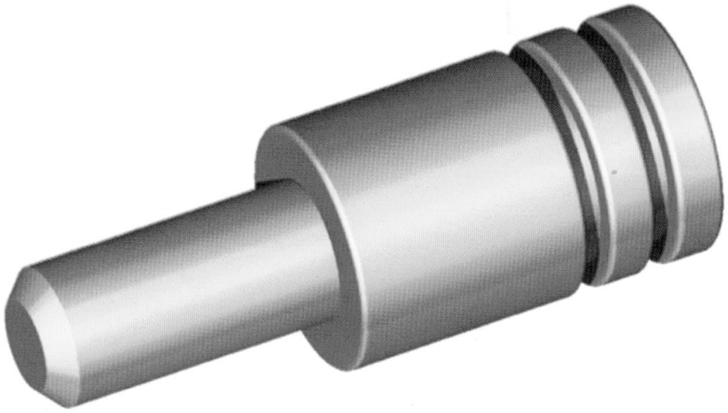

(i) State a functional benefit of adding the grooves to the handle. **1**

The end of the handle was to be threaded to allow it to be secured to the drawer with a nut on the inside of the drawer.

(ii) State a reason for the chamfer at the end of the handle. **1**

(iii) Describe the process of threading the bar. **3**

(iv) Describe one method of checking the thread was a tight fit. **1**

Total marks 24

2. The chair shown below was designed with ergonomic features.

(a) Describe how ergonomics has influenced the design of the chair. **2**

(b) A *scale model* was created during the development of the chair design.

(i) State two reasons for creating a scale model of the chair. **2**

(ii) State the name of a suitable modelling material for the scale model. **1**

(c) An ergonome was used during modelling.

(i) State the purpose of an ergonome. **1**

Total marks 6

3. A desk tidy is shown below.

The manufacturer wishes to carry out an evaluation of the desk tidy.

(a) Describe a suitable user trial to evaluate the function of the desk tidy. **2**

(b) State two key questions that would be included in a survey to evaluate the aesthetics of the desk tidy. **2**

Designers need to find ways of marketing their product in order for it to be successful. The desk tidy was launched under an established brand name.

(c) **(i)** Describe two benefits to the designer of launching a product under a successful brand name. **2**

(ii) Describe two other marketing techniques that may be used to promote the desk tidy. **2**

Total marks 4

4. A child's dinner set is shown below.

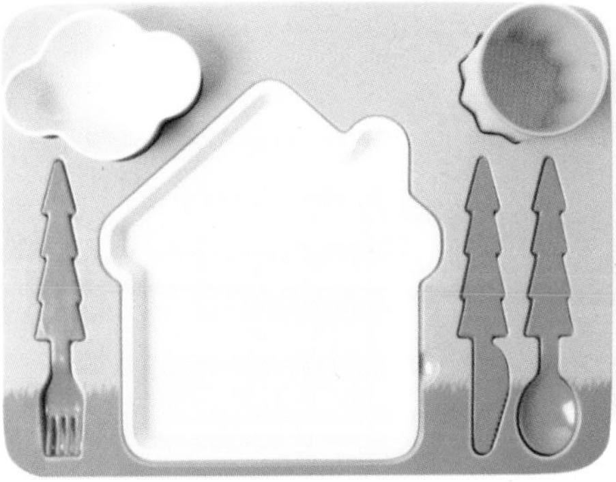

A competitor wishes to carry out an evaluation of the dinner set.

(a) State a method that could be used to evaluate each of the following factors:

(i) function **1**

(ii) materials **1**

(iii) aesthetics. **1**

(b) State **two** more factors which could be used to evaluate the dinner set. **2**

Total marks 5

5. Coffee machines that make hot drinks using 'drinks pods' are increasingly popular.

With reference to the coffee machine explain these terms:

(i) *technology push* **2**

(ii) *market pull* **2**

(b) Describe **two** aesthetic qualities of the coffee machine. **2**

Total marks 6

6. A child's chair is shown below.

(a) Describe a suitable target market for the chair. **2**

(b) With reference to the chair, describe the difference between *primary* and *secondary functions*. **2**

(c) The chair was manufactured by rotational moulding.

(i) State **one** benefit of rotational moulding the child's chair. **1**

(ii) State the name of a material which is suitable for this process. **1**

Total marks 6

7. A designer used idea-generation techniques when designing a playhouse.

(a) State **two** idea generation techniques. **2**

(b) Describe **one** of these techniques. **2**

Total marks 4

8. Designers use a range of sketches, graphic drawing techniques and CAD drawings, like the one shown below, at various stages throughout the design process.

(a) State the stage in the design process at which it would be appropriate to use:

(i) rough sketches **1**

(ii) working drawings. **1**

(b) Describe two advantages of CAD to:

(i) the client **2**

(ii) the manufacturer. **2**

Total marks 6

9. Due to the pollution caused by diesel and petrol, car companies like Renault have recognised the need for electric vehicles.

(a) Explain how the electric-car market has been influenced by:

(i) the rise of consumerism **2**

(ii) consumer demand. **2**

(b) Describe two benefits to the manufacturer when launching a product under a brand name. **2**

Total marks 6

10. A games controller is shown below.

Describe the ergonomic features of the games controller.

Total marks 6

Check your progress

I can:

	HELP NEEDED	GETTING THERE	CONFIDENT
• understand the assignment and how to use the course assignment checklists	◯	◯	◯
• understand the question paper and how to answer the questions.	◯	◯	◯